INTEGRAL SPIRITUALITY:
RESOURCES FOR COMMUNITY,
JUSTICE, PEACE, AND THE EARTH

INTEGRAL SPIRITUALITY

Resources for Community, Justice, Peace, and the Earth

DONAL DORR

ORBIS BOOKS

Maryknoll, New York 10545

The Catholic Foreign Mission Society of America (Maryknoll)
recruits and trains people for overseas missionary service.
Through Orbis Books, Maryknoll aims to foster the
international dialogue that is essential to mission.
The books published, however, reflect the opinions of their authors
and are not meant to represent the official position of the Society.

Published in Ireland by
Gill and Macmillan Ltd
Goldenbridge
Dublin 8
and in the United States by
Orbis Books, Maryknoll,
New York 10545
© Donal Dorr, 1990
Printed in England
All rights reserved

ISBN 0 88344 658 8 (Orbis Books)

CONTENTS

ACKNOWLEDGMENTS

The author and the publishers are grateful to the following for permission to reproduce their copyright material:
SCM Press Ltd, 26-30 Tottenham Road, London NI 4BZ and Augsburg Fortress, Box 1209, Minneapolis MN 55440 for excerpt from Dorothee Sölle, *Choosing Life* [1981]. Peter Kavanagh for the poems 'Worship' and 'Thank you, Thank you' from *The Complete Poems of Patrick Kavanagh*, New York, 1972 [Copyright Peter Kavanagh]. Orbis Books for the poem 'For My Young Comrades' from Dorothee Sölle, *Of War and Love*, Maryknoll NY [Orbis: 1983]. New Society Publishers, 4527 Springfield Avenue, Philadelphia, PA 19143, for excerpts from Johanna Rogers Macy, *Despair and Personal Power in the Nuclear Age*, [Philadelphia, PA: New Society Publishers] 1983. Alfred A. Knopf, Inc., 201 East 50th St, New York N.Y. 10022, and Anthony Sheil Associates, 43 Doughty Street, London WCIN 2LF, for excerpts from Marge Piercy, *Woman on the Edge of Time*, New York [Alfred A. Knopf, Inc.] and London [The Women's Press]. Pádraig Ó Fátharta for the songs 'Light in my Night' and 'Risking'. Pádraig Ó Máille for the poem 'For the Poor Clares, Lilongwe, Malawi'. Ms Frances Croake Frank for her poem, 'Did The Woman Say?' Professor Brendan Kennelly, Trinity College, Dublin for the poem 'Begin' from his book *Good Souls to Survive*, Dublin [Allen Figgis and Co: 1967]. Ms Anne Hope and Ms Sally Timmel for ideas and exercises from *Training For Transformation: A Handbook For Community Workers* [3 vols], Gweru, Zimbabwe [Mambo Press: 1984]. Frank Dorr for permission to use an adapted version of his 'Flower Power' exercise. University Associates, Inc., San Diego, CA: for the exercise 'Prisoner's Dilemmas' in John

W. Pfeiffer and John E. Jones, *A Handbook of Structured Experiences for Human Relations Training, Vol. III*, 1974. Pax Christi, St Francis of Assisi Centre, Pottery Lane, London WII 4NG for 'Cooperation Squares' exercise. Charles Elliot for permission to adapt his 'fishbowls' diagram from *Patterns of Poverty in the Third World: A Study of Social and Economic Stratification*, New York [Praeger: 1971]. Mayfield Publishing Company for use of an adapted version of 'Johari Window', originally published in Joe Luft, *Group Processes: An Introduction to Group Dynamics*, Mayfield, 1963, 1970.

INTRODUCTION

Over the past few years I have been trying to work out an integrated spirituality for my own life; and I have also been looking for ways to communicate to others the relationship that exists between the different aspects of such a spirituality. In a previous book I made use of a famous text from the prophet Micah to highlight three fundamental dimensions of a balanced spirituality. The passage runs:

> This is what Yahweh asks of you, only this: that you act justly, that you love tenderly, that you walk humbly with your God. (Micah 6:8)

I suggested that 'act justly', could be taken to refer to the 'public' aspect of spirituality which has to do with structural justice and option for the poor; that ' love tenderly' could be taken to refer to the interpersonal aspect of spirituality; and that 'walk humbly' could refer to the personal aspect of spirituality.[1]

These different aspects of a holistic spirituality can be grouped under three headings — the personal, the interpersonal, and the 'public'. It is helpful to represent them in diagrammatic form by means of three circles.[2] The top circle represents *structural justice*. The right-hand circle represents *interpersonal respect*. The left-hand circle represents *personal responsibility and integrity*. I shall be dealing with all of these in a variety of ways in the different chapters of this book.

In recent years I have worked on this topic with many groups and this has led me to develop and refine my views. I still consider the three major aspects to be the 'public', the interpersonal, and the personal. But I am now particularly interested in the areas where each of these interlocks with the other two. In the diagram these can be depicted as the

1

Fig. 1

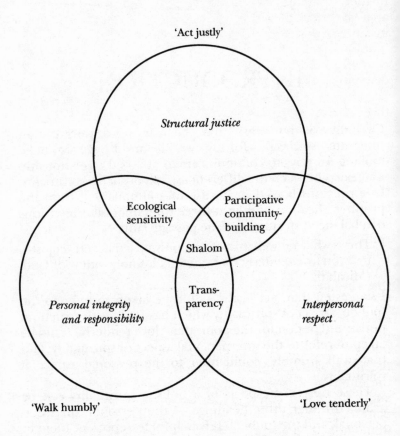

areas where the circles overlap with each other — see figure 1. The result of this overlapping is that the diagram has four further segments of circles. Each of these can represent an area of 'overlap' within an integrated spirituality — for instance, an area that involves both the personal and the 'public' aspects of spirituality. Participants in workshops and courses found it helpful when I displayed a poster of the diagram and began my account of some aspect of spirituality by pointing out where it could be located in relation to the three circles.

I think a major reason why many recent approaches to spirituality are inadequate is that they concentrate exclusively on just one or two of its aspects, without taking account of others — and of how they interlock with each other. In this book I have set out to explore various aspects of a holistic spirituality, with special emphasis on the areas of overlap.

In the nine chapters I explore nine different aspects of spirituality. Each chapter includes my own reflections on one particular topic, as well as practical exercises and resources on the same subject. When one is dealing with spirituality there is no set starting-point or finishing-point. In one sense I can start anywhere, and in another sense I have to start everywhere at the same time. In writing about the various topics there is no clear logical pattern which has to be followed, since all are interrelated and each is dependent on the others. Therefore, in choosing the order in which to treat the different themes, I have been guided by psychological and educational considerations — I tried to work out a pattern that would be interesting for the reader and that would help to build up a rounded picture, bit by bit.

'Down to Earth Spirituality' is the title of the first chapter. In it I set out to deal with the topic of ecological sensitivity. It is an area of overlap between the *personal* and the '*public*' aspects of spirituality. I try to show that respect for the natural world lies at the heart of an authentic spirituality of justice. I also suggest that sensitivity to our environment can mediate to us a personal sense of the loving Providence of God — and this, I believe, is important for our spirituality.

Chapter 2 is concerned with prayer and power. In it I stress the importance of personal prayer — or what is sometimes (mistakenly) called 'private' prayer. I explore how prayer nourishes the deepest part of us; how it enables us to act with greater *personal responsibility and integrity*. Because of this it enables us to relate more authentically to other people. So in this chapter I am dealing with the personal aspect of spirituality — but indicating how it overlaps with the interpersonal.

In the third chapter I set out to explore a key element in relating to others and building community, namely, what it means to be 'open', to share with people at a deep level. I am dealing here with interpersonal respect, participative community-building, and especially with what I call 'transparency'. By 'transparency' I mean a quality of openness in our relationships that enables one's personal integrity to shine through to others. This is the part of an integrated spirituality where *interpersonal respect* overlaps with *personal integrity*. In the second section I give some poems which may be used as resource material for individuals or groups. In the third section I suggest a variety of exercises which can help people to implement the ideals presented in the first section of the chapter; the exercises are techniques which are useful for those who are learning *how* to be open with others and how to share deeply with them.

In chapter 4 I focus attention on community prayer — especially on liturgical prayer. It often happens that liturgy is so formalized that some people find it cuts them off from God rather than offering them a means of finding God as both the goal of their spiritual journey and a companion on the way. So I have devoted this chapter to suggesting how people may be helped to have a more effective and affective experience of God in community prayer or public worship. From my own experience of working with groups of different kinds I share some ways in which faith can be nourished. I pay special attention to the notion of pilgrimage — and how different kinds of pilgrimage may be organized; and I also offer some resource materials for those who wish to plan them.

The fifth chapter offers some reflections on the nature and kinds of power, and on its use or abuse. My main interest here is in drawing out the contrast between the power of domination or coercion and the power of facilitating or enabling others. In the second and third sections of the

4

chapter I outline some exercises and techniques which can be used to facilitate communities in joint decision-making and cooperative planning. All of this concerns the part of spirituality where *interpersonal* respect coincides and overlaps with the promotion of *structural justice* in society. The commitment to build up communities in a participative fashion is a major step towards building a more just world, and at the same time it calls for great sensitivity and respect for the individuals we are working with.

In the sixth chapter I move on to examine explicitly the issue of *structural justice* in society — a subject that is obviously central for anybody who wishes to develop a spirituality that is relevant to our world. The usual approach to this major topic is through economics; and that is understandable since poverty is perhaps the most obvious instance of structural injustice. But on this occasion I situate the treatment of economics within the context of culture. The reason is that I am interested in developing *effective* spirituality; and in recent years I have become more and more convinced that it is only through their culture that people can find the energy to challenge injustice effectively and build alternatives to the present grossly unjust structures of society. Having offered personal reflections on this issue in the first two sections of the chapter I go on in the third and fourth sections to give more practical materials. Section Three outlines a process which can be used to help a group to work out in a very practical way the kind of 'development' they wish to promote in society. Section Four offers exercises and resource materials on the topic of 'Justice for Women'.

Structural justice, interpersonal respect and personal integrity all come together at the heart of an integrated spirituality. The area where they meet may be called *'Shalom'*, the biblical word which means all-embracing peace in every sphere of life:
— the peace of being in harmony with nature and the cosmos;
— peace based on justice and reconciliation in society and the world;
— peace in our relationships with family, friends, and community;
— a deep personal peace arising from being at home with oneself;

5

— and opening oneself up to experience peace as an utterly undeserved gift of God, a peace that passes all understanding in all or any of these areas of life.

In chapter 7, which is entitled 'A Spirituality of Peace', I offer some reflections and resources on 'shalom', with particular reference to the development of a spirituality for those who work for peace and disarmament in the 'public' sphere.

In the eighth chapter I offer material which may be of help to groups or individuals who wish to go deeper into the subject of *personal* growth — and how it relates to the building of *community*, and the transformation of *society*. In doing so I make use of an ancient wisdom called 'The Enneagram' which for centuries provided a basis for the development of spirituality among the Sufi mystics. I propose a way in which the different types of compulsion and personality described in the Enneagram may be explored in a relatively painless way within the space of a few hours. I go on to outline a process by which this material may be used to nourish the life of a group or community. I offer some suggestions for exploring the implications of this material for political activity and for our relationship with God.

Chapter 9 is entitled 'Where Does God Come In?' Having examined different aspects of spirituality in the previous eight chapters I go on in this chapter to offer a framework within which these 'worldly' aspects of spirituality can be integrated with our relationship to God. This is followed by some resource materials related to the same topic.

Finally, I have added an appendix in which I give some very practical guidelines about how a 'workshop' dealing with different aspects of holistic spirituality might be planned and 'got off the ground'. In referring here to a 'workshop', I am speaking about an approach to learning which is 'experiential'. For the benefit of those who may be unfamiliar with this kind of approach I shall try here to clarify briefly what it involves — and I shall illustrate it by referring to my own experience.

Those who use workshops are very aware that lectures or even discussions are not a very effective way of communicating insights about life. So, instead, they set out to design a 'learning event' which may last for just a few hours or may go on for several days — or even for a number of weeks. This 'workshop' includes various practical exercises which are designed to evoke insight in those who take part in them. For instance, the group may be invited to cooperate together in some common task where they have to work under the pressure of a severe time-constraint; immediately afterwards they are invited to reflect on how effectively they cooperated and how the pressure affected their behaviour; in this way they generally learn far more about cooperation and respect for others than they would have learned from a lecture on these topics. A 'workshop' generally includes a variety of such practical exercises, fitted together into a 'package' where all the different learnings come together into a rounded whole. A workshop of this kind may include occasional bits of 'input' — i.e. a talk given by one of the organisers or resource-people. But the most effective way of incorporating such 'input' is not as an opening talk, but *after* a learning event, to help the participants to articulate their insights.

The discovery of such an experiential approach to learning was a major turning-point in my own life. With a sense of unbounded gratitude I recall how I was invited to join with a group of missionaries in the desert in northern Kenya thirteen years ago for my very first workshop. I had previously become disillusioned with the traditional lecture-and-discussion system of communicating ideas; but it was the only approach I knew. During that week in the desert I was introduced to ways of working with groups which were immeasurably more effective. I had the sense that, after much wandering and searching, I had at last 'come home' — I had found what I had been looking for. I was eager to learn these 'new' ways of working with groups (planning and facilitation skills etc.). To my delight I found that I did not have to wait to complete some course in this new approach; as soon as I learned any technique I could immediately make use of it. And I found that this approach enabled me to make use of talents and gifts which I had not previously known I possessed.

Since that time I have been using, and learning more about, all kinds of experiential modes of learning. But I am particularly committed to one particular version of it — the one that is widely called 'The Psycho-Social Method'. It is a

model of experiential learning that is designed to help people work for transformation:
— the transformation of our world into a just and humane society;
— the transformation of groups of all kinds into real communities;
— the transformation of individuals into fully mature and free persons;
— the transformation of the Church into a more effective witness and agent of God's love for the world, for communities, and for each person.

All of the material in this book is designed to fit into such an approach. I do not intend the book as a handbook in the strict sense, since a comprehensive and highly successful handbook on the psycho-social method is already available.[3] But I hope my book may be of help to two different categories of reader:
— The first category consists of people who are hungry for inspirational and practical material on different aspects of spirituality; some of them may be rather intimidated or mystified by talk about 'workshops', 'experiential learning', or 'psycho-social method', but perhaps they would like a gentle introduction to the experiential approach — on a 'do it yourself' basis, which can be used by individuals or small groups.
— The second category of potential readers consists of those who already have some familiarity with the experiential approach — and perhaps even with the psycho-social method — but are looking for a more extended religious-theological underpinning for it, as well as some further resource materials and exercises which may help them in their work.

My hope is that at least some of the readers of this book will wish to make use of the practical materials within the context of a workshop of some kind; that is why I have added an appendix on planning and running the first stages of a workshop. However, those who are not interested in working in this way will still, I hope, find in this book material that will help them in their efforts to develop an integral spirituality in their lives.

Reflections and Practical Resources

I offer three kinds of material to the reader on the various topics with which I deal. I generally begin with some personal reflections of my own on the particular issue. Then I usually suggest some practical exercises which readers may use, either alone or in a group, to explore the matter for themselves. Finally, I offer some other resource materials — for instance some poems or excerpts from helpful writings, with an occasional reference to a video-film which may be found helpful. I have included quite a lot of passages from Scripture — especially from the psalms and the writings of the prophets. I expect people to come to this book looking for resource materials; and I believe some of them would want the translation of the Scripture passages to use 'inclusive language' (i.e. not to be sexist or patriarchal); I am sure they would also want the passages to be suitable for public reading, and to be intelligible even to people who have not had the opportunity to study the background to the Bible. With this in mind I have in most cases made my own translations; on some occasions I have adapted existing translations.

Why combine in one book my own reflections on the different topics with practical resource material and exercises? Because I have found that neither practical material nor theoretical-reflective material is sufficient on its own. On the one hand, I find it very difficult to work through a book which consists entirely of practical exercises and resource materials. Either I get bored or I get intimidated by the sheer number of the exercises and quotations; and I find myself longing to read some of the author's own reflections. But, on the other hand, spirituality is a very personal and practical matter; the extent to which *my* reflections can nourish *your* spirit is rather limited. So there is a value in offering practical material which will help people to explore for themselves, as individuals or in groups, the different aspects of spirituality. Therefore I am offering a combination of the two approaches. In general I give the practical exercises and resource materials *after* my reflective essay. But in cases where it seems more appropriate I change the order or integrate the two kinds of material.

My hope is that my own theological material will serve two purposes. Firstly, it may provide background information and ideas for people working in various demanding ministries. Such people rarely have time or energy for extensive theological reading; and in any case they often find theology somewhat divorced from the reality of life 'on the ground'. I am trying to provide a stimulus and some material for a theology that will emerge from the ground up, rather than from the top down. Secondly, I hope that some of this material may provide the basis for talks to groups of various kinds. Adult education should, of course, be mainly experiential — helping people to learn through reflection on experience. But those who work with adult groups occasionally need to give some 'input', i.e. a talk that gathers together in an organised way some of the things the groups have learned through their reflection. What I have written may perhaps be of help in this regard.

In order to facilitate individuals or groups who wish to use the practical material, I have asked some friends who are well qualified in communications and media work to help me prepare some further resources which can be used in conjunction with the book.[4] These consist of two kinds of material:

(a) A set of cassette tapes on which I have recorded the guided meditations and poems used in the book; these cassette tapes also contain recordings of songs and hymns from the book.

(b) A set of charts on which are enlarged versions of the pictures and diagrams used in the book; these can be employed as visual aids for various 'inputs' or exercises.

I hope the experiment of combining theory and practice will be successful and that readers will make use of the different kinds of material according to their inclination, without feeling obliged to go through every exercise on one topic before moving on to the next.

This book comes out of my experience of working with committed Christian groups over the past five years. A good deal of the writing up and editing of the material was carried out as part of my work for the Mission Institute of the Irish Missionary Union (IMU), under whose sponsorship the book is published. I am grateful to the members of the executive and staff of the IMU and to colleagues in the Institute for encouragement and support. I am also very indebted to my sister Ben Kimmerling who read various drafts of the different chapters and suggested many improvements. Her criticisms and proposals, coming from the perspective of a married lay woman, helped me to avoid the kind of theological jargon or 'in talk' that would have been off-putting to the wider audience to whom this book is addressed.

NOTES:

1. Donal Dorr, *Spirituality and Justice,* Dublin [Gill and Macmillan] and Maryknoll[Orbis] 1984, 8-18.

2. The idea of using three interlocking circles came to me from Anne Hope. She and Sally Timmel have developed the same general conception in a different way in Anne Hope and Sally Timmel, *Training for Transformation: A Handbook for Community Workers,* Gweru, Zimbabwe [Mambo Press: 1984]. Vol 1, 21.

3. This is the handbook referred to in note 2 above.

4. These materials will be available from the Communications Secretary of the Irish Missionary Union, Orwell Park, Dublin 6.

1

Down to Earth Spirituality

To walk humbly upon the Earth: this is an attitude which lies at the heart of an authentic human spirituality. We have difficulty in knowing what it means to be humble. Perhaps that is because we do not pay sufficient attention to the second part of the phrase — walking humbly *upon the earth.* Only one who is 'rooted' in the earth is in a position to avoid the extremes of arrogance and servility. People who are 'grounded', can become aware of how utterly dependent they are not merely on other people, but also on the animals and plants, and on the Earth itself: for water, food, shelter, and the very air that sustains life; how dependent they are also on the Earth for the nourishment of spirit that prevents life from being total drudgery. To be in touch with the Earth is to have the fundamental experience of solidarity with the cosmos, which underpins the solidarity we have with other human beings.

The sense of solidarity with other people is crucial to a genuine morality. Over the past twenty-five years, moral theologians have done remarkable work in rescuing us from a legalistic notion of morality, and from the belief that moral obligation comes from laws that are arbitrarily imposed on us by God. Christians are beginning to see that God put us in a world that has its own in-built basis for morality. For we share the world with sisters and brothers whose very existence calls us to respect and care for them.

But why limit our understanding of 'solidarity with others'? Why confine it merely to other human beings? Obviously, our relationships with other people are a primary component in morality. But there is a lot to be gained from situating these moral obligations within a wider web of relationships. This moral network will embrace, in appropriate ways, our obligations to respect animal and plant life and 'Mother Earth' which is the source and matrix of us all.

Most modern moral theologians seem in practice to hold that morality is essentially a matter of having respect for *humans* — ourselves and others. They do not deny that we have moral obligations in relation to animals and even in relation to the physical world; but they almost always explain these in terms of their effects on humans. For instance, they would say that cruelty to animals or insensitivity to the earth is wrong because it makes *people* cruel and insensitive. I agree that cruelty and insensitivity have these evil effects. But I would wish to go further and say that an adequate account of moral obligation must rest on a more global or cosmic approach, as outlined in the following paragraphs (and the accompanying footnotes).

Each part of the world we live in is in some sense a source of value, calling and inviting us to respect it.[1] This does not rule out human intervention in the world. For intervention is part of the pattern of the world. What is ruled out is mindless or irresponsible or disrespectful interference. We are called instead to participate responsibly in shaping the world — in co-creating it. Normally we rely on our common-sense to tell us what it means in practice to act 'respectfully' and 'responsibly', or 'disrespectfully'. But modern technology gives people the power to change the world in radical ways (e.g. changes of climate) and to damage it irreparably (e.g. the 'nuclear Winter' which could follow a nuclear war). So there is need for ethicians and moral theologians to work in close harmony with specialists in 'the human sciences' and 'the earth sciences' in working out what it really means to respect nature.[2]

It is clear that humans have a crucial role in the world, and the respect due to each human is different from that due to animals. Animals in turn call for respect in a way that is different from the respect due to plant life and the inanimate world. But just because a person is to be respected differently from an animal, a tree, or a lake, does not mean that we have no moral obligations in relation to these nonhuman parts of nature.[3] There is a certain continuity between respect for nature and respect for people. And the one who exploits the environment or animals will be inclined to exploit people as well.

All this has major implications for our spirituality. Modern science indicates that it was not just a romantic flight of fancy that led Saint Francis of Assisi to speak of 'Sister Dove' and 'Brother Ass' — and even of 'Brother Sun' and 'Sister Moon'. We humans are of the same origin and are made of the same elements as these 'sisters and brothers' — and we dare not forget it. We are all woven together into a single fabric composed of waves and atoms and sub-atomic particles — all parts of one 'cosmos'.

The notion of a 'cosmos' is not an outdated myth but a reality solidly established by science. Indeed a number of reputable scientists go much further. They support 'the Gaia hypothesis' proposed some years ago by James Lovelock.[4] 'Gaia' is the Greek word for the Earth, personified as a goddess. 'The Gaia hypothesis' is the idea that all life on the planet Earth can be looked at as though it were a single living organism which carefully regulates its environment and its different parts to ensure its own survival. This would mean that if we humans become a grave threat to the life of the Earth we might find that the Earth gets rid of us and gives our place to animals that are not a threat to the pattern of nature. In other words, we may be risking the survival of humanity by our insensitivity to the Earth, our lack of respect for the patterns of nature on which we depend.

Some enthusiastic ecologically-minded people took the notion of the Earth-goddess more seriously than Lovelock intended; it provided them with a myth around which a new nature religion could be built. In his recent second book he makes it quite clear that he does not intend us to take the word 'Gaia' too literally. He is not really saying that the Earth is a living goddess — or even that we must think of it as a single sentient and rational being, which consciously plans its future as a person would. What he is saying, however, is that it is *as though* the Earth were planning its own survival. Just as a plant might seem to be acting intelligently when it adapts its shape to take advantage of the available sunshine, so the whole complex of life on Earth can appear like a highly intelligent and powerful entity that ensures its own well-being by a wonderful series of adaptations which control and regulate the different elements of which it is composed.[5]

Understood in this way, 'the Gaia hypothesis' is coming to gain a good deal of scientific respectability. Mainstream scientists may never agree to use mythical words like 'Gaia': but they are recognising the close links between human life and the earth on which we live — and the dangers we incur if we exploit the earth in an irresponsible way. Moral theologians and people interested in spirituality must be at least equally sensitive to our links with and obligations towards, animals, plants, the Earth that sustains us, and the universe in which we live.

If our spirituality is to be truly 'rooted' in the earth it is not enough for us to have a theoretical understanding of all this. We need to have a *sense* of being part of the web of the world. In order to help people experience themselves as part of this web, I propose to include here a guided meditation on the subject. It is an adapted version of a meditation entitled 'The Web' devised by the American scholar and educator Joanna Rogers Macy.[6] Her meditation, while very deeply spiritual, is designed for use with people who may not have very explicit religious beliefs. I have been using it in workshops over the past couple of years, while working in Africa and Ireland with people who have an explicit Christian or Muslim faith. Since I could presume that those doing the meditation had faith in the loving Providence of God, I changed parts of it with the aim of evoking this faith and helping people to experience God's care for them manifested in nature and history. After giving the text of the meditation I shall explain why I felt it important to bring out the sense of the Providence of God much more explicitly.

Guided Meditation: 'The Web'

The best posture in which to do this meditation is lying on your back on a rug on the floor. But if you prefer, you could kneel on a prayer stool with your back straight, or sit in a lotus or half-lotus position, without supporting your back and making sure that your knees are touching the floor or a support (so that you feel grounded). (If you feel uncom-

15

fortable or foolish in all of these positions, you can sit upright in a straight chair, making sure that your feet are firmly on the ground.) Play quiet background music which does not have a familiar melody. Listen while somebody reads the meditation, leaving pauses, so that the whole meditation takes about thirty minutes. (If you are not part of a group, you could listen to the meditation on tape or even 'feed' it to yourself bit by bit from the book.)

Relax your body. Be aware of your breathing, and follow the breath, without forcing it . . . If you find tension in some part of the body, direct your attention there while you breathe out, allowing the tension to dissolve as the breath goes out . . . Allow the floor or the seat to support you, and allow yourself to sink into the floor. . . .

Feel the breath gliding into your lungs, filling them, stretching them . . . in . . . out . . . Allow the breathing to happen, allow the life-giving air to flow into your body, to nourish and sustain you . . . The air you breathe is shared by others in the room. The breath in your lungs at this moment was in your neighbour's lungs some minutes ago. Yesterday it may have been in the lungs of somebody a hundred miles away. The air you now take in may be the air breathed out last week by a refugee in the Sudan, by a starving child in Bangladesh, by a soldier in South Africa, or by somebody in a submarine with a finger ready to press the button that will launch a dozen nuclear bombs . . . This air sustains life in all of us, the gift of life which none of us has earned. . . .

Visualise the air entering your lungs . . . imagine each molecule of oxygen being drawn into the blood-stream . . . see how it sparks off there a little explosion of new life and energy. Picture a thousand of these tiny explosions of energy taking place in your lungs every second. See them as pinpoints of light, so many of them that they link up into streams of light. See them as filaments or threads of light and energy circulating in the blood-stream and being carried into every corner of your body, bringing you the gift of life moment by moment. . . .

See the threads of energy stretching out even beyond your body, forming a kind of aura around you. Visualise this aura of life-energy as formed of a million filaments of

16

light stretching out from you, and intersecting with the aura of those around you. Together, these filaments form a delicate web of light, of energy. Through the web you are linked to those around you . . . to the people among whom you work . . . to men, women, and children several miles from here . . . even to people in remote parts of Asia . . . Africa . . . Latin America . . . Australia . . . the Pacific . . . The web carries love and care . . . it carries pain and sadness . . . hope and joy. Open yourself up to the energies flowing in the web of life . . .

This web in which we live is not just made up of spiritual energy; it is made of the stuff of the Earth — electrical impulses, light-waves, gravity . . . all the interactions of atoms and molecules, and the emanations given off by every living being. The web links you to animals, for they are made of the same material as yourself, and breathe the same air as you. Your life has been nourished by eating the flesh of cows and sheep and pigs . . . You have made their flesh your own. . . .

The web of life links you to the plants as well. The bread you ate this morning was made of wheat which drew moisture and nourishment from the Earth; it grew and ripened and was harvested, ground and baked. It brings you minerals from the soil and energy from the sun . . . And when the time comes you will give back your body to the Earth, to provide nourishment for other living beings which will in turn give back their life, to continue the cycle of life . . . We come from the womb of life . . . we will give back our bodies to be remoulded in that womb and passed on to others . . .

The web of life existed before you; you were born into it. It extends back through time, linking you to your mother and father, your grandparents . . . and their grandmothers and grandfathers . . . Back through thousands of years . . . back to the first communities of humans who came to this land . . . Back to the very first men and women . . . and beyond them to our remote ancestors swinging in the trees . . . And beyond them to the creatures that first crawled out of the sea . . . to the very earliest forms of life. . . . The web links us to our sisters and brothers whose evolution took a different

17

direction from ours — to the birds in the air, the strange fish in the deeps of the ocean, the little insects that scurry through the grass and burrow in the Earth . . . All these are our sisters and brothers, sharing with us the bounty of our common mother, the Earth . . .

The web of connectedness existed even before life developed on Earth. Reach back along it to the time when the solar system first took shape . . . And back millions of years further, to the time when the universe first came into being . . .

Now glide forward again along the web, noticing the pattern, the direction . . . Have a sense of how the universe has taken a shape that made life possible. You may wish to picture the Spirit of God brooding over the primeval waters . . . giving pattern . . . drawing forth life . . . directing the whole process of evolution, according to the creative, loving plan of God . . . Have a sense of that mysterious power that is beyond and above and beneath the world, shaping it with utter delicacy and total respect . . .

By faith you know that God loved you before you came to be, and showed that love by shaping your pre-history . . . God had you in mind when forming the world . . . The divine power was at work in the million coincidences that brought your remotest ancestors together . . . that gave you the unique genetic heritage you carry — the legacy of millions of years . . . Allow yourself to appreciate the loving Providence that chose for you a country and a home . . . that was present at the meeting of your great-grandparents . . . that smiled for you when your parents were born . . . that was present in the love that drew your mother and father together . . . that understood the coincidence that allowed your mother to conceive you at that particular moment . . . that gave you your own unique place in the web of the world and the web of life . . .

Open yourself once again to the energies flowing in the web — the light, the excitement, the creativity constantly at work . . . And do not close yourself off from the pain that comes along the strands of the web . . . For if you shut out the pain, you are shutting out the life . . . Grieve with the mother whose baby has starved to death in the Sudan . . . Feel the frustration of the lion locked up in a zoo . . .

18

Sense the pain of the Earth as the tropical forest is burned away . . . Allow yourself to experience the threat of the nuclear weapons that lurk in the oceans and spin in orbit around the Earth . . . Let in the pain, the danger, so that it will not be blocked and turn sour . . . If it flows it may touch the love and the creative power that flows in the web . . . Perhaps the pain and the danger can be transformed . . . For the Earth has its own deep springs of life and hope . . . And we believe that there is a Providential power at work in and beyond our world, a power that draws life out of death, good out of evil . . .

We who are part of the web at this critical time, we are called to be agents of healing and hope . . . agents of the providence that brings hope where all seems dark . . . We open ourselves once more to our sisters and brothers who share the web with us . . . to the tears and the laughter of our friends and of all humanity . . . to the movement of the whale through the ocean depths . . . to the power of the storm as it lashes the mountain-tops . . . to the energy locked deep in the heart of the Earth . . . to the slow shift of the continents . . . to the spinning energy of the molecules all around us and within us . . . and to the loving Providence that works through them all.

This is a dark time . . . a time of fear . . . but also a time to hope . . . a time to face the darkness and reach out beyond it in confidence of new life . . . For we do not face the dark alone . . . We are part of the web and from it we draw strength . . . We give ourselves into it, allow ourselves to be cradled within it, nourished and sustained, and led into the future . . .

Still sensing our connection with others and with the web of the world, we return to this room . . . stretch . . . and, when we feel ready, slowly open our eyes . . .

Providence

The reason why I have adapted the meditation on 'The Web' to focus it especially on the loving plan of God is that the experience of being in the hands of Providence is at the heart of my own spirituality. It is not a matter of some kind of abstract belief but a matter of fact: I experience events in my life as coming from God. I talk to God about them: I

19

complain, I argue, and sometimes I shout. After such 'dialogue' I usually end up smiling ruefully — but occasionally the smile is one of real joy.

This vivid and explicit sense of providence sometimes makes me feel oddly out of place in our secularised world. I know many good people — even deeply committed Christians — who do not share the experience. So I examine my conscience: could it be just an escape, a way to avoid facing up to the full horror of the Holocaust of the Jews under Hitler, to the atrocities committed in defence of apartheid in Southern Africa, and to the glaring injustices in my own country? I don't think so; in fact my sense of God's providential care seems rather to fortify the commitment to resist such evils.

The sense of providence is such a gift that I wonder how I might share it with others. I can locate elements in my own life-story that must have helped to foster it. For instance, I grew up a stone's throw from the Providence Woollen Mills where my father worked. This factory was opened nearly a hundred years ago to give employment in an impoverished West of Ireland village — opened in the face of impossible odds by a religious Sister whose motto was: 'Providence did provide, Providence can provide, Providence will provide'. But what of all those typically 'modern' people who have never lived in a situation where faith in Providence was embodied so strikingly? If the sense of Providence is to be central to their spirituality, they need some experience in which God's care is 'incarnated' or embodied before their eyes.

We see this in most of the great religions. The Jewish people looked at their own *history* and could see at work in it the powerful hand of God. The life and words of the human person *Jesus* were experienced by the first Christians as convincing evidence of the presence of God in their midst. The indigenous peoples of North America experienced the presence of the Great Spirit in the *land* over which they roamed. The traditional 'primal' peoples of Africa and elsewhere experience the power and presence of God in *nature* — the fertility of the soil, the gift of rain, and the unpredictable power of lightning. The Hindu believer experiences the One in and through the many human *consciousnesses*.

Unless we in the Western (or Westernised) world find something that mediates to us the sense of God's care for the world, we are in grave danger of losing the world entirely. We may lose it in a quite literal sense — in a total nuclear war, or in the slow death of the life-supporting systems of the world. Alternatively, we may lose our world in a more psychological and cultural sense — losing our way through the loss of meaning and the erosion of values; and there are indications that this is happening in some sectors of the Western secularised world. But where can 'modern' people find a mediation of the presence of God similar to that provided by world religions? What could provide them with a conviction of the care of God at work in a very concrete way in their lives and world?

Some would say that to ask this question is simply to pine for a past pre-scientific world; science, they say, has secularised us and banished God from the world. But I believe with Teilhard de Chardin that our sense of God can be nourished by science rather than undermined by it. The secularization which genuine science brings is one that allows God to be really God. The God we can now find is not 'a God of the gaps', used as an explanation for the things that science has as yet failed to account for. A proper understanding of science removes God from being just one of the many secondary causes at work within the world. This sets us free to realise that God is transcendent, beyond our world; and for that very reason God is able to be immanent, present in the whole process of the cosmos rather than just in some parts of it.

Our best way forward is to grow in our understanding of the processes at work in nature — the development of the universe and of the solar system over countless millions of years, the emergence of life on earth and its slow evolution, and so on. In the past, believers experienced God's presence especially in *particular events* of life — for instance, in the coming of rain as an answer to prayer, or in the bolt of lightning that strikes inexplicably. Today, we must experience God at work in the very *processes* of the world — for instance, in the rhythm of nature by which life leads to death, and death to new life. My hope is that 'modern' people can come to have a sense of God's care for them in each event, precisely because they have learned to appreciate God's presence to the world first of all in the whole process — in the web of life and the very fabric of the world. We do not have to limit God's presence to our inner 'spiritual' life, since God is equally at work in the 'public' world. For those who have eyes to see it, 'the world is charged with the grandeur of God', to use Gerard Manley Hopkins' phrase.

My understanding of a 'down to earth' spirituality is not one where communion with Nature is substituted for communion with God. Rather it is one where we grow in a sense of the personal loving care of God according as our understanding of the natural world increases and our sensitivity to what is going on expands and deepens. This requires a twofold move forward:

— Firstly, we need to move out from our familiar and limited world — by learning more and more of the marvels of the universe[7] which range from the birth of galaxies to the complexities of the genetic codes that determine the patterns of living beings. We can do this by keeping in touch with developments in science, not confining attention to the technological implications but focussing especially on the 'cosmological' aspects, i.e. those that affect our overall conception of the world.

— Secondly, we need to go deep — pausing to reflect, to explore the personal implications of these marvels, to contemplate them and allow them to touch and nourish the depths of our spirit. We can do this by taking time alone, especially in some 'wilderness' place where we can have a sense of the wonder and beauty of nature. We can also make use of meditations such as the one on 'the Web', given above.

These are ways in which we can develop a spirituality which is not merely 'down to earth' but is also characterised by the quality of 'ecological wisdom'.

SECTION TWO: ECOLOGICAL WISDOM

By ecological wisdom I mean a deep *awareness* of myself as part of the web of life here on earth and a fundamental *respect* for the patterns of nature. This is present in an unreflective way in primal peoples all over the world. But the modern Western pattern of living has replaced it with an exploitative attitude to our environment. There are four main reasons why ecological wisdom is a crucial part of any genuine Christian spirituality today:

— Firstly, it is a matter of justice. When we use the resources of the earth wastefully we are stealing from future generations. Furthermore, the wasteful use of resources by rich nations and classes takes place at the expense of poor nations and people. For instance, land that is badly needed by the peasants of Kenya and Brazil to grow their corn or rice is taken to grow coffee for export to the West.

— Secondly, we need to be in touch with unpolluted earth and sea to nourish our spirit. We cannot survive long unless we are in touch with the beauty of nature, and experience at times the freedom and space of a wilderness place. These are not luxuries but necessities of the human spirit.

— Thirdly, when I come into touch with nature I may begin to 'walk humbly' as God calls us to do (Micah 6:8). Then I may come to realise that I am not the only important thing in the world — and even that there is beauty and majesty and power in the world that is beyond any human measure (Job 38, 39).

— Fourthly, the balance of nature and the survival of life on the planet are now under threat. This last point is one which I shall treat in the following pages.

A World Under Threat

There is a great fragility of the balance of nature. The web of life is being undermined by modern so-called 'development'. Last year I listened to a woman from Ghana telling the story of the dreadful economic crisis which shattered her country a few years ago. She pointed out that one key factor in that disaster was the indiscriminate cutting down of the forests in the name of economic development. The country needed the 'hard currency' gained from selling the timber; and the plan was that the land would be farmed once the forest was cleared. But when the trees were cut down the soil became eroded and the climate changed, so droughts became more common — and the result was food shortages and the impoverishment of millions of people. Variants of this story come from all over the Third World. Just to give one more example: we now know that the 'fast food' hamburger industry of North America and Europe has led to a massive burning down of the rain forests in Central America, to provide land for cattle ranches; within a few years the soil becomes eroded and is incapable of growing either grass or trees.[8]

The Use and Abuse of Science

Why does modern 'development' lead to such ruthless and reckless behaviour? Behind the destruction lies an attitude of exploitation which has been a basic ingredient of Western culture in recent centuries. Western scientific achievements and the scientific mentality are often cited as an explanation for our exploitative attitude to nature.[9] Western science has promoted a mechanistic outlook: it treats the universe as a kind of machine that is there to be used and controlled purely for our own benefit. The technology which is based on the sciences of physics and chemistry enables people to 'exploit' the resources of nature; and it is significant that in this context this word 'exploit' is still used widely and unashamedly.

But I think we need to look even more critically at Western *economic* science, both in its capitalistic and its Marxist versions. For it is economics that provides the more immediate justification for the exploitative mentality. Both capitalist and Marxist economics promote and justify an attitude of aggression in relation to people:

— Capitalist economics explicitly reduces human labour to a commodity to be bought and sold; in this way it provides a justification for the widespread exploitation of workers.

— Marxist economics can also encourage a ruthless attitude towards others — by laying great emphasis on the inevitability of class-war.

This attitude towards *people* is closely linked to the attitudes these models of economics inculcate in relation to *nature*. What both have in common is an assumption that nature is simply a resource to be used or even plundered for the benefit of the present generation of humans. Just to give one obvious example: there is nothing that I know of in either capitalist or Marxist economics that shows up the folly of the incredibly wasteful way in which the limited oil and gas resources of the world have been exploited; untold

24

amounts of natural gas are burned off in order to allow the oil to be reached more conveniently.

I conclude from this that we are in dire need of a new version of economic science. It must be one that puts a true economic value on *all* our resources — for instance on clean air and water, and on the reserves of gas and oil that are still underground. Once this is done it will be easier to demand that those who introduce high technology should pay its *full* cost, rather than leaving that to be paid by the community or future generations.

This revised economic science must also take far more account of values which at present become gradually eroded because the economists largely ignore them or take them for granted — such values as the dignity of individuals, the sense of being rooted in a particular location and community, harmony and cooperation in communities and regions, the meaning and sense of purpose given to a whole people by a common culture and tradition. To this list I would add other items which people need to recognise as values — for instance, the traditional partnership that existed between humans and farm animals until mass-production techniques led human 'producers' to think of poultry, pigs, or cattle purely as 'products' to be exploited; another example is the value of living near some kind of 'wilderness' (e.g. a woodland, a mountain, a lake or an ocean) which is not seen simply as a place to be exploited.

Such a revised economic science would underpin a more authentic model of economic development, linked to appropriate political and social policies. These would be designed to promote a pattern of life that we will find attractive and worth striving for — but one that is also sustainable. All this must take place at the local level and the national level. But it also requires a much higher degree of *international* solidarity than exists at present.

An example may help to bring home the urgent need for greater international cooperation. It is now clear that the cutting down of the tropical rain-forests is depriving the Earth of its main source of oxygen; this may quickly lead to severe ecological disruption, caused by what is called 'the greenhouse effect' i.e. a build-up of carbon dioxide in the atmosphere. But governments of poorer countries committed to 'development' say they cannot afford to forbid the cutting down of the forests. The most just and practical solution to this problem would be for every country to dedicate a certain amount of land for forests, so as to ensure that the world as a whole has enough oxygen. Most countries would grow the forests on their own territory. But a country like Holland could negotiate with, say, Indonesia to provide Holland's share: the Dutch would pay the Indonesians to preserve an extra share of their forests. Such international cooperation is no longer just a pious aspiration. It is an urgent necessity if the Earth and its inhabitants are to have a future.

The ecological issue cannot, of course, be understood or tackled in isolation. It is intimately related to three other vital issues:
— There is the question of the destruction of thousands of traditional cultures which have endured for centuries, giving meaning in life to millions of people; this fund of experience of ways of being human, which had seemed to be inexhaustible, is now dwindling rapidly — and whole nations and peoples are losing their sense of identity.
— There is the issue of social justice — the ever-widening gap in wealth and power between classes, races, countries and whole continents.
— Finally there is the threat of obliteration which hangs over our world from the nuclear and bacteriological arms-race — an arms-race which is also gobbling up the resources needed to overcome poverty and protect the environment.

In other chapters of this book I have something to say about these three issues that are so intimately related to the ecological question.

Christian Basis

The exploitative element in the Western attitude to physical and economic science reflects the Western 'cosmology' or world-view. If this exploitative attitude towards nature and people is to be replaced by one of partnership, the new attitude will have to be rooted in a different world-view.

A key figure in the attempt to replace the older Christian cosmology with a 'new story' of creation is Thomas Berry — a cultural historian and theologian, former professor of the history of religions, president of the American Teilhard

26

Association, and founder of the 'Center for Religious Research' in Riverdale, New York. A good deal of his work consists of what one might call 'clearing the undergrowth'. By this I mean that he is pointing out the inadequacy of the world-view out of which most Western Christians have been living in recent centuries. Berry maintains that the older Christian cosmology is inadequate because it is too static; and in any case this creation cosmology was largely replaced by a very deficient redemption mystique — the idea of escaping out of the world.[10]

Berry and his disciples believe that the Judeo-Christian tradition has played a considerable role in justifying an exploitative attitude to the natural world. One has only to think of the emphasis we have laid on God's mandate to the first humans: 'conquer the earth' (Gen 1:28). In a fairly recent book, Sean McDonagh points out how such a biblical outlook is conditioned by the situation in which the Jews lived: for them life was a constant battle against the elements'.[11] In other parts of the world, by contrast, life can be experienced in the main as a partnership with nature rather than a struggle; this would give rise to a different mindset, one that is far more appropriate for the Christian today. Berry himself argues that the strong biblical stress on montheism and the transcendence of God had an unfortunate effect: 'the natural world was to some extent despiritualised and desacralised'.[12] He also points out that the Bible gave rise to the notion that a perfect 'millennial' state is to come about as part of human history; in recent Western history, says Berry, this notion has been transformed into the commitment to transform the world totally through technology — even if this means despoiling the earth in the process![13]

Some biblical scholars feel that Berry is rather too sweeping in attributing to the Bible the inadequacies of the present dominant Christian world-view. It would be more accurate, it is claimed, to blame the European historical context in which the Bible has been read.[14] But whatever about these nuances, the central point remains: we need to rethink our easy assumption that the Bible and our Christian faith give us a mandate to exploit the earth.

There is some basis in Christianity for 'the new story'. It has not yet been developed at any great depth, but some of the elements are already available to us. Within the Christian community the new emphasis on 'creation-centred spirituality' is an important contribution. A central element in this approach is the idea that 'original sin' is not the fundamental human reality; far more basic is 'original blessing' — the fact that each of us, and humanity as a whole, have been given marvellous gifts which we have to learn to recognise and use. Another important contribution towards 'the new story' can come from the Christian feminist theology which is developing so rapidly today. A major strand of feminism seeks to put us more deeply in touch with Mother Earth and its rhythms. This strengthens the links between Christian faith and an attitude of ecological sensitivity.

If we are to develop a theology that evokes respect for the Earth then we must do so in dialogue with other religious traditions. They, too, have their inadequacies, as Berry points out.[15] But there is so much that we can learn from the Hindu and Buddhist traditions; think, for instance, of the understanding of the unity of the cosmos that lies behind the notion of Karma and re-incarnation. More difficult, but perhaps even more important, is being open to the 'primal' religions of tribal societies; for many of them are cults of the Earth.

It is not enough for us in the West to have dialogue with the religious traditions of other parts of the world. We need also to listen to the poorly articulated religious yearnings of people in the Western world who do not find much nourishment in our version of Christianity. In recent years even in 'Christian Ireland' I have met hundreds of people who are spiritually hungry. Some are people who have drifted away from the Church or have rejected it decisively. Others are still Christian but they find the Church too cold, too logical, too scared of affectivity, too much out of touch with the human body and with nature. They are looking for an experiential type of religion — one that will teach them to meditate, that will open them up, perhaps, even to mystical experience.

Such people are looking for a spirituality of the body as well as of the spirit. Some deep instinct leads them to reject the kind of dualism that separates the spirit from the body and the individual from the world. They want a faith that brings a sense of wholeness, a healing of the total person — the embodied spirit. They feel the need for religious practices that will put them in touch with the rhythms of nature; that will open them up to prayer and in this way help them to tune in to their own inner sources of life and energy; then they can find a sense of direction, even a sense of being guided from within.

All these are deeply religious people, dissatisfied with the triviality and exploitativeness of modern society. They should be able to find themselves at home in the Christian community. Yet the Church has not been able to offer them much help — perhaps because Church people tend to be too limited in their vision and too complacent about the adequacy of the present model of Christianity. Christian preaching and teaching does not offer these 'searchers' the kind of guidelines they need for their search. No wonder then that many of them remain lost, or confused, or pulled from one fad to the next. I believe that a Christian theology that has been radically transformed by becoming thoroughly sensitive to the ecological question is the kind of faith that many are looking for. In this situation there is a really urgent need for many Christian theologians to read the signs of the times and get in touch with the deep religious currents that are flowing through the lives of so many men and women in our apparently secularised world. We need a theology that corresponds to, and underpins, the work being done by activists like Petra Kelly of the Green Party in West Germany, Mary O'Donnell of 'Earthwatch' in Ireland, and Johanna Macy in the USA.

It would be great if we now had available to us a clearly articulated Christian theology that was integral, 'grounded', and cosmic. But to expect to have such a developed theology at this stage is quite unrealistic. It can only emerge 'from the ground up' (literally), i.e. from a new commitment and spirituality of action in the world. If we can get our Christian attitudes and commitments right, then the theological vision will follow. This is not to say that the theology is mere 'icing on the cake'. Theology has an important role to play. It will serve the faith by providing a coherent and inspiring articulation of our beliefs. But the main breakthrough will have to come 'on the ground'. Christian communities and individual Christians must develop a spirituality which combines belief in God's providence and human salvation in Christ with a deeper sensitivity to the beauty, the energy, and the fragility of our world. In this way we can play our part in saving the world.

Saving the World

'To save the world' — that is a phrase that has become such a Christian cliché that we seldom stop to think what the words really mean. The phrase conjures up, perhaps, a notion of all people becoming Christians. I want here to suggest that nowadays we need to take the words more literally. The world, the Earth, needs to be saved from destruction. There is some basis in the Scriptures for this idea. Look carefully at the following passage from St Paul's letter to the Romans:

> . . . creation still retains the hope of being freed, like us, from its slavery to decadence, to enjoy the same freedom and glory as the children of God. From the beginning until now the entire creation, as we know, has been groaning in travail, in birthpangs, and not only creation, but all of us who possess the first-fruits of the Spirit, we too groan inwardly as we wait for our bodies to be set free. For we must be content to hope that we shall be saved — our salvation is not in sight, we should not have to be hoping for it if it were — but, as I say, we must hope to be saved since we are not saved yet — it is something we must wait for with patience (Rom 8:20-25).

This is an extremely rich passage, but there are just three points I would like to stress here:

— Firstly, creation itself, our world, is enslaved to decadence and is groaning in pain.

— Secondly, in the light of our faith we can interpret this decadence and pain in a hopeful way; the pain may seem entirely negative but our faith gives us the sure hope that this is the pain of childbirth — a new and better world is being brought forth, out of the present decadence.

— Thirdly, *we* are part of creation, sharing its pain, its hope, and the process of the new birth.

In recent years the words of St Paul seem more true than ever. Our world is indeed sunk in decadence and groaning

30

in travail. The air we breathe is becoming polluted, the sea around us is being poisoned, forests are dying or being slaughtered. No wonder our world is in anguish. The whole web of life is under serious threat — the threat of the slow death of decadence as life withers away as a result of poisons and lack of nourishment. Furthermore, our creation, our world, is also under threat of a more sudden death brought about by atomic war or nuclear accident. All this has come about as an inevitable consequence of the model of development which is being imposed by the Western world on the whole world. It is a type of development that is intrinsically exploitative — it exploits people who have little power, and it ruthlessly exploits the planet which, by God's power, has brought forth and sustained human life.

In this situation we can see that 'saving the world' doesn't just mean bringing about the 'conversion' of far away peoples but also, and perhaps above all, the salvation of our threatened planet. This means committing ourselves to the search for a model of human development that is fundamentally respectful — of people and of the earth that nourishes us. It is not enough to denounce the exploitation of people and nature. We must also be actively involved in developing a more just and more sustainable model of human living to replace the present decadent and exploitative one that is killing people and raping our planet. What we need is a model that enables us to live as part of nature and in partnership with the rest of our world.

SECTION THREE: RESOURCES AND EXERCISES

In this section I shall offer first some passages from a modern novel which may be used as a basis for personal or group reflection. Then I shall suggest a practical exercise which may be used by a group to foster their sense of respect for nature.

Partnership or Utopia?

Some of the most effective accounts of what the world might look like if it were organised in an ecologically sensitive manner are to be found not in scientific books and articles but in novels of fantasy or science fiction; and I think it is no coincidence that some of the best of these are by women writers.

In her novel, *Woman on the Edge of Time*,[16] Marge Piercy offers a deeply moving and sustained account of the contrast between life 'at the bottom' in our present world and life in a possible future that takes ecological issues seriously. Here I offer some quotations to indicate the kind of conversion of attitudes that is involved in what some people are beginning to call 'deep ecology' issues.

Luciente, a woman from the future, is explaining to Connie, a woman from our time, the fundamental outlook or 'religion' that permeates the life of the people of the future who try to live in partnership with the world:

'We have limited resources. We plan cooperatively. We can afford to waste nothing. You might say our "religion" makes us see ourselves as partners with water, air, birds, fish, trees.'

'We learned a lot from societies that people used to call primitive. Primitive technically. But socially sophisticated. . . . We tried to learn from cultures that dealt well with handling conflict, promoting cooperation, coming of age, growing a sense of community, getting sick, aging, going mad, dying, — '

[Connie:] 'Yeah, and you still go crazy. You still get sick. You grow old. You die. I thought in a hundred and fifty years some of these problems would be solved, anyhow!'

'But Connie, some problems you *solve* only if you stop being human, become metal, plastic, robot computer. Is dying itself a *problem*?'.[17]

Later on, Connie is brought to see an old lady dying by the river-bank and she protests:

'If she was in a hospital she might not die.'

'But why not die?' [replied Luciente]: 'Sappho is eighty-two. A good time to give back . . . Everybody gives back. We all carry our death at the core — if you don't know that, your life is hollow, no? This is a good death . . . Connie, your old way appears barbaric to us, trying to keep the rotting body. To pretend we are not made of elements ancient as the earth, that we do not owe those elements back to the web of all living . . . For us a good death is one come in the fullness of age, without much pain, and in clear mind. A full life is a used life! . . . You should sit in on the wake with us! You'll see. It feels beautiful, it feels good'.[18]

32

On another occasion, the people from the future describe to Connie their approach to work, explaining that, apart from emergencies and the times of planting and harvesting, there is plenty of time for leisure and for being with children:

' . . . after we dumped the jobs telling people what to do, counting money and moving it about, making people do what they don't want or bashing them for doing what they want, we have lots of people to work. Kids work, old folks work, women and men work. We put a lot of work into feeding everybody without destroying the soil, keeping up its health and fertility. With most everybody at it part time, nobody breaks their back and grubs dawn to dusk like old-time farmers'.[19]

'You eat well here, anyhow,'

'Very important! Enough food, good food, nourishing food. We care a lot that all have that. Nobody born now anyplace on the whole world, Connie, is born to less . . . Instead of competing for a living, for scarce resources, for food, we try to cooperate on all that'.[20]

'Coffee, tea, sugar, tobacco, they all took land needed to feed local people who were starving. Now some land is used for world luxuries, but most for necessary crops'.[21]

In this future world the people are willing to use advanced technology when that is appropriate — for instance, in computers and for really unpleasant or dangerous kinds of work. But they use it with a great deal of restraint because they are very aware of the limits to the resources and energy that are available:

'We have so much energy from the sun, so much from wind, so much from decomposing wastes, so much from waves, so much from the river, so much from alcohol from wood, so much from wood gas.' Luciente checked them off on her fingers. 'That's a fixed amount . . .'[22]

If one community were to use too much of the limited resources, they would leave others short. Therefore, communities negotiate about the use of resources; and in this dialogue they appoint one person as 'Earth Advocate' to speak 'on behalf of the total environment', and another person as 'Animal Advocate' to speak on behalf of the animals. Local decisions are taken locally, but decisions affecting other areas have to be brought to regional councils.[23]

People take turns to represent their area; and special efforts are made to ensure that the political power which people are given does not 'go to their heads'. Luciente explains about a person called 'Grey Fox' who held an important position for some time:

> 'Last month that person was chairing the economic planning council of Massachusetts-Connecticut-Rhode Island . . .
>
> But after a year on the economic council and nine months chairing it, Grey Fox may come to identify with that job . . . May come to feel that it's part of the essence of Grey Fox to make big decisions while others look up . . . So right now Grey Fox is on a six month shepherding duty. After we've served in a way that seems important, we serve in a job usually done by young people waiting to begin an apprenticeship or crossers atoning for a crime . . .[24]

With a view to helping committed groups or individuals to do some serious reflection based on the above excerpts from Marge Piercy's book I suggest the following questions:
— What are the feelings you experience as you read the passages (or, better, the whole novel)?
— Do you identify with the disappointment of Connie about the way the people of the future accept death? What are your own views about the use of high technology to prolong life? Would you have different priorities?
— How do you react to the idea that people who have exercised a lot of power over others should spend time, like 'Grey Fox' doing simple work that brings them close to the Earth?
— Do you think the whole pattern of life described in the book is a good one? Is it unrealistic? If so, why? If it is realistic, how do you think we might work towards it? What are the major obstacles, and how could they be overcome?

If these or similar questions are being used in a group, try not to get into arguments or theoretical discussion; stay, as far as possible, at the level of sharing of personal feelings, attitudes, and convictions — with a lot of respectful listening.

Ecological Trust-Walk

I conclude this chapter by outlining a practical exercise which can help people to develop a spirituality that incorporates sensitivity to the environment. It is an adaptation of an exercise that is commonly used in groups to build up the level of trust in the group. This modified version of the exercise should also lead to an increase of trust; but its primary purpose is to put people in touch with the wonder of the world around them. The original exercise is usually called a 'Blind Walk' or a 'Trust-Walk'; so this variant may be called an 'Ecological Trust-Walk'. Note that the usual 'Trust-Walk' can be a very amusing and exciting event, leading to a lot of hilarity; but if you are organizing the 'Ecological Trust-Walk' try to evoke instead an atmosphere of quiet and reverence.

Begin the exercise by explaining its purpose briefly (as above) and checking out whether the members of the group would like to take part. If some of the people present have done the usual 'Trust-Walk' previously, tell them that their experience may be different on this occasion. If the members of the group want to undertake the exercise, ask them to divide into pairs. Each member of the pair has an opportunity to be led blindfold by the partner for about fifteen minutes; then, after a short pause, the roles will be reversed, so that the person who had been the leader is now blindfold and led by the other. The whole exercise is done in silence.

While the blindfolds are being put on, speak to the 'leaders'. Suggest that they steer their blindfold partners out into the open air and find interesting experiences for them — allowing them, for instance, to feel the breeze on their faces, to explore the texture of the bark of a tree, or of a blade of grass — using not only their hands but also, perhaps, their bare feet, or their faces. Remind them to make the journey safe for the partner, not trying to give them a fright or a surprise, but enabling them to use all their senses, except sight, to experience the variety and wonder of nature. The way they lead the partner should inspire reverence and a contemplative attitude.

Each 'leader' should keep track of the time. When the fifteen minutes are nearly over, the leaders very quietly steer their partners back to the room, or to some quiet place where the blindfolds are gently removed — while still maintaining a reverent silence. The person who has been blindfolded may need a few moments for reflection; then the roles are reversed. At the end of the second fifteen minutes the partners may quietly share what the experience meant to them. Afterwards, the whole group may share a little, and perhaps take time to be silent together as well.

NOTES

1. I should note that in some ways my position is very similar to that of the well-known moralist James M. Gustafson; but there are also very significant differences. The following references illustrate the similarity: *Ethics from a Theocentric Perspective, Vol.1: Theology and Ethics*, Chicago and London (University of Chicago Press: 1981), 82: 'Man is always the *measurer* of all things . . . But to be the measurer of all things does not necessarily imply that all things are to be in the service of man.' *Ibid.*,88: Gustafson suggests that we should ask not just 'What is of value to human beings?' but 'What is good not only for man but for the natural world of which man is a part?' *Ibid*, Vol. 2 (1984) 135: Gustafson adapts Kant's practical imperative to extend beyond the human sphere — 'Act so that you consider all things never only as a means to your own ends or even to collective human ends.' Cf 'A Theocentric Interpretation of Life', *The Christian Century* XCVII, No 25, 1980, 755: Many contemporaries feel the need 'to enlarge the range of considerations involved in ethics . . . to see our actions in relation not only to historical events, but also to the wider natural world.'

There are two main points on which I disagree with Gustafson. Firstly, he presents this moral approach as *more theocentric* than the approach which bases moral obligation more or less exclusively on the value of humans. In my opinion each of these approaches allows morality to have a certain autonomy; and each of them can become theocentric when inserted in a larger religious context. Secondly, Gustafson seems at times to play down the centrality of humans in the cosmos to an extent which I find unacceptable.

(I am greatly indebted to Martin Reilly, of St Patrick's College, Kiltegan, Ireland, who in conversation and by allowing me to use his doctoral dissertation on this subject, has helped me to understand and critique Gustafson's position).

The position I have outlined finds some support from Gustavo Gutiérrez. This viewpoint is implicit in his book *On Job: God-Talk and the Suffering of the Innocent* (Maryknoll, Orbis: 1987). More recently, in his lectures, he has stressed the point that passages such as Chapters 38 and 39 of the Book of Job bring out the fact that humanity is by no means the sum total of creation, so our outlook on the world should not be totally human-centred.

2. Cf Gustafson, *Ethics* . . . Vol 2, 295: 'The patterns and processes of interdependence of life in the world are a *basis, foundation or ground* upon which ethical reflection is further developed, and which must be taken into account in determining the values and principles that are to guide human ends and action . . . [But] the patterns are not sufficient to determine what we are enabled and required to do.'; *ibid.*, Vol.1, 92: ' . . . material considerations for a normative ethics are to be derived not only with reference to man, but with reference to the place of human beings in a larger ordering of life and nature in history.'

3. Cf James M. Gustafson, 'A Response to Critics', *Journal of Religious Ethics*, 13 (1985), 208: ' . . . since human beings are part of a larger whole, I necessarily have to give fairly high priority to issues which threaten the nonhuman world and not only for the sake of the preservation of human life.'; idem, *Ethics* . . . ,Vol. 2, 243: 'Persons who develop resources for the human population have to be sensitive to the natural needs for the sustenance of the rest of nature both because of human dependence on it and for the sake of nature's own flourishing.'; cf *Ibid.*, 112 and 284.

4. For a brief popular outline of 'the Gaia hypothesis' see, for instance, Frank Barnaby (general editor), *The Gaia Peace Atlas: Survival in the Third Millennium,* London, Sydney and Auckland (Pan Books: 1988), 10, 233-4. See also Norman Myers (general editor), *Gaia: An Atlas of Planet Management,* New York (Doubleday: 1984) and London (Pan Books: 1985).

5. See James Lovelock, *The Ages of Gaia* (Oxford University Press: 1988).

6. Joanna Rogers Macy, *Despair and Personal Power in the Nuclear Age,* Philadelphia Pa. (New Society Publishers: 1983), 128-130. With the permission of the publishers, I have adapted the material considerably.

7. See for instance the cosmological account of the universe in Stephen W. Hawking. *A Brief History of Time: From the Big Bang to Black Holes.* London and New York (Bantam Press: 1988).

8. *cf* Sean McDonagh, *To Care for the Earth: a Call to a New Theology,* London (Chapman: 1986), 35.

9. e.g. McDonagh, *op. cit.,*

10. See, for instance, his booklet, *The New Story (Teilhard Studies Number 1. Winter 1978),* Chambersburg (Anima Books: 1978).

11. *Op. cit.,* 112.

12. Thomas Berry, 'Economics: Its Effect on the Life Systems of the World', in Anne Lonergan and Caroline Richards (editors), *Thomas Berry and the New Cosmology,* Mystic, Connecticut (Twenty-Third Publications: 1987), 15.

13. *Ibid.,* 16-17.

14. See, for instance, Donald Senior, 'The Earth Story: Where Does the Bible Fit In?' in Lonergan and Richards, *op. cit.,* 41-50. Senior blames, not the Bible, but 'the worldview of Greek thought and the urbanised context of later European experience' for the emergence of an exploitative attitude to the earth (*ibid.,* 48).

15. Berry, 'Economics: Its Effect . . . ', 25: 'My own view is that . . . the existing religious traditions are too distant from our new sense of the universe to be adequate to the task that is before us. We cannot do without the traditional religions, but they cannot presently do what needs to be done.'

16. London (The Women's Press: 1979); New York (Alfred Knopf: 1976).

17. *Ibid.*, 125. Punctuation slightly adjusted.

18. *Ibid.*, 156-7, 162.

19. *Ibid.*, 128-9.

20. *Ibid.*, 174.

21. *Ibid.*, 195.

22. *Ibid.*, 129.

23. *Ibid.*, 150-2.

24. *Ibid.*, 251-2

2

Prayer and Power

In the previous chapter I looked at one of the ways in which the personal dimension of spirituality overlaps with its public dimension. In this second chapter I propose to focus attention on another such area, namely, the way in which personal prayer has an effect on the power we exert in our relationships with others.

SECTION ONE: THE POWER OF PRAYER

One of the major difficulties in developing a holistic spirituality is that, in modern Western society, prayer and other 'spiritual' affairs have been largely confined to a 'private' world. Prayer is seen as a personal matter — or at most as a domestic affair. There seems to be an almost un-bridgeable chasm between prayer and political activity. Therefore prayer and spirituality appear to be quite irrelevant to the shaping of the wider world.

In recent years, liberation theology has gone some way towards remedying the split between prayer and politics, by developing a spirituality of political activity. In doing so it has a solid foundation in the fact that for the peoples of Africa, Asia, and Latin America, religion has not been privatised. It is not surprising, then, that the sermons preached by Archbishop Romero were political events as well as religious ones; so too are the funerals of people murdered by 'security forces' in South Africa. But the more secularised Western world has, for the most part, remained quite resistant to this development. (Exceptions are the spirituality of the peace movement and the 'sanctuary' movements in North America, the emergent spirituality of ecology, and the spirituality of reconciliation of those who work for peace in Northern Ireland and elsewhere. I touch on these elsewhere in this book. Here

39

I just want to note that as yet they have touched the lives of only a very small number of people in the Western world.)

In this chapter I shall try to show what a mistake it is to imagine that prayer belongs to the private sphere only. I shall examine how personal prayer can nourish one's power and how it can help us to use this power properly in our relationships with others. Human relationships of all kinds, from the international level right down to the family level, involve the use or abuse of power. I shall focus attention here mainly on the use of power in our everyday interpersonal relationships, where we normally try to cooperate with other people, but sometimes find ourselves engaged in a power struggle with them. If we can appreciate how relevant prayer is to such domestic struggles, then we will see that it is equally relevant to the power struggles which take place on the larger scale in local, national, or international politics. Prayer is relevant to all such politics because it nourishes our personal power and helps us use it wisely.

Personality and Power

When I look at two dogs facing up to each other I see that their relationship is not determined purely by size or brute strength. Each of them has a certain 'presence' which seems to be a compound of strength, courage, restraint, and a sense of self-worth. This 'presence' is picked up by the other; and it determines how the other reacts. I think much the same happens when dogs meet people, and also when people meet each other. The influence we exert on others has far more to do with our 'presence' than with logical arguments,

Some people have a stronger presence than others, so their opinions and proposals are more likely to be heard and accepted. Are they then *dominating* others? To call it domination is to give a moral label to something that is pre-moral; at this stage it is simply a psychological fact that some people are more convincing, more credible, than others. How one uses this power is a moral matter. Do I take advantage of my credibility to convince people of something that is less than the whole truth? Do you use the force of your personality to persuade people to do something that is not in their best interests? Here is where we must examine our consciences.

40

But we are under no obligation to switch off our persuasive power; that is a gift from God that should not be hidden or stunted but used and developed.

This power of personality is much more complex in us than in animals. There are many different modes in which it can be present. We are all familiar with 'the strong silent type' of person who commands immediate respect when he or she chooses to speak. A very different mode is that of the person who is light, lively, and charming — and often very convincing. The variants are endless so I won't bother listing any more of them. What they have in common is that they are all ways in which we can lead others.

Politicians are people who make use of this power in order to get things done in society. The more successful politicians are often people who can switch modes to suit the situation. When they operate at the local level they may exude an easy charm and warmth — and this must be combined with a sensitivity to the nuances of the 'presence' of those with whom they are dealing. Those who enter politics at the national or global level need a more commanding presence — a kind of charisma that will attract large numbers of people and give the would-be politician a lot of public credibility.

If you or I engage in politics it is certain that at some point we will become involved in confrontations and struggles with individuals or groups whose policies are different from ours. It may seem that political struggles are fought out primarily in parliament, or at the ballot box, or at times on bloody battlefields. But *all* political struggles are first of all battles of the spirit. For the enemy always seeks to crush one's spirit. That was the aim of those who oppressed the People of God long ago (Ex 1:11). And leaders like Gandhi in India, Steve Biko in South Africa, and the Irish patriot Arthur Griffith saw clearly that the battle of the spirit has to be won first of all. Indeed this becomes obvious to anyone who reflects on the experience of playing football or chess or any other kind of game; you have to want to win and to believe you can do so — and you must not allow the opponent or the audience to undermine your faith in your own ability.

In the light of what I have just said I want now to suggest that prayer is not accidental to the way we relate to others, either at the domestic level or in the public sphere of politics.

Rather it nourishes in us a spiritual power that is central to all our interactions with others. This spiritual power has to be examined from two distinct points of view.

— First of all there is the purely *psychological* dimension, independent of any overt moral considerations: do I have the strength of character to stand up for myself and my convictions; or do I let myself become hassled, or browbeaten or worn down, so that I give up the struggle?

— Secondly, there is the strictly *moral* aspect: are my convictions based on a commitment to justice, respect, truth, and other moral values and to a sincere moral evaluation of the situation? I propose to examine each of these aspects in turn.

I begin with the psychological aspect — the issue of personality power or strength of character in the *pre-moral* sense. This power is the human equivalent of the animal's determination to stand its ground. It lies at the heart of all struggles with others, whether they be interpersonal or political. For it is this inner strength that gives us both tenacity and credibility. We need tenacity in order to campaign for what we believe in without losing heart in difficult moments of the struggle. We need personal credibility if we are to persuade others of the value of the course of action we are proposing.

Prayer in a Storm

In order to illustrate what I am talking about I want now to evoke the experience of a personal struggle of the kind that occurs at one time or another in everybody's life. Not an earth-shaking conflict by any external standards. But, like any such tangle, this power-struggle can feel, at the time, like a matter of life and death. It gives me the opportunity to convey the role of prayer in the form of a 'report from the battle-front':

> After that bruising tussle, what I need this morning is space. So I am not drawn to pray in a cozy chapel or in the quietness of my room. I need to breathe, to be buffeted by the elements. It's lashing rain and my head says it is crazy to go out. But I know that just now I have to get in touch with the welter of disturbed emotions inside me. The storm outside mirrors the storm within me; I sense that walking in

42

the storm will help me look a bit more objectively at what's happening inside. So out I go, a first small victory, breaking away from the cycle of futile remembering, fantasizing, and plotting.

(Walking through driving rain: can this be prayer? I don't want to argue the point. If you like, you can simply call it a preparation for prayer — certainly the best preparation I can make in this situation. I think it *is* prayer — trying to become present to myself so that I can allow God to be present to me.)

As I walk I begin to breathe . . . to breathe *again.* So I come to realise that I have scarcely been breathing since this confrontation. Yes, that's it, I've been squeezed, constricted, I've allowed 'them' to do this to me. Anguish, *angustia,* a sense of being hemmed in; that is what they've done to me. How dare they? By what right . . . And now I'm beginning to unfreeze, to get in touch with the anger I had blocked off, the anger I had turned in on myself, the anger that was eating me up, knotting up my stomach — and which I hadn't even noticed until now.

Look at what she did to me — got right inside my defenses, and began to 'press my buttons'. That patronizing way in which she 'put me down' pressed a button that called up old painful memories and attitudes — a childhood sense of being helpless in the face of adult power. This was heavy primal pain, a legacy of early childhood, which came to ride 'piggy-back' on the present pain which on its own would have been just a minor irritation. No wonder, then, that I felt so hurt, so helpless, as though sunk in a swamp with no solid ground under me. But now I am beginning to feel angry instead.

So I breathe deeply and look coolly at this anger. Coolly? No, it is too soon to be cool. I must really let the anger in before I can let it go; otherwise it will go underground again, devouring me and souring my relationship with 'the enemies'. Enemies? Yes, there is a part of me that sees them as enemies for now. 'Fierce bulls of Bashan surround me . . . a gang of evil people surround me, roaring and tearing at me'. (Ps 22). I experience what seems like a burst of hatred. My God, do I really hate them? How awful!

43

But I cannot deal with the torrents of emotion that are running through me unless I am willing to acknowledge what is there.

I look more closely. Is it really hate? No, it is just hurt and anger. I'm sinking in deep mud, there is no solid ground. (Ps 69); 'my strength is gone, spilled out like water on the ground' (Ps 22). 'Those who want to hurt me threaten to ruin me; they never stop plotting against me'. (Ps 38). Now I find myself, like the psalmist, beginning to cry out against God: Why did You let it happen? Where were *You* when they were plotting to pull me down? What about your promise to throw down the mighty from their seats of power? (Lk 1:51-2). Why don't you keep your promise? Yes, I am angry with *You* also . . .

I breathe again and stay with this for a while. Slowly the atmosphere begins to change. Is that a little snort of laughter I heard from God? Laughing at my puny anger? Yes, but nevertheless allowing me to be angry, and acknowledging my cry. Laughing too at the futile power of the enemies — from your throne in Heaven You laugh and mock their feeble plans (Ps 2:4). So this is Your answer. I breathe it in and feel myself led on to hear more: 'I remember the days gone by; I think about all that you have done, I bring to mind all your deeds' (Ps 143). Well then, let me bring to mind some of the things you have done for me, for us, in the past. Yes, marvelous . . . Can I then raise my hands to You in praise and thanks? Let me try it . . . and continue to breathe in this wild air which is bringing me your peace . . .

Prayer and Personality Power

At this point I suspend the 'report from the battlefront' to reflect on the effect of this particular bit of praying on this instance of a struggle for power. The first and most obvious effect of the prayer is that it is giving me space to stand back and get some overall impression of the struggle — and especially of what it has cost me.

This inspection of the damage has begun to lead on to the next step — healing of the spirit. There is no need for me to give a blow-by-blow account of all the elements in this healing, especially since the process will vary from one

44

person to another; and, even in the life of any individual, no two instances will be the same. But it may be helpful to note three points:

— This kind of prayer in the midst of a power struggle cannot heal my spirit unless I allow in the negative emotions such as fear, hurt, and anger. So long as I refuse to acknowledge them, they will crowd the door of my spirit, blocking the entrance of God's healing and strengthening power.

— When I let in the anger and hurt I can then begin to find out how much of them truly belongs to this situation and how much is old emotion, the legacy of childhood or infancy, touched off by something that was said or done today.

— I must not allow my head to determine the movement or pace of the prayer; it is essential to 'stay with' the hurt or anger until that part of me feels heard. The flow is interrupted if I feel so guilty or uncomfortable with the negative emotions that I push myself too quickly on from anger to love. 'There is a time for tears, a time for laughter, . . . a time for loving, a time for hating, a time for war, a time for peace.' (Eccl 3).

A further effect of this kind of prayer is that it restores my strength. But it is important to note that the Judeo-Christian notion of strength of spirit is notably different from the usual understanding of strength. What prayer gives us is not the power of the mighty ones, the dictators or arrogant rulers who care nothing for the views of ordinary people. But on the other hand it is not simply a blind trust in a kind of magical power of God — though the difference is hard to put in words. I think it goes back to the issue of justification so hotly debated at the time of the Reformation. God's saving power at work in each of us has a *real* effect; it transforms the spirit. It won't make me feel powerful in the conventional sense but it will give me a sense of inner strength, a strength that is quite compatible with a keen awareness of fragility. David put it well: 'You are coming against me with sword, spear, and javelin, but I come against you in the name of the Lord Almighty' (I Sam 17:45).

Prayer and Morality

So far, I have been fighting for survival. The effect of my prayer has been directed towards renewing my psychological power, countering the experience of being totally crushed in spirit. I have now reached a point in the prayer where I was touched by the laughter of God both at me and at the enemy. I have begun to smile a little at my hurt and anger. Now, and only now, I can perhaps begin to move on to a second stage where I can try to look objectively at the *ethical* aspects of the struggle, reviewing it in terms of who was right or wrong. So let me return to my 'report from the battlefront'...

The storm within me is subsiding a little and I begin to be more objective. Now I feel the need to seek out the truth — and face up to it. I look more closely at the text where David feels ready to take on Goliath; David says, 'I come against you in the name of the Lord'. Can I echo his words? By no means — or at least not yet. I shall have to pray my way towards such a position. It is time now to begin to see whether my struggle for survival coincides with fighting 'in the name of the Lord'.

I feel God is inviting me, and challenging me, to pray the final words of psalm 139:

'God, examine me and know my heart,
probe me and know my thoughts;
make sure I do not follow pernicious ways,
and guide me in the way that is everlasting.'

Yes, perhaps I was somewhat hasty; maybe I didn't make allowances . . . and I suppose those I felt were 'the enemy' may be praying to You at this very moment, calling for help against *me!* Can I be sure You are on my side? . . . No, I can only be sure that I am in your hand, with my name carved on your palm (Is 49:16). And even if I was hasty or wrong You forgive me and love me just as much or more than ever. So now I can try to look again at the struggle, to review the different phases — this time through your eyes and ready to acknowledge where I have been wrong . . .

Once again I suspend the 'report' in order to reflect on the pattern of the prayer. God has been leading me to seek and follow the truth, a truth that will set me free. And the only way to see the truth is to have 'a pure heart'. This is a gift — but one I must be willing to receive, and to work for in prayer. It is not all-or-nothing, but comes in varying degrees. If I have a fair measure of purity of heart in my

46

review of the struggle, then the next step should become clear. I may be called to make contact with my opponents, to admit my faults and seek forgiveness. On the other hand I may become convinced that I have been fighting a just cause, and doing so with integrity. Then I can say with David (though with due trepidation) that I am fighting in the name of God. That does not absolve me from looking for reconciliation; but in seeking it I shall feel obliged to hold my ground on matters of principle.

At first sight it might appear that the moral effect of prayer pulls me in the opposite direction to the psychological effect — in other words, that morality involves being gentle and yielding whereas being psychologically strong means being firm and unyielding. But, far from being opposed to morality, strength of character is an essential element in it. I need to be quite strong in order to acknowledge my mistakes and my sinfulness — even to myself. So when I am in the midst of a painful political struggle it is pointless to begin my prayer by looking at the moral issues without first tending my psychological wounds. Not to do so is dangerous both psychologically and morally.

If I do not allow my spirit to be healed, strengthened and nourished I may find myself touchy and aggressive; or, on the other hand, I may be so insecure that I would compromise my principles in an effort to please others. In either case I will not be able to deal with the moral issues. If that happens, I will be failing to act in a fully human way. After all, we are not dogs squaring up to each other, but humans called to shape a world where truth, respect, and compassion take priority over brute power. Respect for others is a crucial aspect of an integral spirituality.

Integrity and 'Transparency'

There is a further way in which the psychological and moral effects of prayer are closely linked: prayer helps people to develop a certain integrity and transparency of spirit. To have 'integrity' is to be 'pure in heart'. This involves a wholehearted commitment to fundamental values such as truth and respect for others — and therefore a willingness to acknowledge and eliminate those inconsistencies and half-conscious compromises which we so easily tolerate. Such wholeheartedness leads to what I am calling 'transparency' — by which I mean the way in which a person's integrity shines out to others.

'Transparency' is one of the most priceless gifts anybody could have. It adds enormously to the person's credibility, making his or her attitudes and policies seem very convincing and attractive. Furthermore, it greatly reduces the conflicts in which one becomes embroiled. For most disagreements, whether domestic or political, come from personality clashes rather than from issues of policy; and the person whose sincerity and integrity is evident to others arouses admiration rather than frustration and hostility. This is one situation in which 'honesty is the best policy'.

Prayer is almost essential for anybody who wishes to avoid the twin temptations that beset anybody who becomes involved in a power-struggle of any kind: the temptation to deceive oneself and the temptation to manipulate others. When I stand naked before the God who 'knows all my actions' (Ps 139) I begin to become aware of the myriad subtle ways in which I am guilty of such deceptions. This invites me to a conversion which has different dimensions:

— Conversion to the truth: being willing to seek it resolutely even at the cost of eliminating the comfortable inconsistencies in my attitudes and arguments.

— Conversion to the value of emotional honesty, so that I avoid deceiving myself or others about what is going on inside me.

— Conversion to respect for others — and a large part of this is a consistent effort to look at issues from the other person's point of view.

— 'Political conversion', by which I mean full acceptance of the fact that social justice requires changes in the structures and rules of society rather than just *ad hoc* remedies to correct particular abuses.

Talking to Jesus

To open up some final reflections on prayer and power, I return once more to the 'battle-front':

As I review my present struggle, I find myself invited to compare it with the battles in the life of Jesus. This gives rise to a sense of invitation to talk to Jesus: Yes, You found

48

yourself misunderstood by the people who liked power. They wanted to catch you out. They set traps for you — about paying tax, about punishing the women caught in adultery, about keeping the Sabbath. They misinterpreted you about the destruction of the Temple and the nature of the Kingdom. The Gospels show you defending yourself vigorously against Pilate, going on the attack against the pharisees, and simply staying silent before Herod. How did you know how to deal with them? Did you plan a strategy beforehand, or simply play it by ear — and as your heart led you? How did you hold your ground, remain true to what you believed in, and still keep yourself genuinely open to Nicodemus, to Simon the Pharisee, and to Judas?

What do you want to say to me here and now? Is it something about my *moral* stance — about some element of self-deception or some way I'm manipulating my allies?.... Am I lacking in the kind of compassion you showed? Am I willing to allow myself to be vulnerable as you were, trusting not in the power to dominate others but only in the power of truth? Am I willing to wait, as you did, for the vindication of the Faithful One whom you called Abba?

As I try to listen, I realise that maybe what you want to say to me just now is not about my moral behaviour. You can see that I'm not even ready to hear your word on that. So all you want to do is simply to reassure me, comfort me, strengthen and heal me. I try to stay with that. It is not easy. It is rather humbling to realise that I'm running away from you just now if I move on to look at the morality of my behaviour! That can come later. For the moment,

I am not concerned with great matters,
or with subjects too difficult for me.
But I am content and at peace.
As a child lies quietly in its mother's arms,
so my heart is quiet within me. (Ps 131)

I stay with the quietness for the remainder of this period of prayer . . .

Listening to Jesus

What does it mean to listen to Jesus in prayer at a time of struggle? It would be a serious mistake to expect Jesus to give me advice or instructions on a particular issue, in the way I

49

might get them from a friend. I have no 'hot line' to God or to Jesus. To ask 'advice' from Jesus about how I should act is to seek to get in touch with a barely accessible part of *myself*—the part that is 'conformed' to Jesus, that is committed to listen to him, willing to be challenged by him.

While I don't expect to get explicit instructions from Jesus, I do hope for comfort or challenge from him — or some deeper insight about how best to nourish and use my power in the present situation. For I believe that when I get in touch with the deepest part of myself, then the Spirit of Jesus speaks to and through my spirit. Of course I can have no guarantee that I will be able to overcome my own bias and correctly understand what the Spirit is saying to me. But that is not a good reason for giving up the effort. It means rather that I should endeavour to be more open to 'the voice of God'.

As a Christian committed to prayer, I do not expect my prayer to provide me with some domestic or political policy that is not available to others. For that very reason I can be content to stay as long as seems right at any point in my prayer; I'm not missing anything vital by failing to move on. There is a certain analogy between this kind of prayer and a session of non-directive counselling. God, and Jesus, trust me to come to my own conclusions; but those conclusions are likely to be radically different from the ones I would have come to if I had not given the time to prayer!

It is true that at times I need to go through a process of discernment in which I ask the Spirit of God to enlighten my spirit, so that I may be led to the truth, the right decision, the will of God. But even then I have no excuse for trying to rush God — even if the decision I have to take is urgent. For Jesus assures me that it is alright to be unprepared:

> 'When they hand you over, do not worry about how to speak or what to say; what you are to say will be given to you when the time comes'. (Mt 10:19)

If it is acceptable to be unprepared about what to *say*, then I take it that I may also be unprepared about what to *do*. More accurately, it is alright to act on a sense of call to spend the available time in allowing my spirit to be nourished and challenged by the Spirit of Jesus rather than in pushing for an immediate decision. Prayer of that kind strengthens me to go forward with faith in God and myself, trusting that the

50

right decision will emerge at the right time. (Of course, in matters like this I need to know my own character pretty well; for my delay in making the decision might be due to some compulsion or some neurotic element in my personality; that is where I can be helped by the Enneagram — dealt with elsewhere in this book — and by other techniques that may give me a better understanding of my character.)

There are many issues about power and struggle which it would be helpful to explore in personal prayer with Jesus. There's so much I'd like to learn about his use of power of various kinds. About how he resisted the temptation to dominate others by the sheer force and charm of his personality. Or how he combined integrity with compassion. Or how he developed the leadership potential of his followers, facilitating them rather than imposing his will on them. But I suspect that these are questions to which there is no general answer. Each one of us needs to spend time in prayer looking for the answers that meet the particular situation in which we find ourselves. To try to generalise our answers would be to turn them into platitudes.

There are also some more profound political-religious questions that I need to look at with Jesus. About what it means to 'love to the end' (Jn 13:1) — facing death when there's no other way; and yet not anticipating that final confrontation, but instead taking any way out that is compatible with one's integrity (cf Lk 4:29-30). About how Jesus knew when 'his hour' had come? And what that says about the pattern of my life. These are questions which I shall have to face at some time, since the Gospels warn me that as a disciple of Jesus I must expect to have to follow him all the way (Jn 15:18-20; cf Lk 21:12).

This seems to indicate that some day I may find myself in a struggle where purely human strength or moral rightness are not enough. For, if I am following the pattern of Jesus' life and death, then in that final 'Hour' of confrontation, no matter how strong or how right I may be, I cannot hope for success or vindication on this side of the grave. But that 'Hour' will come in its own time. It cannot be rushed. All I can do is wait. As the poet Patrick Kavanagh says:

Lie at the heart of the emotion, time
Has its own work to do.[1]

SECTION TWO:
PRAYER AND MEDITATION RESOURCES

In this section I offer three passages from Scripture and a short excerpt from the writings of the poet-theologian Dorethee Sölle. Then I offer a guided 'breathing meditation'. I believe these resources fit in well with the kind of situation described in Section One of this chapter.

In Time of Betrayal

Some time ago I was conducting a workshop in Africa for a development group who had been betrayed by one of their own members. They were very hurt. Before taking up the main theme of the workshop we spent some time in prayer and faith-sharing. The text I proposed to them for their prayer was from Psalm 55. It proved to be very powerful for them, enabling them to get in touch with their hurt and anger so that they could then move on towards healing and new hope. So I offer the text here for use by others who may find themselves in a similar position.

Hear my prayer, God;
    do not turn away from my plea!
Listen to me and answer me;
I am worn out by my worries.
I am upset by the threats of my enemies,
    by opposition from the wicked.
They bring trouble on me;
    they are angry with me and hate me.

Fear fills my heart,
    and the terrors of death are heavy on me.
I am gripped by fear and trembling;
I am overcome with horror.
I say, 'I wish I had wings, like a dove!
    I would fly away and find rest!
I would fly far away
    and make my home in the desert.
I would hurry and find myself a shelter
    from the raging wind and from malicious tongues.'

Violence and discord stalk the city
   surrounding it on all sides day and night.
The city is full of crime and trouble;
   there is destruction everywhere;
   the streets are filled with oppression and fraud.

If it had been an enemy that did this
   I could endure the taunts.
If it had been a foe
   I could have gone into hiding.
But it is you, my own companion
   Who had been my very close friend.
We walked together in harmony
   And went together to the house of God . . .

So I cry out to you, Yahweh God, for help,
   and you will come to my help.
My groans and my protest go up to You
   morning, noon, and night —
   and I know you will hear my voice . . .
My former companion proved faithless
   and we were betrayed.
The traitor's conversation was smooth as cream
   but it concealed the malice of the heart.
The words seemed smooth as oil
   but they cut like swords.

Hand over your burden to God
   and God will support you.
God will never let down
   the one who maintains integrity and faith.

You, God, will put to shame the bloodthirsty traitors
   before they have lived out half their lives.
And so, Yahweh God, I put my trust in you.

Gratitude for Healing
   The following passage from Psalm 73 is helpful when one
is in need of healing of spirit:

When my thoughts were bitter,
   and my feelings were hurt,
I was stupid, and did not understand;
I acted like an animal toward you.

Yet you are always present to me,
  and you hold me by the hand.
You guide me with your advice,
  and at the end you will receive me with honour.
What else do I have in heaven but you?
  since I have you, what more do I want on earth?
My mind and my body may grow weak,
    but God is my strength;
    God is all I ever want.

Surely, those who abandon you will die,
  and you will destroy those who desert you.
But my joy lies in being close to God.
I have made you, Yahweh God, my refuge,
And I will proclaim your marvelous deeds
  to all the world.

The following lines from the book of Jeremiah can be very nourishing for somebody who feels broken and pulled in many directions. The person who reads the passage in time of trouble can experience it as a promise of peace of spirit, of healing and restoration:

I alone know the plans I have for you,
  plans of peace not of disaster,
  plans to bring about the future you hope for.
When you seek me you shall find me,
  provided you seek with all your heart.
I will restore your fortunes
  and bring you back from the places
  where you have been scattered.
I will bring your exile to an end. (Jer 29:11-13)

The following short excerpt from *Choosing Life* by Dorothee Sölle[2] fits in well with the passage from Jeremiah:

There are times when we feel nothing of his resurrection — times of pain and torture, times of many crosses. In spite of that, let us not be among those who suppress the news of the resurrection, or no longer believe in it ourselves. In times of many crosses we should go on telling what we have heard and understood. We should talk in such a way that Christ is missed, that he is even present as someone who is missing. We should express the pain we feel when we don't perceive his victory; we should utter our longing.

54

A Breathing Meditation

In the early part of this chapter I mentioned the importance of *breathing* in order to allow oneself really to get in touch with what is happening inside. One of the great weaknesses of Western spirituality in recent centuries is its failure to take sufficient account of the role of the body. It is only within the past decade that we are coming to realise that a crucial aspect of learning to meditate is learning to breathe properly; without that it is almost impossible to do serious meditation.

The purpose of this meditation is to give one a sense of being rooted, of being present to oneself, of being tranquil and at peace. Some people may find it very easy to do this meditation. But for people whose minds and imaginations are very active it can be very difficult. However, these are the very people who can benefit most from it. Even if you find it very hard, if you get distracted and lost, you may still notice that this effort to be more present to yourself in the 'here and now' has a calming effect on you. It is better not to judge the effectiveness of the meditation simply in terms of whether or not you were able to 'stay with it'; judge rather in the light of whether, over a period of several days, you feel it has helped you to feel more at home with yourself, more in touch with your centre. Hopefully the meditation will help you to be more in touch with the part of yourself that is more interior and centred, rather than with the part of you that is totally scattered, pulled this way and that.

Kneel on a prayer stool with your back straight, or sit in a lotus or half-lotus position, without supporting your back and making sure that your knees are touching the floor or a support (so that you feel grounded). Allow about thirty minutes for the meditation. You may spend the first five minutes or so listening to the following introductory remarks, read by a friend, or heard on a tape-recorder (or simply recalled from memory). After that, simply stay with the breath (or keep returning to the breath) for the remaining time:

> Allow the body to breathe naturally, without forcing or controlling the breath . . . Gently bring the attention to the point where the breath makes contact with the nostrils as it passes in and out . . . Hold the attention at that one precise point, like somebody standing on a bridge looking

down at the water flowing underneath, noticing the water flowing by but not carried along with it . . .

Notice the sensation that accompanies each breath as it flows in and out of the body . . .

There may be sensations in the body . . . Just notice them as sensations present in the background . . . But hold the attention gently on the breath as it passes in and out through the nostrils . . .

If the attention strays, bring it gently back to the point where the breath passes through the nostrils . . .

If thoughts arise, just notice that there are thoughts, but do not let them carry the attention away . . . The thoughts are allowed to flow under the bridge while the attention remains steady in the same place . . .

The body is relaxed . . . the shoulders are dropped and loose . . . the face is relaxed . . .

The attention is stationed at the point where the breath passes in and out . . . observing each breath, each new breath, moment by moment . . .

No need to force anything. Just be aware of the breath . . . surrender to the breath . . .

A Poem

I end this chapter with a little poem I wrote some time ago. I think it follows on nicely from the breathing meditation; and it also echoes some of what I was saying towards the beginning of the chapter about learning to 'stand your ground':

Alone

And so I stand alone
The gantries all drawn back
And clearly there's no railway line to use
To travel out to God, or you,
Or to the me I'm called to be.

And is it nice?
Well, is it 'nice' to stand alone
Upon the highest board of all
Before the final dive?

No, 'nice' is hardly quite the word.
A word like 'true' is closer to the mark —

56

The piercing truth that sends a shiver down the spine.
And if I launch myself with dignity and grace
There could emerge an act of sheerest beauty.

Yes, here I stand alone,
Yet not alone as lonely,
But as free.

NOTES

1. From, *Patrick Kavanagh: The Complete Poems* (Collected, Arranged and Edited by Peter Kavanagh), New York (The Peter Kavanagh Hand Press: 1972), Newbridge, (The Goldsmith Press: 1984), 256.
2. London (SCM: 1981), 96-7; and Minneopolis (Augsburg Fortress).

3

Sharing and Community

The building of Basic Christian Communities has become one of the most talked-of topics in Church circles in recent years. Interest in the question is not confined to those who are working in what were traditionally called 'mission areas'; a lot of people who would like to have a more relevant and dynamic Church in the secularised areas of Europe and North America think that the 'BCC' approach could offer new hope where other methods have failed. In the first section of this chapter I offer some reflections on the self-giving that is the deepest element in community-building. In the following two sections I offer some resource materials and practical exercises related to community.

SECTION ONE: SELF-GIVING

How does one go about starting such a basic community? Those who ask this question seem mainly to be looking for some guidelines about *techniques* they can use. The main point I want to make here is that something much more basic than technique is involved. Those who want to build basic communities successfully must have a fundamental openness of heart and mind, a willingness to risk sharing themselves with others. There is no real community unless the members of the group are sharing not just their food or their religious insights but themselves. Anybody who wants to develop a basic Christian community — or any truly human community — has to lead the way by modelling this kind of self-sharing. Some of those who want to adopt basic communities as a pastoral strategy already have the kind of openness that enables them to share themselves; but for others a major change of attitude — a real conversion — may have to take place. In the pages that follow I shall try to outline what is involved, why it is costly, and what we have to learn about it from the Gospel accounts of the life of Jesus.

Simon is a priest who took part several years ago in a training workshop which I helped to run for lay leaders, sisters, and priests. In the workshop there were very few talks; we spent a lot of the time doing fairly simple sharing and listening exercises. Our aim was twofold: to help the participants to have a sense of community during the workshop itself; and at the same time to communicate to them an approach they could use afterwards, with the various groups of people among whom they were working. I've kept in touch with many of the group and I have learned a lot from seeing the effects of the workshop in their lives.

As always, the results were mixed. For about half of the participants the workshop was a major turning point. Their whole approach to others and to their ministry changed quite significantly as a result of what they learned; and several of them have gone on to become outstanding leaders. Simon, on the other hand, was one of the people whose long-term approach changed very little as a result of the workshop. He came back to his parish full of enthusiasm, and the very next day he was making use of the exercises he had learned. But it soon became clear that what he had brought home from the workshop was 'a bag of tricks'. He felt he now had a set of 'games' or exercises which he could use to 'jolly along' the members of the parish council and other parishioners. But he had no notion of relinquishing to them any of his power to make the decisions that really mattered. Worse still, it didn't really occur to him that he could share his personal worries and pain with them; he still carried them alone. In the next few years he plunged deeper and deeper into his work. Eventually, having driven himself to a standstill, he had some kind of breakdown. As he comes through this he is painfully learning to expose himself, to share with others his weakness as well as his gifts.

This incident helps to illustrate the main point I want to stress about improving communications and building community. The learning of new techniques is not the heart of the matter. Techniques may be helpful, but the essential thing is learning to share myself. For there is really only one genuine form of communication — the giving of self. Even the most minimal form of communication, such as my nod to you in the street, involves offering you a little of myself. So I'm hurt if you fail to acknowledge my greeting — because I feel you are rejecting *me*. One might imagine that the teaching of chemistry is the communication of purely objective facts. But even chemistry teachers communicate as much about themselves as about their subject; we often remember the teachers long after we have forgotten the facts.

We come to a deeper level of communication when we move from sharing information to the sharing of our personal feelings. When I meet my family and friends after a long absence I find that we are interested not so much in the facts about what we've been doing, as in our reactions and feelings. That is because facts are things I know about, whereas my feelings are part of *me*; so when I share them I'm sharing myself in a more obvious and intimate way.

At the top end of the scale of communication between humans is the attempt of lovers to give themselves totally to each other, to break down all the barriers of suspicion — and even of privacy. There is a mutuality in this kind of communication: each feels a desire to be dissolved into the other, and to accept the other's desire for complete self-giving. The passion of the body is fully human when it expresses the passion of the spirit for perfect openness and communion with the other person.

Ultimate Need, Ultimate Fear

What I have been saying about the desire for perfect self-giving may sound somewhat unreal. That is not because it is untrue, but because I have not yet taken account of the greatest block to human communication. When I look back on some peak moments of my life, times when I really felt myself in near perfect communion with another person, I find that in the midst of such experiences I was occasionally pierced by an awareness of an utter inability to give myself fully or to receive the other. I find in myself an aloneness that even the most intense human love cannot overcome; in fact the experience of intimacy makes me even more aware of being isolated. This is not just a quirk in my character; it seems to be part of the human condition.

When I try delicately to probe this primal loneliness I find that the major element in it is an ambivalence deep within me. At the very core of my being lies a hunger for acceptance. But alongside it is a deep fear of being rejected. These two pull me in opposite directions. I can only be accepted if I am willing to give myself to another; so one part of me wants desperately to let go, to entrust myself completely to the other person. But the fear of rejection inhibits my desire to give myself, and at times swamps it entirely. I'm afraid to let go, to admit my utter need for acceptance and love; for I have a dread that a rejection at this fundamental level would be equivalent to condemning me to death. I'm afraid that it would hurt me beyond all hope of healing.

When I look at the eyes of the people around me I often see something of the same mixture as I find within myself: a primal need to reach out and be loved competing with a primal fear of rejection. The first time I noticed this was in a growth workshop some years ago. One of the participants was a young man who seemed to me to have retreated *behind* his eyes for most of the time. Occasionally he risked coming out a little and then his eyes came alive as he became present to us through them. Then suddenly he would be gone again. It was clear that he needed and wanted to stay 'out' more, to be with us for more of the time. All we could do was try to provide an atmosphere where he felt safe enough to do so. What he had to learn was to trust us — but more particularly to trust himself.

As far as I can see, much of what passes for communication between people — even between friends — is really an acting out in public of the ambivalence that lies deep within each of us. We are frantically looking for ways to reach out to others, but constantly checking to make sure we have not left ourselves too exposed. Each of us has built various defenses because we are afraid of being wounded if we reveal too much of ourselves. Occasionally we venture out from behind the ramparts, seeking the comfort of meeting another fearful person who has taken the same risk at the same time. If a real encounter takes place it brings a marvelous sense of warmth and satisfaction. So, most of us are willing to take some risks to achieve that sense of communion — even if it is only for a short time.

61

Such communication is tentative and fragile. One or other of us may become just a shade more defensive or more brash than the other can bear. This slight hitch will send each of us scurrying back, eager to hide the fact that we had ever exposed ourselves. Just the other day, in the middle of a very interesting conversation with a teacher of religion, I suddenly noticed that we had begun to play with words. I sensed that some remark of mine had come across to him as too threatening or too revealing. So, quite unconsciously, he had retreated and had subtly drawn me into light banter.

Another reason why our communication may break down is misunderstanding. In conversation with you I may not be clear about what I really want; so I may be sending you mixed signals at the subliminal level. Some of my signals may be saying 'please help me' while other signals may be giving the message 'keep away'. No wonder then if you fail to respond in a way that I find satisfactory! On the other hand, your reception of my signals may also be somewhat defective — either because of your fear or because of the very intensity of your desire to be accepted.

Cover Up

When I first began thinking about the problems of communication I was living in a remote African village where letters took four weeks to arrive (if they arrived at all) and an effective phone was hundreds of miles away. Yet even there I became very aware that the major difficulties we have in communicating with others are not technical but psychological. Even the most advanced technology of communication does nothing to heal the fear of rejection that makes us wrap up our messages in face-saving camouflage and causes us to misinterpret the signals of others.

Different societies develop safeguards to minimise the risk and the hurt when people try to reach out to each other. An obvious example is the convention by which members of the upper-classes in Britain replace 'I' with 'one' when speaking about their feelings, e.g. 'one felt rather embarrassed when one spoke with the local people'. In other English-speaking countries this sounds rather affected; but people in these areas frequently replace the word 'I' with the word 'you', e.g. 'you don't like it when you are treated that way'. Another way of avoiding saying 'I' is common in many countries: a person in a group says '*we*' instead of 'I' — thus making a quite unwarranted claim to speak on behalf of a whole group.

I find it a very helpful discipline to avoid using such escape hatches. I try to say 'I' when I mean 'I'. By doing this I take personal responsibility for my own thoughts, feelings, and demands. Whenever I help to run a workshop we try gently to encourage people to use 'I' if they are sharing their own feelings or insights. But it calls for a good deal of sensitivity to be able to choose the right time to invite somebody to rephrase what they have just said, using 'I' instead of 'one' or 'you' or 'we'.

At some half-conscious level people seem to sense that speaking in the first person singular leaves them more vulnerable. So they often devise little stratagems of their own to avoid it. One of the most obliging and competent people I have ever met had the odd habit of scarcely ever using the word 'I'. So her conversation or letters often ran like this: 'Went for a walk today; felt great; decided to take more exercise in future. . . . ' This 'editing out' of the personal pronoun must have been more costly than she imagined; for — quite unexpectedly — she had a break-down. She is now recovering — and slowly learning to reveal herself, learning to be able to say 'I'.

There are subtle differences between cultures as regards the degree of directness that is considered good manners. Last year, when a Nigerian Sister, an Irish Sister, and myself were running a workshop, we got into a tangle about this question. The Nigerian said; 'We Africans are much more direct than Europeans; we say straight out what we think and feel, without beating about the bush'. And she gave a number of convincing examples. The Irishwoman countered by quoting instances where she felt quite brash compared with Nigerians, whom she found to be more sensitive and cautious about expressing negative reactions to others. The exchange helped me to realise that each culture is more 'permissive' in some situations, more restrictive in others. This can be a source of misunderstanding when we try to communicate across cultural boundaries. But I must add that, in my experience, such cultural misunderstandings are relatively minor; the major blocks to communication are

63

personal-psychological. If people are willing to take the risk of trusting each other, cultural differences, even though they make communication somewhat more difficult, can actually enrich the interchange.

The Experience of Jesus

Any worthwhile Christian spirituality must take account of the basic tension we find within us. And where better to look for a model than at the life of Jesus. Since he was a fully human person, Jesus had to cope with the experience of feeling himself pulled in two directions. Like us, he felt drawn to share himself fully with others; but, like us, he also found himself fearful of being rejected, hurt — and even condemned to die.

How did Jesus react to the ambivalence, the mixture of desire to reach out and fear of doing so? The Gospels make it clear that he opted to trust others, to leave himself open and vulnerable. In fact that was precisely the way in which he *gave* himself to others. His giving of himself in death was simply the culmination and the obvious consequence of his daily self-giving in communication and trust to those around him — friends and enemies. And it was this entrusting of himself to others that revealed most clearly how the one whom he called 'Abba' is always reaching out to us: 'He said to them: "Now that you have known me, you will know my Father also, and from now on you do know him and you have seen him . . . Whoever has seen me has seen the Father." (Jn 14:7,9).

Jesus held nothing back. The only limits to his self-giving were in the people with whom he tried to communicate. The ones who responded more eagerly to his trust were formed by him into a little community. With them he shared his time ('they spent the rest of the day with him' — Jn 1:39), his meals (the common purse — Jn 13:29), his journeys (e.g. Mt 20:17), his glimpses of the future that awaited him ('He will be handed over to the Gentiles, who will mock him, insult him, and spit on him; they will whip him and kill him' — Lk 18:32), his hopes ('If the grain of wheat does die then it produces much fruit . . . when I am lifted up from the earth I will draw everyone to me' — Jn 12:24,32) and all that he was learning from Abba ('"Lord, teach us to pray . . . ";

"when you pray, say this . . . "' — Lk 11:1-2; '"I have told you everything I have heard from my Father"' — Jn 15:15).

The followers of Jesus were jealous of each other (Mt 20:24). But that did not inhibit Jesus from being particularly intimate with those who could respond more fully to his trust and love. He had an inner group of three special confidants ('Jesus took with him Peter, James, and John, and led them up a high mountain . . . as they came down he ordered them, "Don't tell anyone what you have seen . . ."' — Lk 9:2,9). Apparently he did not even hesitate to allow one of them to be known as 'the disciple whom Jesus loved' (Jn 13:23).

Even more shocking was the fact that Jesus did not allow the social conventions of his time and culture to limit his openness to all with whom he came into contact. Prostitutes were welcome to his meals, and so too were the despised tax-extorters (Mt 11:19). John's Gospel depicts him talking freely with a Samaritan — and a woman Samaritan at that! (Jn 4:7-26). Jesus also took the risk of reaching out in friendship and trust even to members of those groups who were most opposed to him — to Simon the Pharisee (Lk 7:36) and Nicodemus, one of the ruling elite (Jn 3:1ff).

The willingness of Jesus to entrust himself to others shows that he consistently opted for one pole of the basic human ambivalence: he chose to reveal his yearning for the acceptance and love of others, and he refused to be held back by fear of being rejected. Could it be that he, being who he was, did not really experience this primal fear of rejection? That I cannot believe. For in that case he would not have been fully human, 'like us in all things except sin'.

He Paid the Price

In fact the Gospels bring out the point that Jesus was keenly aware that his love and trust were being spurned by many — and was deeply hurt by it: '"Jerusalem, Jerusalem, . . . how many times have I wanted to put my arms round all your people, just as a hen gathers her chicks under her wings, but you would not let me!"' (Mt 23:37); 'many of the followers of Jesus turned back . . . so he asked the twelve disciples, "Do you also want to go away?"' (Jn 6:66-7). Jesus had to endure the pain of being turned down by the rich young man (Mk 10: 21-2), and of being misunderstood by

Peter just when Peter had made his greatest act of faith (Mt 16:22). He was grieved by the failure of his special friends to respond with greater trust in him: 'Why are you so fearful? Have you still no faith? (Mk 4:40); "Did I not tell you that that you would see God's glory if you believed?"' (Jn 11:39).

So the self-giving of Jesus was costly from the beginning. And, as the opposition became more intransigent and violent, the pain for Jesus became greater. Eventually he had to pay the ultimate price — his life. It is worthwhile looking closely at how this came about.

Jesus had not come to condemn people but to set them free (Jn 12:48). His offer was unconditional and was open to all. But this was precisely what made it seem a threat to those who held power of one kind or another. Caiphas and Herod and Pilate had all erected their own defenses against insecurity — and their primary defense was their exercise of power over others. They were not willing to let go their power and leave themselves vulnerable. And they did not dare allow Jesus to teach the ordinary people his way of coping with primal fear — by entrusting themselves in openness and vulnerability to others; for that would be a fundamental challenge to the customary use and abuse of power. So those who relied on power felt they had to use it to quench the light that Jesus had thrown on the human dilemma; then they and their subjects could remain in the darkness of suspicion, fear, and whatever futile security they had been able to work out for themselves. They made Jesus pay the price for holding nothing back, for witnessing to the truth that sets people free from tyranny and fear.

In general, the Gospels tell us very little about the inner life of Jesus. But there is one notable exception: the Agony in the Garden. There the evangelists show Jesus prostrated by fear and sorrow. As he faced the utter loneliness of the death of a criminal and heretic, he was overwhelmed by primal terror. Mark's account is very graphic: 'Distress and anguish came over him, and he said to them, "The sorrow in my heart is so great that it almost crushes me." ' (Mk 14:34). Luke adds: 'His sweat was like drops of blood falling to the ground.' (Lk 22:44). These accounts of the agony of Jesus make it clear that the drama of his rejection did not take place merely in the public arena of the judgment halls of the rulers and the place of execution. Prior to that it had already been acted out in the heart of Jesus. He had allowed himself to experience a primal sense of terror and anguish, sparked off by his awareness of being repudiated by religious and civil authorities, grossly misunderstood by the ordinary people, and betrayed or abandoned by his friends.

This cold sweat of terror is very important for us. It shows clearly that Jesus was *fully* human and it encourages us to embrace our own humanity fully. Jesus chose to take on our humanity by sharing not merely our bodily life and our deepest hopes, but also our most basic fears and tensions. In doing so he assures each one of us that it is alright to allow ourselves to experience them. There is nothing wrong about finding myself torn between the ultimate need to give myself and the ultimate fear of letting go. That is part of the human situation which was taken on by Jesus. So I do not have to block it out — to find an escape from it in hyperactivity or triviality or alcohol.

The Way Forward

It is true that in our sinful world each of us is very vulnerable. Those who follow Jesus in opening themselves fully in trust to others soon find that they have to endure rejection and even hatred from those who find that attitude too threatening. Jesus shows us the way forward. It is to *acknowledge* the fear and pain of rejection but not to *yield* to it. If I deny the fear and refuse to allow it into consciousness, I am stifling a profoundly human experience and blocking access to the deepest part of myself. I must allow the fear in, as Jesus did when he admitted to his friends that he felt weighed down 'unto death' (Mk 14:34). But I must not lie under that fear indefinitely: 'Arise, let us go.' (Mt 26:46). Jesus teaches me to take the ultimate risk, to face up to the ultimate pain, hoping against hope to follow him to the fullness of life even when the way seems blocked by death.

How was it that Jesus was able to choose consistently to open himself to others? How was he able to take the risk of rejection by others so total and devastating that it evoked the primal fear that is 'unto death'? How could he 'let in' that fear without being utterly swamped by it? It is far too glib to respond to these questions by saying: 'He was divine.' For we are concerned here with his humanity. Can we find anything in his *human* life that would help to account for such an almost superhuman pattern of behaviour?

There is one outstanding experience in the life of Jesus which, I think, provides an answer to these questions: his baptism. That was a moment when he had an overwhelming conviction of being totally accepted by God as 'the Beloved One': 'As soon as Jesus came up out of the water, he saw heaven opening and the Spirit coming down on him like a dove. And a voice came from heaven, "You are my own dear Son, I am pleased with you"' (Mk 1:10-1).

It is likely that this was just one particularly outstanding instance out of many such experiences. In any case it is clear from the Gospels that this one had a profound effect. It gave Jesus a deep security at the very core of his being. Evidently it left him with a clear sense of being called, and an equally clear sense of the purpose of his calling. He then found himself with two things to do — and he set about them at once:
— First he had to discern *how* he was to carry out his mission; and that is what the temptations were about. His prayer and fasting enabled him to see that his mission would be compromised if he tried to impress people as a wonder-worker, a man of power (Mt 4:1-10). There were to be no short-cuts, no easy ways. It was himself that he had to give; nothing less would do.
— Next he had to find people with whom he could share himself and his sense of mission. So the evangelists show him soon afterwards calling his first followers (e.g. Mk 1:16-20).

What comes through in the Gospels is the deep sense of assurance that Jesus had, both in facing his temptations and in calling his followers. All through the years of his public ministry, even in his failures and the changes of strategy they required of him, his readiness to give himself did not falter. It was nourished by his sense of being totally accepted and cherished. His assurance remained unshaken until the Agony and the crucifixion. (Presumably that is why Luke says: 'When the Devil finished tempting Jesus in every way, he left him *for a while*.' Lk 4:13). And even in those moments of abandonment Jesus was able to endure the primal fear and anguish by drawing on the conviction that he was still 'the Beloved One', who could still cry 'Abba' into the darkness.

You and I are each offered some experiences like that of Jesus, some occasions where we find ourselves totally loved and accepted. At times this may seem to come 'directly' from God. At other times it may be mediated through the unconditional love of a human friend. But always these experiences come as pure gift. Indeed they may be so unexpected and so undeserved that we are tempted not to believe them. We may shut them out or run away from them as a threat to whatever fragile security we have built up. But if we wish to follow Jesus in his total openness to others and the vulnerability that requires, then we must learn to recognise and welcome such moments of grace. If we reject them or fail to savour them, we shall never be able to reach out unconditionally to others in the love that creates and nourishes friendship and community.

A Basis for Sharing and Community

The example of Jesus provides us with a basis and a model for community-building. It is clear that we, like Jesus, have to resist the temptation to look for easy short-cuts. We cannot evangelise, we cannot build community, simply by *doing* things for people, or *giving* them things. We have to give ourselves — to open ourselves in our weakness and fear of rejection. If we want to follow Jesus we cannot, in principle, set a limit to our degree of openness, to our giving of self; there must be no limit to its depth and no limit to the number of people with whom we are willing to share. Like Jesus we are called to give all — and to the uttermost (Jn 13:1).

In practice, of course, it is necessary and right to hold back on occasion, to operate within the limits of restraint or convention. But when we do so it must not be primarily because of our own fear or embarrassment or self-interest. Rather it should be mainly out of respect for 'where the other person is at'. For instance, it is not truly respectful to 'swamp' a person with intimate confidences the first time we meet. Nor should I set out to break down the defenses of others without regard for their feelings. But that is no reason for taking refuge behind a chilly wall of politeness, or for covering up my sense of inadequacy or my shyness by assuming an air of superiority. There was a refreshing direct-ness and honesty in the conversation and manner of Jesus, a bluntness in his criticism of his enemies (e.g. Mk 12:38-40; Lk 13:32) and his friends (Mt 16:23; 20:25-7), and even in his eloquent silence before Herod (Lk 23:9). The Gospels tell us that he asked his followers to be equally direct: 'All you need say is "yes" if you mean "yes", "no" if you mean "no"; anything more than this comes from the evil one.' (Mt 5:37).

There were times when Jesus adopted the strategy of speaking publicly only in parables, reserving the full explanation for his personal friends (Mk 4:11-2). This suggests that each of us may sometimes find it necessary for strategic reasons to reserve some part of our most cherished beliefs for those who are open to them. I have said that we may at times have to hold back out of respect for the limits of *others*. Now I must add that we may also have to take account of *our own* limits as well. Certain restraints may be imposed on my openness by the fact that I can find no ideally human way to deal with a particular situation or person. But these are just temporary and strategic limitations. In principle I must remain open to all, as Jesus was. The test of sincerity is whether I am trying constantly to extend my limits, to take the risk of being more open than a self-interested prudence would allow.

The Right to Participate

John's Gospel tells us that when Jesus was accused of preaching heresy or subversion he was able to respond: '"I have always spoken publicly to everyone . . . Question the people who heard me."' (Jn 19:20-1). This openness challenges us to avoid any kind of 'cover up' in our relations with our communities. Probably the greatest obstacle to true community is the 'hidden agenda', the attempt to manoeuvre or manipulate people — even for the best of motives. It indicates a failure to trust others, to involve them in deciding the policy of the community and the shaping of its vision. So, whenever I have responsibility for promoting community I am obliged to share information and decision-making with others.

Corresponding to this obligation I also have the right — and even the duty — to claim from various authorities that I not be marginalised in the community through lack of relevant information or of the chance to take part in policy-making. In this, as in all other aspects of community-building the following of Jesus invites me to take risks. For the ultimate value in a Christian community is not security but respect. The greatest respect I can show to others is to offer them the gift of myself. This means that, like Jesus, I must be willing to pay the price for trusting others. The price, like the gift, is myself. What the techniques of community-building offer me are effective and respectful ways to pay that price.

SECTION TWO:
RESOURCES: CHOOSING LIFE — OR DEATH

In this section I want to quote from two poems, which may indicate the fundamental choice each of us has to make — to open ourselves to others or to close ourselves off around our pain and loneliness. The first is part of a poem which expresses very powerfully how important it is for each one of us to feel 'heard' and appreciated — to have, as the author says, 'a holy hearing audience':

Thank You, Thank you
— by Patrick Kavanagh[1]

. . . We are not alone in our loneliness,
Others have been here and known
Griefs we thought our special own
Problems that we could not solve
Lovers that we could not have
Pleasures that we missed by inches.
Come I'm beginning to get pretentious
Beginning to message for instead
Of expressing how glad
I am to have lived to feel the radiance
Of a holy hearing audience
And delivered God's commands
Into those caressing hands,
My personality that's to say
All that is mine exclusively.
What wisdom's ours if such there be
Is a flavour of personality.
I thank you and I say how proud
That I have been by fate allowed

71

To stand here having the joyful chance
To claim my inheritance
For most have died the day before
The opening of that holy door.

The second poem I wish to quote here is one I wrote a few years ago to help myself understand what was going on in a rather difficult situation. I had a lot of contact with somebody who seemed to be doing a good deal of harm because of his combination of very high intelligence with a great amount of hurt and bitterness. He was so locked into his pain that he seemed incapable of reaching out to others in simplicity and vulnerability.

Pain-World

Bright butterfly, now pierced and pinned
with spike of pain that nails you to the past.
Despite the mortal wound you brilliantly devise
the perfect ploys, the master plan
that hide the wound — at least from you —
by making it the centre of your world.
So, circling round the pain,
exuding threads of anti-life, you weave an anti-world
and restlessly patrol the border posts
between it and the dull and placid world
where we mere humans live.

Some victims blunder blindly in,
they stumble past the raw nerve wire
and never know their fate
until they feel your cruel sting.
For fools like these you need no fine finesse,
a bludgeon, or a blunderbuss soon blots them out
and may provide a nervous laugh for those beyond your reach.

But there are some who freely share your world
— poor rabbits fascinated by your verve,
or wounded souls who think that you have found
a way to cope with inner hurt.
With these you seem to show a strange restraint;
at times you teach them simple steps
in your St Vitus dance of pain,
or stroke them gently as a cat the mouse,

while slyly you inject your venom in their veins,
spread poison pollen on the springs of life
to fertilize the cancer cells.
And so you colonise our world
with offspring spawned in ecstasies of pain.

What drives you on to drill so deep
to tap the inmost springs of pain?
Is loneliness the hidden goad?
Is comradeship a need so strong
that, lacking saner fellowship, you aim
to build communities of anguished souls?
Or do you fear the emptiness of life
and use your pain to prove you still exist?

My brother I have heard your scream,
but find no way to reach inside your shell.
Admit, go limp, ask help, accept my outstretched hand.
Then we can weep warm tears to melt
the spear of ice that pins you to your past,
dissolve your Snow-Queen sparkling frozen world,
and so allow the glacier to unlock
its long stored seeds of life and simple joy
in some high Alpen valley in the Spring.

SECTION THREE:
LISTENING AND TRUST-BUILDING EXERCISES

In this section I propose a series of exercises which should be of help to a group who want to deepen their sense of community with each other. Some of the exercises can also suitably be done by individuals on their own; they may wish to use them with a group later on. It is not, of course, necessary to make use of all these exercises. You can pick and choose. But it would be a mistake to assume that 'well educated' people can skip the 'easy' exercises. Intellectual people may understand the exercises in theory; but in practice these 'simple' exercises may be both very necessary for them and quite demanding on them.

1. Johari's Window
The name 'JOHARI' comes from the fact that the idea of this 'window' came from two psychologists called Joe and

Harry.[2] The Johari Window is a simple diagram which illustrates different aspects of the personality. We have found it a very useful introduction to exercises that have to do with listening and sharing. It only takes about 20 minutes to present and explain it. But the presentation is of little value unless it is followed immediately by practical exercises such as those outlined below.

Display a large poster with a drawing of a window with four panes (Fig. 2). The top left-hand pane is marked 'OPEN'. It represents the part of my personality that is *known to myself and to others* and is therefore open to people, not hidden in any way. Give some practical and topical examples — preferably amusing ones, such as well-known facts about your own personality e.g. that you are cheerful, etc.

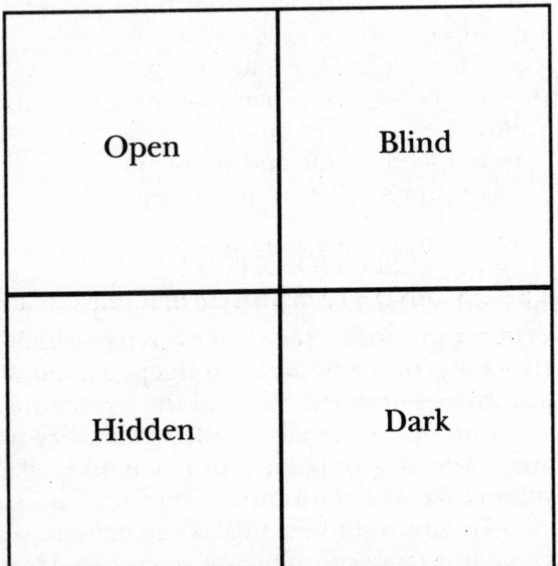

Open	Blind
Hidden	Dark

Fig. 2

The lower left-hand pane of the window is marked 'HIDDEN'. It represents the part of my personality that is *known to myself but not known to others*. Give two or three examples from your own personality. The first example could be something light and amusing e.g. your age. But then you might share with the group something sad or painful about yourself that they hadn't known before. This will evoke a more serious and sympathetic kind of listening from the group and will prepare the ground for the kind of sharing you will be asking them to engage in before long — and will even 'model' it for them (— but do not distract them by speaking, at this point, about the exercise which is to follow).

The top right-hand pane of the window is marked 'BLIND'. It represents the part of my personality that is *known to others but not known to myself*. It may be seen as a 'blind spot' — some fault or quirk of mine that I am not aware of. (You could give an amusing example about yourself e.g. some odd facial expression which you had not been aware of). But, much more importantly, it could be some gift I have, but which I am scarcely aware of, or am unwilling to admit. By way of example share with the group some really valuable discovery you made about yourself through working with others — some talent you had not been aware of until a friend or team-member pointed it out to you. This sharing should evoke real interest in the group — an eagerness to discover their own hidden talents. If you tell the story in a simple way, avoiding the extremes of boastfulness and mock-humility, you will be modelling for the group the kind of sharing that helps to build community.

The lower right-hand pane of the Johari Window is marked 'DARK'. It represents the part of my personality that is *not known to myself and not known to others*. Only God knows this part of my personality. It probably contains some frightening things — e.g. buried memories of childhood hurts and terrors. But, more importantly, it also contains deep sources of life and energy — the basis of many rich and powerful gifts which will be revealed to me in the future. You could give an example of some gift which, until recently, neither you nor anybody else knew you had — perhaps the gift of being fully present to others, or a healing gift, or the gift of making peace. Then explain briefly how you became aware of this gift. The example should if at all possible be of some important experience in your life, which you can speak about with feeling and conviction. All the better if you find it a little embarrassing or costly to share it with the group. This is far more powerful than a concocted example: and it will give the group a model to follow.

The second part of the explanation of the Johari Window can be quite brief. Draw a horizontal line a couple of inches below the line that marks the boundary between the 'open' pane and the 'hidden' pane (see Fig. 3). Explain that this means enlarging the area that is 'OPEN' by sharing with others some of what was previously 'hidden'. Recall the examples you have already given when explaining the 'hidden' area. Point out that this kind of sharing, when carried out with sensitivity, is one of the most important ways of building up trust in a community. We are sharing something of ourselves, opening up to others. Write the word 'SHARING' in the area between the old boundary and the new one.

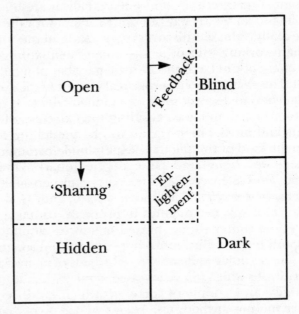

Fig. 3

Now draw a vertical line about two inches to the right of the boundary between the 'open' pane and the 'blind' pane. Explain that this means a further enlargement of the area that is 'OPEN' to others. This time the enlarging is done, not by my sharing with you something I already know about myself, but rather by you giving me what is called *'feedback'*. This jargon word is now used widely to mean that you tell me something about my character or behaviour — generally something I hadn't previously known about myself. (Write in the word 'FEEDBACK' between the old and new boundary — as in Fig. 3). Recall the examples you have already given of such 'feedback'. Point out that this is another way of building up trust in a group. Those who receive the 'feedback' are allowing themselves to be judged by others — even at the risk of being embarrassed or hurt. Those who give the feedback are taking the risk of being rejected. Explain that 'feedback' is not so easy to handle as 'sharing'; we need to learn ways of making sure that people do not give feedback when it is not invited or appropriate.

Next you extend the two new lines slightly so that they meet. This creates a small square in the top right hand corner of the 'dark' pane. Explain that when we extend the 'open' area through sharing and feedback it often happens that elements of the 'dark' area come into the light. Suddenly or gradually we may get a whole new light on our personality and our gifts: this comes unexpectedly and is experienced as a gift from God. So it is a kind of revelation or enlightenment. (Write the word 'ENLIGHTENMENT' in the small square, as in Fig. 3). Recall the personal example you have already given; and you could perhaps give a further moving example — from your own life or (with due discretion) from the life of a friend. Add that one of the wonderful effects of building up a community is that it helps each of its members to grow and develop, to discover unexpected gifts that bring joy and fulfillment into their lives. These gifts can be shared with others to enrich the community and help bring about the new world in which we believe.

After this presentation it is best to hand over to another member of the team who will facilitate any discussion and lead it briskly into a practical exercise of sharing. The first thing is to allow a few moments for people to ask for clarifications about any points that they did not grasp. At this point, try to confine the discussion to short clarifications. If necessary, explain honestly that the team considers it more important to help the group to make *practical* use of the Johari Window than to get into a general discussion of the theory.

NOTE: If you are working with the same group over a considerable period of time you will probably find it very helpful to repeat the presentation of the Johari Window after some months or years. At that stage the group will be quite advanced; they will have had a lot of experience in listening and sharing. Then they will appreciate more than ever how the Johari Window model provides a framework which integrates what they have learned through their own experience. The presentation should then be followed not by the rather elementary exercise of 'simple sharing' described below but by some more advanced sharing or feedback exercise — perhaps based on the Enneagram material which I shall discuss in a later chapter.

2. A Simple Sharing Exercise

The first practical exercise is one which we call 'SIMPLE SHARING'. The whole group should be sub-divided into groups of four — and the members of the facilitation team should mix around to join in with the other participants in these little groups. If you wish, you may form the groups by numbering people off. But it is more challenging and more helpful to ask the participants to form their own groups, asking them to choose people whom they do not know very well. Make sure that each little group forms a tight circle of its own so the members can listen attentively to each other. Ask the participants to take a few minutes to recall some interesting experience they had recently; when they feel ready, each member of a small group is allowed five uninterrupted minutes to share his or her own experience with the three other members of the group. The other members of the group do not interrupt by asking questions or making comments, even if the person goes silent; for the silence may be quite fruitful. When the five minutes are up, another member of the group will share his or her experience. Then the turn of the third and fourth person will come around. Explain that by 'simple sharing' we mean offering each person the opportunity to share with people who undertake to listen without question or comment; people who are sharing feel more safe when they know they will not be probed or challenged. Stress the point that this is not only a sharing exercise but also a listening exercise.

The over-all facilitator may have to check occasionally (but not obtrusively) to ensure that in the various small groups each member is getting a fair amount of the available time. If there are experienced facilitators in the different groups they can quietly ensure that the time in their own group is fairly distributed. You may have to allow a few extra moments to give time for all the groups to finish their sharing. Then ask all the participants to form one large circle and facilitate a light general sharing for about fifteen minutes. This can be sparked off by asking: 'What helped you to listen attentively?' It is likely that somebody will bring out the point that it is easier to listen if the speaker is sharing personal feelings — especially 'negative' feelings of hurt, fear or anger.

You may go on to ask: 'What helped you to speak openly of very personal experiences?' This will probably lead to a recognition of the importance of trust and respect in the group. Another point that may emerge is that, when we are speaking of very personal matters, we feel a person is really present to us if, when we look up, we find the person looking (but not staring) at us. This is an opportune time for one of the team to stress the importance of 'eye contact'. This can be linked with 'I contact' — the importance of the speaker using the word 'I' rather than 'one' or 'you' or 'we' (as I pointed out in Section 1 of this Chapter).

3. 'The River of Life'

This is a very valuable exercise which serves two purposes. Firstly, it offers individuals an opportunity to reflect on the pattern of their lives, in a way that can be very moving and can in fact be a deeply religious experience. Secondly, it can contribute greatly to the development of a deep sense of community in a small group; for it provides a wealth of material which members of the group may share with each other in varying degrees. So it is important that the exercise be given plenty of time and that everything be done to ensure that it takes place in a non-threatening and friendly atmosphere.

Invite the participants to relax and centre themselves while you play some quiet meditative music. Then introduce the exercise as one which offers members of the group an opportunity to reflect on their lives. Display a large sheet of paper on which you have sketched a wavy line to represent your own 'river of life'. Share with the group one or two of the significant turning points in that 'river', and mark them on the drawing in various colours or with some symbol. Explain that this is just a very brief sample of the work you are now inviting each person in the group to do. Ask the participants to spend half an hour reflecting on their own 'river of life', noting the major developments and turning points, and drawing or painting them in symbolic form. Distribute sheets of typing paper and leave plenty of markers, crayons, and pastels in the centre of the room where they can be easily picked up. Emphasise that this is not a test of one's skill in art; even a very poor drawing may represent a very rich life.

If the members of the group are interested in religion, then you might invite them to look particularly at the places where they feel God touched their lives. But you may decide that this is such a rich topic for reflection that it should be held over until another occasion, when the group may be invited to look again at the river of their lives, this time in terms of God's action in it.

After half an hour invite the participants to form groups of five. Suggest that, in these small groups, each member in turn takes six minutes to share with the others whatever parts of the 'river of their lives' they feel free to share. The exercise is one of 'simple sharing', so the others do not interrupt or probe.

Allow enough time for everybody to be heard in the small groups. Then invite everybody to come back together and form one large circle. Gently invite a few comments in response to some such question as, 'how did you find that experience?' Round off the session by inviting a couple of short spontaneous prayers from members of the group.

4. 'Feedback'

As I have already explained, if you give me 'feedback' this means that you tell me something about my character or behaviour — usually something I hadn't previously known about myself. I begin with a cautionary note. Most of us have met people who are strongly opposed to group work. A little sympathetic listening often shows that this opposition is linked to some bad experience of group work which the person has had, or has heard of. And such 'bad experiences' are nearly always associated with inappropriate 'feedback'. A poorly facilitated exercise of 'feedback' may have left the person the victim of some deeply hurtful remark — and, worst of all, such offensive comments may have been presented as justified in the context of 'group dynamics'! No wonder that such people have become suspicious. My conclusion is that in this matter it is better to move very slowly, and if necessary to err on the side of caution. In order to build up trust in a group it is better to have a lot more sharing exercises than feedback exercises; and to have positive rather than negative feedback most of the time — especially in the early stages.

It is easy to organize an exercise where people give each other positive feedback. But it is not always easy to ensure that this is done in a way that avoids artificiality or insincerity. The context and atmosphere have to be right if such exercises are to work well. I can illustrate this by giving an example which took place recently. A group of eight or nine of us had organized a weekend conference for almost one hundred and fifty people. After the final closing prayer and ritual we were all about to rush off home. But, before leaving, we in the organizing group gathered in a little circle to say goodbye to each other. Just as we were about to break up, one of our members spontaneously proposed that each of us should be offered a little affirmation by one or two others in the group. So, without any prior planning, each of us congratulated one of the others with such remarks as: 'I liked the way you handled that crisis', or 'I was touched by what you said on that occasion', or 'I was very impressed by the time and energy you gave to preparing the lists of participants', or 'I was very moved by the prayer you led'. In less than ten minutes each of us had been given some very heart-warming feedback, and we went home feeling more alive and linked to each other in a warm bond of affection.

81

5. A Faith-Sharing and Feedback Exercise

I have found that exercises of sharing and feedback usually have more depth when they are linked to periods of prayer. So what I am suggesting next is a simple faith-sharing exercise followed by some sharing and feedback. The time given to the exercise may be anything from about forty minutes to over two hours; I shall indicate below how much time may be allotted to each part of the exercise.

Ask the group to form a circle, and to sit with their backs straight and their feet firmly planted on the floor. Play some quiet meditative music, or one of the Taizé chants. Do a short centering exercise. Then have two members of the group read out slowly the following texts (or similar ones which would be more appropriate for the group):

> There are different kinds of gifts, but it is the same Spirit who gives them all. There are different ways of serving, but the same God gives to each of us the power to carry out our own particular service. The presence of the Spirit is shown in a special way in each person for the good of all. The Spirit gives one person a message full of wisdom while to another person the same Spirit gives a message full of insight. One and the same Spirit gives faith to one person, healing power to another, and wonder-working power to yet another. Some receive a gift of speaking God's prophetic word while the same Spirit gives to others the gift of discerning which word is truly God's word. Some are given the gift of praying in the Spirit while others have the gift of relating that prayer to daily life. It is the self-same Spirit who is at work in all this, freely distributing to each one of us our own special gifts.
>
> (I Cor 12:4-11 paraphrased)

> It was you who created my inmost self
> and put me together in my mother's womb
> for all these mysteries I thank you
> for the wonder of myself, for the wonder of your works.
>
> (Ps 139)

> Yahweh God has taught me what to say
> so that I can strengthen the weary.
> Every morning Yahweh makes me eager
> to hear what God is going to teach me.

God has given me understanding
and I have not rebelled
or turned away.
                    (Is 50:4-5)

Now distribute to the group photocopied or cyclostyled copies of these texts. Suggest that each person should reflect and pray on the texts for thirty minutes. (If they are people who are used to extended prayer periods you may propose that they take an hour for this personal prayer. On the other hand, the period of personal prayer may be shortened to fifteen minutes if there is a shortage of time or if the members are not used to this kind of prayer. You will probably find, as we did, that the longer the time of personal prayer, the deeper will be the sharing that follows.)

Suggest that at the end of the period of personal prayer the members come together in groups of four. (An easy way to form these groups is to write beforehand a group number and location on each of the distributed sheets of paper containing the Scripture texts.) Suggest that in these little groups each person be given five uninterrupted minutes to share on some or all of these questions (especially the first and third):

— What *touched* or moved me in the text or prayer?
— Did I receive any *insight?*
— Did I feel called to any *action?*

After about twenty-five minutes suggest to the different small groups that they go on to do the following sharing and feedback exercise. Still in the same little groups, each in turn is invited to listen for three or four minutes to each of the others as they tell that person of just *one* gift which they see in her or him. The person who is receiving this positive feedback is asked not to comment or evaluate the feedback there and then, but to hold it for personal reflection later on. Instead of responding directly to what the others have said, the one receiving the feedback is asked to reply by sharing briefly with the other members of the little group about some *one* gift which s/he believes her/himself to have, and about how it could be used for the benefit of the community.

This second part of the work in the small groups should take about twenty minutes. After that time, ask the members of all the small groups to form one large circle (perhaps gathered around a lighted candle and some flowers or vegetation on a hand-woven cloth) and ask if anybody would like to say a few words about how they found the exercise, or perhaps to say a short prayer. Try to keep the atmosphere very quiet and prayerful, avoiding, if possible, any theoretical discussion or debate about the process. You should draw the whole exercise to a close after about ten minutes in the large group — unless the group gets into some very rich and powerful sharing; and even if that does happen, remember that there is a very thin line between 'long enough' and 'too long' — and it is better to err on the side of brevity!

6. *Sharing of Character Types*

Most people like to explore their own characters, and to share this with others whom they trust. In a later chapter, on the Enneagram, I shall offer guidelines for doing this in some depth. But before that it is useful to do the following simple exercise of reflection and sharing.[3]

The Story of the Gift

Mrs Cardoz was the local community health nurse in the village of Tura. She announced her retirement, so five of the local women gathered to plan a farewell which would include giving her a gift.

Fatima was full of ideas: 'We could give her a handbag, or some hand-woven cloth, or a pair of earrings, or an ironing board'. She went on to consider the pros and cons of each of these as a possible gift.

After a little while Ruth intervened to say that they should decide quickly rather than spend the morning exploring all possibilities.

At this point Rebecca intervened and made a strong case for choosing the hand-woven cloth. She maintained strongly that it was the only proper gift to give to somebody like Mrs Cardoz.

While the others were speaking, Maria had been looking around the group, trying to weigh up who was in favour of which gift, worrying that the gift might become a divisive issue, and wondering what was going on in the mind of Deborah, who had said nothing so far. She said: 'I am sure we all know that the cloth would be beautiful, but I feel that most of the group would find it too costly. I had the impression that nearly everybody was impressed by Fatima's description of the handbag. Could we agree on that?'

Ruth cut in quickly: 'Why waste all this time? Let's have a vote. Will those in favour of the handbag put up their hands.'

Rebecca said: 'Mrs Cardoz already has a fine handbag. So we really don't have much choice. We must give her the cloth.'

Maria said: 'We haven't heard anything yet from Deborah; I'd like to hear your opinion.'

Deborah said very quietly: 'I'm not sure. I haven't yet made up my mind.'

And so the discussion went on . . .

Having told the above story (or some variation on the same theme), point out the different character types:

Fatima: a 'head' person, full of ideas, wanting to explore all the possibilities and all the arguments.

Ruth: a 'task-centred' type, anxious to get the decision made quickly, inclined to be impatient with the long discussion.

Rebecca: a 'strong and forceful' type, with definite ideas which she wants the others to accept.

Maria: a 'heart' type, mostly concerned about how the others in the group are feeling, sensing their views, anxious to have agreement of all.

Deborah: a 'quiet and thoughtful' type, holding back, thinking her own thoughts, reluctant to share them with the group.

Have five large sheets of paper, each with the title of one of these five different types ('task-centred' etc). Put up the sheets of paper on the walls in different parts of the room. Ask each member of the group to reflect for a moment to see whose behaviour in the story did he or she identify with, and which of these kinds of behaviour is nearest to the way he or she usually behaves in a group; are they 'strong and forceful' like Rebecca, or 'quiet and thoughtful' like Deborah etc. Then ask each of them to gather under the sheet of paper which best describes her or his behaviour. Each of these small groups is then asked to discuss for about twenty minutes: 'What is helpful about this way of behaving in a group? What is not helpful about it?' They can then go on to consider what is helpful about other ways of behaving in a group.

After about twenty minutes the participants are asked to form one large group, in which the members of the smaller groups are still sitting near each other. Each group in turn shares the conclusions they came to in the small group.

This group exercise can provide the basis, later on, for a good deal of informal interpersonal sharing and feedback between the members about their own and each other's characters. In this way it promotes personal growth and the build-up of trust in the group. Those who find the whole topic very rewarding can be invited later on to go much deeper by studying the Enneagram and doing the exercises on it which I outline in another chapter of this book.

7. Critical Feedback

I don't think it is a good idea to introduce negative or critical feedback simply as an *exercise*. But any group that works together for a while will soon find that irritation and frustration builds up between individuals or between certain categories (e.g. the younger members in relation to the older ones, or the women in relation to the men). When this happens it is helpful to have a fairly structured way of relieving the pressure. What I outline here is a process which, when working on various teams, I have found very useful; it is a process which can be adapted to suit different circumstances. The teams I worked with used it mainly to help different *groups* to give positive and negative feedback to each other. But it can also be used when there is on-going tension between two or three *individuals*.

On one of our workshops for Church leaders we had three distinct groups — lay-people, Sisters, and priests. As they reflected on their work for the Church it became clear to us that the lay leaders felt somewhat frustrated about their position. Eventually we proposed this process: the people in each of the three categories were asked to form a distinct group. So the laity, the Sisters, and the priests went off to separate rooms for about an hour. The lay leaders were given the task of bringing back to the whole group large sheets of paper giving their answers to the following questions:

— What do we *appreciate* about the Sisters?
— What do we find *difficult* in the conduct or manner of the Sisters?
— What do we *ask of* the Sisters?
— What do we *appreciate* about the priests?
— What do we find *difficult* in the conduct or manner of the priests?
— What do we *ask of* the priests?

The Sisters' group was asked to answer the same questions about the priests' group and the lay group; while the priests' group was asked to reply about the lay leaders and the Sisters. When the whole group came together, each sub-group was asked to listen in silence while the responses were read out. Questions for clarification were allowed, but we asked everybody not to defend their group or even to comment on the feedback or to probe what had been said.

Having positive feedback made it easier for people to listen to the negative feedback. And the third question was very important, because it encouraged people to scale down their expectations of the other groups to a manageable level. The exercise gave people a lot of food for thought. It also caused quite a bit of pain; but the participants felt it was better to endure that pain than to live in a false paradise while anger and frustration were building up in people whom they imagined to be content. Honesty is essential if one is to build up a true community spirit.

A Poem

Working with groups, I have often used this little poem by Dorothee Sölle. Most of them have found it very inspiring. It has helped them to bridge the wide gap that people often experience between working with a small group and working to change the world. The poem has brought home to them the public and political implications of building small communities and networks.

For My Young Comrades
— by Dorothee Sölle[4]

One plus a friend plus a friend plus a friend
don't say that makes four
the whole is greater than the sum of its parts

small numbers mean friendship
large ones revolution

Begin with what you can count on your fingers
for a friend does not dominate
a friend always has time
or knows someone else who does
a friend always finds an answer
or knows someone else who will
a friend is always competent
or will find someone else who is

Small numbers provide a network
large ones build the new city.

NOTES

1. From 'Thank You, Thank You' (Epilogue to a series of lectures given at University College, Dublin), *Patrick Kavanagh: The Complete Poems* (Collected, Arranged and Edited by Peter Kavanagh), New York (The Peter Kavanagh Hand Press: 1972), Newbridge (The Goldsmith Press: 1984) 350-1.

2. From *Group Processes: An Introduction to Group Dynamics* by Joseph Luft by permission of Mayfield Publishing Company. Copyright (c) 1984, 1970 and 1963 by Joseph Luft. I have slightly adapted the original version of the 'window' which was designed by Joe Luft and Harry Ingham.

3. The exercise is an adapted version of the 'Multiple Role Exercise' in Anne Hope and Sally Timmel, *Training for Transformation: A Handbook for Community Workers*, Gweru, Zimbabwe (Mambo Press: 1984) Vol 2, 65. The idea of adding the story came from members of the group with whom I worked in West Africa. So far as I can recall, the story was worked out by Steve 'Lani Adeleye, Maura Ramsbottom, Berne Eyewan Okure, Felix Obanubi, Noel Bradley, Mary Anthony Ogunkorode, Kehinde Silva, and Tina Enamhanye. Here, I have adapted the story.

4. *Of War and Love*, Maryknoll (Orbis: 1983), 143.

4

Liturgy and Life

Some of those who are most committed in practice to transforming the world according to the Christian vision are people who have very mixed feelings about the Church and about the traditional forms of Christian worship. This may be because they have been hurt or angered by the behaviour of some Church leader or by the style of worship services they have had to put up with. So we cannot take for granted that the celebration of the Eucharist will automatically be a nourishing and unifying experience for all of those who work with us in 'justice and peace' groups or similar gatherings. The best way forward is to enable such people to experience liturgies which speak to their hearts.

It takes a lot of creativity to find ways of doing this. In the various workshops which I helped to design and facilitate over the past ten years we came to realise that a prayer service must not be planned on its own; it is most important that it be closely related to whatever is going on in the workshop itself. This relationship may be a *direct* one in which the topic of the workshop session is taken up again in prayer. Sometimes it is even more effective to design the worship service as a *counterpoint* to the material that is being dealt with in the working sessions; for instance, if one is dealing with oppression and struggle the prayer service might be a very quiet one in which the participants are helped to become aware of the healing power of God. This counterpoint effect may come about by chance. But I think it is important for those who are working with groups not to rely entirely on providential coincidences. In each workshop we run, we ask for a volunteer group to coordinate the prayer services. But we appoint one member of the facilitation team to liaise with this 'liturgy team', making sure that the prayer group know in good time the topics that will be covered in the working sessions. And on special occasions we ask that we on the facilitation team be allowed to prepare the liturgy.

Such 'special occasions' arise when we design a 'working session' that is at the same time a worship service. For instance it may be a pilgrimage of some kind, varying in length from an hour or two to a whole day or longer. The pilgrimage is an excellent way to bridge the gap between liturgy and daily life. And many of those who take part are affected at a very deep level. I suppose this is partly because the pilgrimage involves the body and the heart even more than the head. But I am convinced that the real source of the power of the pilgrimage to move people is that it puts them in touch with part of the tradition in which their spirits are rooted — even when they are scarcely aware of these roots.

A pilgrimage event within a workshop should be carefully designed to suit the spiritual needs of the particular group. Obviously one should use traditional elements in so far as they are appropriate; but I think it is necessary at times to make adaptations — even considerable ones. Rather than theorise about this I propose to give some examples of things we have done, in the hope that this may spark off the creativity of my readers to design their own pilgrimages or adapt what they find here.

The Holy Mountain

Last year a group of us, about fourteen in all, from a wide variety of locations and backgrounds, spent about ten days together in a big old house beside the sea in the west of Ireland. Our time together was partly a holiday and partly 'work'. By 'work' I mean here a variety of different activities and exercises designed to nourish our spirituality and improve our skills. Our activities ranged from guided meditation to bioenergetics, from gestalt work to exploration of ecological issues; and each evening we celebrated the Eucharist together in a very participative manner.

The house we were staying in was near to the foot of the holy mountain Croagh Patrick, where St Patrick is reputed to have spent forty days and forty nights in prayer. So we arranged that our time there would include the pilgrimage day on the last Sunday of July. On that day every year almost 70,000 pilgrims climb the mountain in the traditional pilgrimage — which, though now Christian, goes back three or four thousand years to the pre-Christian Celtic sun worship.

Traditionally, the pilgrimage took place at night. I remember thirty years ago when I first climbed the mountain, we started at midnight and waited on top until dawn when the first of many Masses was celebrated in the little chapel on the moonscape surface of the summit. In recent years the Church authorities changed the time of the pilgrimage to the day-time. But there is little or no change in the format of the pilgrimage; there are two or three points on the way up where the pilgrims walk round a little mound of rocks seven times saying the Lord's Prayer; and many people say Rosaries almost continuously as they climb.

We adapted the pilgrimage so that it would be more nourishing for our particular group. We met for a couple of hours the evening before, and together we designed an event that retained most of the traditional pattern but gave it a much more Scriptural character. We saw *our* pilgrimage as a symbolic reenactment of the Exodus of God's people and their return to the Promised Land. We resolved to start climbing the mountain in the dark, shortly before dawn. But we decided to begin our pilgrimage on the night before the climb, by reading, in a liturgical setting, the biblical story of the escape from Egypt.

On Sunday morning we got up after 4.00 a.m. and had a hasty breakfast, standing round the kitchen table carrying the sticks we needed to help in the climb. Meanwhile we listened to an adapted version of chapter 12 of the Book of Exodus:

> Each family or community is to prepare food and each person is to eat it with staff in hand and dressed for the journey. You shall eat it in haste before you depart. This is a paschal meal, celebrating our rescue from slavery and our journey into a land of promise. It is a passover meal, recalling how God chooses those who wish to be liberated, leading us out of darkness into the light of life. This is the Word of God.

As we left the house two women of our group prayed over each of us in turn, invoking a blessing of the four elements — Earth, Fire, Air and Water.

Soon we were struggling up the pilgrim path in the semi-darkness. When we stopped for breath a few hundred feet above sea level we gathered together to listen to the Word of God:

> When Pharaoh had let the people go, God did not allow them take the road to the land of the Philistines, although that was the nearest way. Instead God led the people by the roundabout way of the wilderness. . . . Yahweh went before them, by day in the form of a pillar of cloud to show them the way, and by night in the form of a pillar of fire to give them light: thus they could continue their march by day and by night. The pillar of cloud never failed to go before the people during the day, nor the pillar of fire during the night (Ex 13:17-22). This is the Word of God.

By this time the new day was dawning so we walked on with renewed hope and a sense of the presence of God in our midst. But some of us were breathless and tired by the time we reached the shoulder of the mountain. We were glad to stop and gather for another reading:

> When the ruler of Egypt was told that the people had made their escape he said: 'What have we done? We have let them go free so they are no longer our slaves!' So he and his army set out in pursuit and they caught up with the people of God where they had camped near the sea. God's people were terrified and cried out to Yahweh. Then they turned on Moses, saying: 'Why did you have to bring us out here in the wilderness to die? Did we not tell you beforehand this would happen? We told you to leave us alone, to let us go on being in Egypt. Better to live there as slaves than to die out here in the wilderness.' Moses replied: 'Do not be afraid! Stand your ground and you will see what Yahweh will do to save you this very day. Yahweh will fight for you; you have only to hold on.' (Ex 14:5-14). This is the Word of God.

We moved on again and before long we were swallowed up in heavy driving rain which turned the track into a stream. Just before the final steep and dangerous slope leading to the summit we huddled together for one more reading — a very short one this time:

God said to Moses: 'Why are you crying out for help? Tell the people to move forward; they will be able to go on dry ground. The enemy will know, when I defeat them, that I am the sovereign God.' (Ex 14:15-18 adapted)

We scrambled to the top of the mountain but could see nothing through the storm which was blowing. The chapel on the summit had not yet been opened, so there was no sheltered place where we could celebrate the second part of our Liturgy. Very quickly we set off again, this time taking a different route — easier underfoot but more risky because we could easily lose our way. As we struggled forward through the storm, we wandered off the track. When it became apparent that we were lost, our three leaders conferred about the route. Each of the three proposed a different direction, and each was afraid that the other proposed routes would lead us over a cliff!

The crisis began to affect our morale and our sense of communion with each other. One of the women abruptly called the group to a halt and proposed that now was the time for the Eucharistic Prayer; even though there was no shelter we could not afford to wait any longer for our 'viaticum' ('food for the journey'). So, standing there in the rain, we celebrated as our persecuted ancestors had often done in the past when they gathered around the Massrock. Nourished by this Eucharist we finished in better spirits — and just at that moment, the storm abated and, like 'a rumour of angels', we heard the voices of climbing pilgrims coming to us from the other side of the gully in which we were gathered. Greatly encouraged and fully in communion with each other — and with our fellow-pilgrims — we resumed our descent. Within ten minutes we came out of the rain and clouds and could look down with new eyes on the beauty of the bay with its hundreds of little islands stretched out below us.

Less than an hour later we were home again, drinking hot soup and listening to our final Scripture reading:

I sing to Yahweh who has won a glorious triumph,
Yahweh, my strong defender, the one who has saved us.
This is my God and the God of my ancestors,

93

This is the one whose glory I sing.
Yahweh is the name of my God,
A God who is present to defend me.
Your right hand, O God, is majestic in its power.
You cleared a path for us through the waters.
Your righteous anger shrivelled up the enemy,
breaking the power of evil.
The enemy said: 'I will track them down and catch them,
I will take all that they have and leave them broken.'
But just one breath from you and they sank like lead
In the terrible waters.
Who is like you, Yahweh, among the gods?
Who can compare with you, in your majesty and holiness?
Who can work wonders and mighty deeds like you?
Faithful to your promise you led the people you had saved,
And by your strength you guided us safely home.

                              (Ex 15:1-13 — adapted)

Another Pilgrimage

On that occasion we were fortunate to have a 'ready-made' pilgrimage which we could adapt to suit us. But if that is not possible one can make creative use of the possibilities that are at hand. On another course last year we proposed the idea of a pilgrimage to the group. They decided on a walking pilgrimage to a 'holy well' located in a beautiful gap in the hills of Donegal.

The group chose a series of biblical texts, somewhat on the pattern of the Easter Vigil readings. On the evening before the pilgrimage we listened to a beautiful passage from the book of Ezekiel — God's promise of a new heart for the people (36:24-30), followed by psalm 121: 'I lift up my eyes to the mountains, where will my help come from?'. Next morning before setting out, we read the story of the passover meal (Ex 12:1-14). At our first 'station' we listened to the account of the offering of Isaac and God's promise to Abraham (Gen 22:1-18). At the second 'station' the reading was from Deuteronomy 26:1-11 — the acknowledgement of God's goodness and power in leading us into the promised land. The reading at the third 'station' was the story of Elijah's journey to the holy mountain and how he heard the voice of God in the whisper of the breeze (I Kngs 19:3-13) —

ending with God's challenging and evocative question, 'what are you doing here?'

When we arrived at the traditional holy well we contemplated the living water for a little while. Then we celebrated the Eucharist during which we listened to two further readings — Gen 1:12-31, which tells how we are made in the image of God, and the account of the beatitudes of Jesus from chapter 5 of Matthew's Gospel.

Past, Present and Future

Some time ago we were running a workshop for experienced facilitators. Towards the end of it there emerged in the group a strong sense of the need to devote some time to the question of an integrated spirituality. The easiest way for us as organisers to respond to this need would have been to schedule a talk and discussion on the topic. But we felt that this was such a generative issue that what was called for was something both deeper and more participative — an event designed for the heart more than for the head.

So we proposed that the group take an hour for a 'walking meditation' on the theme of spirituality. We suggested that during the first half-hour — the outward journey — each would reflect on 'where have I come from in my journey up to the present?' During this period the participants walked quietly into the chapel, then out through the grounds (in bare feet if they wished), past the buildings of a large missionary seminary, then down to the cemetery, and past a shrine with a statue of the Virgin Mary, and so into a clearing in deep woodland. There we formed a circle and held hands, still in silence, for a short time, before beginning our return journey.

The topic proposed for meditation during the return journey was, 'where am I being led now, in my spiritual journey?' It was interesting to note that several participants chose to return by a different route. When we gathered together after our return, each person had the opportunity to share with the rest of us some of the fruits of the meditation. We suggested that the participants might use some symbol to express what they had learned — for instance, a little mime or dance to represent the movement from the past through the present and into the future; or some symbolic object picked up on the journey. After this, one of the participants shared the following beautiful poem by the Irish poet Patrick Kavanagh:

Worship

To your high altar I once came
Proudly, even brazenly, and I said:-
Open your tabernacles I too am flame
Ablaze on the hills of Being. Let the dead
Chant the low prayer beneath a candled shrine,
O cut for me life's bread, for me pour wine![1]

Following on from this sharing we invited members of the group to think briefly about two key elements of official Christian spirituality — the Bible and the Eucharist — and to say what these meant to them. This in turn led on to an invitation to the members of the group to say under what conditions they would like to celebrate the Eucharist together. We asked these questions because we sensed that several members of the group were carrying hurt and anger about Eucharists in which they had taken part in the past. We did not want to gloss over these feelings too lightly; there was a danger that we might have ended up with a celebration which would be nourishing for most of the group but could have increased the sense of alienation of a minority. By taking the extra time to allow people to express their reservations, we were able to move on all together; and the whole group created a Eucharist which responded to the needs of all.

Pilgrimage as Workshop

What I have been describing so far in this chapter is the use of a pilgrimage as an integral part of a workshop, which itself would normally be one element in a training programme for community leaders. But the more I reflect on the notion of pilgrimage, the more I realise that *the pilgrimage itself* can and should be a kind of workshop in its own right. The medieval pilgrimages served roughly the same purposes as we would have for a workshop nowadays — the creation of an experience of community as a nourishing and prayerful ambience within which the participants can stand back a little from their daily lives to reflect on their faith and learn more effective ways of living it out.

96

In places like South Africa and Latin America where the struggle for human dignity and liberation is very much to the fore, major religious events like funerals or festivals can be among the most effective means of building awareness and cohesiveness in the ordinary people, and a means of nourishing their faith and commitment. I am inclined to think that for certain groups in Europe or North America a pilgrimage can serve the same purposes. This would apply to people who have a strong folk religion in which the notion of pilgrimage is an element. One such group in Ireland is 'the Travellers'.[2]

Last year I was a member of a group involved in helping people explore the relevance of liberation theology to the situation of these, the group in Irish society who are most deprived and discriminated against. We had the exciting experience of organizing a workshop in which Travellers and people who work with them explored together aspects of the life of Travellers and their relationship with 'settled people'. This workshop was the culmination of some months of work on the ground in a number of areas where an effort was made to carry out the first stages of a social analysis related to the lives of Travellers.

Some months later, we pondered on the question 'where do we go from here'. Our conclusion was that a national pilgrimage of Travellers, under the slogan 'Let My People Go', could be a significant liberation event for them. The Travellers have a strong awareness of the presence and power of God: this pilgrimage could help them to deepen this and understand it more consciously in a fully biblical sense. It could enable them to experience themselves as people loved and chosen by God, people with a sense of their own dignity, people called by God to be agents of change in society, taking charge of their own destiny, challenging oppression and injustice. It could also offer other committed Christians — including, perhaps, well-known national figures — an opportunity to show effective solidarity with the Travellers in their struggle for justice.

Is this expecting too much of a pilgrimage? Not if the preparation for it is adequate. What we envisaged in this case was several months of preparation, with varying degrees of involvement by groups and individuals from different parts of the country. Leaders drawn from the Travellers themselves would have to pay a central role in planning the details of the pilgrimage and the preparation for it.

As I write, the preparations are well under way. A lot of work has been put into the choice and study of relevant texts from Scripture, to be used during the pilgrimage itself. These have been chosen to fit in with the theme of the pilgrimage, 'Let My People Go'. Key texts have been taken from the biblical account of the Exodus. Study of the texts and a careful comparison of their context with the present situation of the Travellers has become a very effective evangelising process: the Travellers who are involved are becoming more conscious of their own dignity; they are experiencing their Christian faith as a power for liberation. At the same time those who are working with the Travellers are coming to a greater appreciation of the faith of the Travellers and the special role to which they are called by God. All who are involved in the preparation are coming to have a richer and more concrete understanding of what is involved in those challenging phrases 'option for the poor' and 'solidarity with the poor'.

Because of overseas commitments, I have only been marginally involved in the pilgrimage preparations in recent months. It has been a very exciting experience for me to rejoin the group and see the remarkable commitment and creativity which has developed in those who have been involved week after week in the preparation. Particularly rewarding is the progress they have made in working out effective models of adult education for people who may have had very little formal schooling. For instance, I have spoken of 'study' of the biblical texts. But this study is not a matter of listening to scholarly explanations of the text. Incidents from the biblical account of Moses and the Exodus have been put in the form of drama, in which Travellers play the key parts. These playlets are followed by discussions in which all participants share their insights about the meaning of the biblical stories and their relevance to the present situation of the Travellers.

There are solid grounds for believing that the pilgrimage, including the period of preparation for it, will help all those involved in it to make their own the words of Mary in the *Magnificat* (Lk 1:46-55):

My whole being proclaims the greatness of the Almighty One
and my spirit rejoices in God my Saviour,
who has remembered me, a lowly servant of God.
From this time onward people of all ages will call me blessed,
because of the marvels done for me
by the Almightly One whose name is holy.
The divine mercy is shown from age to age to all who respect God.
The All-powerful One has stretched out a mighty arm,
to shatter the plans of the arrogant,
to pull down mighty rulers from their seats of power,
and lift up the little people.
God has filled the hungry with the best of food
while the rich are sent away empty.
This is the One who in the past
came to the help of the people of Israel, God's people,
fulfilling the promise made to those who went before us,
a promise of mercy made by God to Abraham and Sarah
and their children's children down through the ages.[3]

Gospel Truth

Some time ago I was involved in running a two-week workshop under the auspices of the 'Partners in Mission' programme in Ireland. This brought about a very fruitful (and at times painful) interaction between people who had been working in the Third World and people who worked in demanding situations on the home front. During our time together we shared something of our life stories, using the 'River of Life' Exercise described elsewhere in this book. We had a memorable outing to the river Shannon, to visit the ruins of Clonmacnoise, one of the ancient monastic seats of learning. Some days later we went on a kind of pilgrimage in a woodland area where we gathered around an old Massrock, where two hundred years earlier a persecuted people had gathered together to celebrate the Eucharist in secret.

All of these experiences touched something deep within me and they must have formed a pattern in my unconscious mind. For when I woke up on the morning of the last day of the workshop, I sat down immediately and, almost without thinking, I wrote out the following passage, which I shared with the group after Communion in our final Eucharist together:

A Reading from the Continuation of the Holy Gospel according to the Tradition of Luke
(— a newly discovered fragment, which forms a small part of chapter 1988 of the Gospel)

At that time a group of the followers of Jesus came from their homes to a place that might be called Emmaus, a journey of half a day or half a lifetime. They were accompanied by Emmanuel; but they were so preoccupied by their own hopes and fears — and so deafened by too many words — that at first they found it hard to hear his voice. And in any case they were not expecting him to share their journey, since they thought he spent his time mainly in a large house with stained-glass windows.

When they gathered to share his bread they thought that they could faintly hear his voice. But the voice of Emmanuel was not heard most clearly in the breaking of bread.

Then they shared with each other the waters from the river of their lives. And the voice of Emmanuel was heard more clearly in the voice of the calm and troubled waters.

They were led out to visit the ruins that survive from their glorious past. And in that sacred place the voice of Emmanuel was heard strongly by many of them, opening to them a history and tradition that they had almost lost.

They went as pilgrims to a quiet glade. There they heard distinctly the whisper of Emmanuel in the trees — and in the echoes of a persecuted people gathered round a broken Massrock.

During their days together they often heard the voice of pain. And they began to listen to that pain as they stood at the foot of each others' crosses. And for them the voice of Emmanuel was heard most clearly not in the waters or the broken bread, not even in the broken stone, but in the brokenness of each others' hearts and lives.

This is Gospel truth.

For those who may be looking for further resource material on life and liturgy — perhaps for use during or after a pilgrimage, or on other liturgical occasions, I give here the text of a poem written some time ago by my friend Pádraig Ó Máille, after a visit he paid to the contemplative Poor Clare Sisters in Lilongwe, the capital of Malawi. This is followed by the text of a beautiful Offertory hymn, written by Joe Wise. Finally, I suggest reflection on a video-film called 'Babette's Feast'.

For the Poor Clares, Lilongwe, Malawi
— by Pádraig Ó Máille

God gave us hands to raise in prayer and praise
God gave us tongues to sing and lips to kiss
God gave us feet to dance
All these He gave and saw that they were good
And yet in all my years these gifts lay fallow
My hands have failed to raise themselves in praise
My feet have never danced
I have not kissed the beauty of the world
I sang no song — until today
I came upon you, hands upraised in love
I heard you sing and as you danced
To sacred tunes you caught me up
My hands entwined in yours beyond the grill
Gave thanks
My lips dared taste the searing of
His beauty
My tongue which never sang until today
Bore witness to a love but dimly felt
And magnified the glory of His name.

Offertory Hymn
— Joe Wise

Chorus:
Here is my life, myself, the bread that I bring.
Here is my soul, my wine, the song that I sing.
Take it for gift and take it for granted,
Sprung from the seeds that I've washed and I've planted,
So long ago, and even till now, and even till now.

101

Bread from the fields, from my friends, and bread from
the lean years,
Bread from my youth and my loves and bread from the
green years.
This much is ready now (x 3)
Take it as your own . . .

Wine of my joys, my dreams, and wine of my good times,
Wine of my won't and my will, my did and my should
times.
This much is ready now (x 3)
Take it as your own . . .

Bread from the highlands of life and bread from the valleys,
Bread from the good things we've known that nobody
tallies.
Now we are ready, Lord (x 3)
Take us as your own . . .

Final Chorus: . . . and even till now (x 3).[4]

Reflection on a Video-Film

A recent and very beautiful Danish film called 'Babette's
Feast' (now available on video) could provide the basis for
some very useful personal or group reflection on the
relationship between life and Eucharist. The story is very
simple. A French refugee woman is welcomed into the home
of a deeply religious family in Denmark. They have no idea
that she had been the most famous cook in Paris. After many
years, she inherits, quite unexpectedly, a lot of money. She
spends it all on a feast which she cooks for the members of
the community who accepted her. This very 'secular' feast
leads to the kind of effects which religion is supposed to
bring about, but seldom does.

Perhaps the best way to use the film to evoke group
reflection would be to show it one evening, purely as an
aesthetic experience, without trying to 'use' it in any way.
The following morning some key passage (perhaps the end
of the feast) could be shown again; this would be followed by
some questions for reflection and sharing, e.g.:

— Was there something in the film, or this part of it, that
touched you or moved you?

— Do you think those who took part in the feast prepared by
Babette learned anything from it?

102

— Does this scene say anything to you about our religious celebrations? About our 'secular' celebrations?
— Does the film or the discussion suggest anything practical that we might do?

NOTES

1. *Patrick Kavanagh: The Complete Poems* (Collected, Arranged and Edited by Peter Kavanagh), New York (The Peter Kavanagh Hand Press: 1972), Newbridge, (The Goldsmith Press: 1984) 16.

2. The Travellers or Travelling People are a distinct group who have their own culture and a language of several hundred words. Traditionally, they lived in caravans and moved around, camping at customary halting sites. Modern 'development' has forced them to diversify from their traditional occupations as tin-smiths and horse-traders; they have coped quite well with this change. But 'development' has also deprived the Travellers of many of their traditional camp-sites, and forced them into shanty-town situations in the cities, where they are victims of very serious harassment and discrimination.

3. I have ventured to add the name of Sarah to that of Abraham in this translation. This represents, of course, an effort to transcend the patriarchalism which permeates much of the Bible. But there is a solid basis for it in the biblical account of the promise; the text of Genesis makes it clear that the promise was made to Abraham and Sarah (since in fact Abraham and Hagar were already the parents of Ishmael); see Gen 17:15-21.

4. I have not been able to discover who are the publishers of this hymn.

5

Power and Participation

This chapter deals with the area where the interpersonal aspect of spirituality converges with, and overlaps, its 'public' dimension. In the first section I offer some reflections on power and ways of exercising it. These reflections follow on from the treatment of prayer and power in a previous chapter. I hope that what I have to say here will provide a theological foundation both for the second section of the present chapter and for several other parts of the book — especially the next chapter which deals with structural justice. The second section of this chapter is more practical. In it I propose some exercises and background explanation which may be of help to people who wish to promote participation in decision-making in Church and society.

SECTION ONE: DIFFERENT KINDS OF POWER

I find it useful to distinguish between four different kinds of power — so different from each other that it would be misleading to apply the same word 'power' to all of them without indicating which kind of power is in question in any particular case.

Personal Power

The first kind of power is the one about which I wrote in chapter 2 — the personal power or 'presence' which enables us to believe in ourselves, and to hold our ground in our relationships with others, by standing up for our own beliefs and values. It is a certain psychological strength of character which all of us have in some degree. But some people have a very weak character, while others have great inner strength. (It is worth noting that people who are loud and 'pushy' may in fact be trying to 'cover up' for their lack of inner strength.

On the other hand, really strong people may often appear to be quiet and self-effacing; they may show the steel that is in them only when others push them too hard.)

At its strongest, this kind of power amounts to a *charisma*, the kind of quality found in people like Joan of Arc, Gandhi, Martin Luther King, Helder Camera, Mother Teresa of Calcutta, and above all in Jesus. It involves a type of personal magnetism that attracts and charms people. It is the quality that makes one an obvious leader, somebody whom disciples gather around.

I do not think this is some further power added on to one's personality. Rather it is part of what it means to be human — and the more we grow into full humanity the more we will have of this power. In fact I suspect that it is precisely that part of the human person which makes each of us an 'image of God'; for it is a share in the 'marvellous and fascinating mystery' that is God.[1]

From Jesus we learn how to use and develop this power in a fully human way. It is clear that many were attracted to him by the sheer power of his personality. He welcomed the disciples who gathered around him. But he did not abuse their confidence in him. He showed the utmost respect for them, supporting them when they needed it and challenging them when he felt this would help them to grow. He trusted them, educated them — and when the right time came he departed, leaving them his own Spirit and the task of continuing his mission.

Those who, like Jesus, develop and use 'personality power' in a truly moral and respectful way will grow to have a certain quality that I can only call 'luminosity'. It is as though their inner light were shining through to the outside world, bringing life and warmth to those who are open to receive it. This luminosity is really a high degree of the quality I described as transparency in a previous chapter — the way in which personal integrity becomes evident to others. This kind of personal light does more than bring brightness to those who accept it; it also shows up the darkness that lurks in our world and in human hearts — and then it evokes implacable opposition from those who prefer the darkness. (I pointed out in chapter 3 that this is what happened to Jesus.)

Personality power of this kind may be developed and used in a manner that is less than fully moral. The person may become selfish, closed, and secretive, nourishing an inner strength that can be used as power over others. This can result in a style of leadership that is autocratic, where the behaviour of the leader tends to enslave the followers rather than bringing them freedom and responsibility. It is particularly dangerous if this takes place in a religious leader. The result at best is that the disciples become uncritical devotees of the leader; at worst they become religious fanatics.

Domination

The second type of power can be called 'domination' or 'coercion'. It is the power to control others. It may take various forms, such as:
— physical force,
— the threat of force or punishment,
— psychological domination or intimidation,
— indoctrination.

The power of domination or coercion may be exercised over individuals, groups, classes, nations, or even whole races of people.

I have never heard of any government that was able to renounce *entirely* the use of such power. All governments find themselves compelled at times to coerce some people, both to ensure that the state is not attacked from outside, and also to restrain criminals within the state. But some governments rely almost exclusively on the power of domination. This necessarily involves a good deal of repression. Citizens are deprived of fundamental human rights such as freedom of conscience, the right to free speech, the right to be tried according to just laws and by just judges, and the right to some meaningful 'say' in choosing the government.

In the future, to which the Christian looks forward with sure hope — a future to which we give the biblical title, 'the Reign of God' — human communities will no longer have any need for repressive, dominating power. We believe that humanity is called, with the help of God, to bring this future into being; and that it is already present in our world in some degree. Therefore, the ideal towards which every government is called to move is to have all its citizens participate freely and

106

actively in working for the common good without any need for repressive measures. Consequently, a most important test of the extent to which a government is fulfilling its role is the extent to which it can evoke the willing cooperation of the people, rather than relying on domination.

Repression by force or the threat of force is not the only way in which an individual or a government may exercise the power of domination over others. People may be cowed, broken in spirit, by a domineering individual, or a repressive state — or by a tradition, culture, or religion that classifies them as inferior or outcast or 'untouchable'. They may have internalised this image of themselves, to a point where it does not occur to them to question the will of the dominator. Furthermore, people may be manipulated by being deprived of the knowledge necessary to make an informed judgement about issues, or even by being deceived into believing things that are not true. Governments sometimes engage in this kind of domination by controlling the flow of information in society, through ownership or censorship of the mass media. If this kind of deception and manipulation occurs on a large scale it amounts to indoctrination.

I believe that a major element in an authentically Christian spirituality, for individuals and for groups or communities, should be the relinquishment of the power to dominate or coerce others, leaving that power to be exercised *only* by the State, and then only when absolutely necessary. If we do this we leave ourselves quite vulnerable, since we shall have to rely on the civil and criminal law (and on those who make laws and those who enforce them) to protect us against domination by others — and governments and law-enforcement agencies are often weak, incompetent, or even corrupt. It would be difficult to show that renunciation of the power to dominate others will always bring about the best result in the short term. To justify it as the truly human response it is necessary to consider the long-term effects for the community as a whole. If we choose this path we have the example and the words of Jesus to encourage us: 'Put your sword back in its place . . . All who take the sword will die by the sword.' (Mt 26:52). I shall return to this point later.

What about the case where the government is simply a *tyranny?* In such situations Christian spirituality does not require one to collude with repression. The Christian is called instead to work for the replacement of the tyranny by a more just authority. That involves submitting oneself to those elements of a true authority that are already being created by the people engaged in the struggle for liberation.

May Churches or Church organizations exercise the power of coercion or domination? In the past, they often did so. Nowadays, I believe, Churches, Church leaders, and all Church bodies, should be quite explicit in their renunciation of such power. Only in this way can we ensure that there is a clear distinction between faith and political activity, and between Church and State.

At first sight it may not seem much to ask of Church authorities that they relinquish the power to dominate people. Certainly they would scarcely wish to make use of physical force or the threat of it. But it is by no means easy for anybody in a position of authority to give up trying to control or influence the flow of information and the free expression of opinion; and that is another form of domination. It is particularly difficult for Church authorities to relinquish this power, because they feel responsible for bringing 'the truth' to people. All of us can probably remember occasions when people with religious authority insisted on limiting our freedom, on the grounds that the question at issue was a matter of God's law. What they failed to take into account was the fact that the conflict was not between you and God but between your view about what God wanted and the view of the person in authority!

Those who hold authority in the Church need to be quite courageous, and very trusting of others, in order really to accept in practice that people have the right to make their own decisions — and even to make mistakes about religious matters. It becomes somewhat easier for them to do so once they realise that there are other kinds of power besides the power of domination. They may come to understand that the giving up of such power does not necessarily lead to anarchy. On the contrary, it may actually increase the person's genuine authority. As a result of my experience of training community leaders over several years, I have come to these two conclusions:

(1) Leadership is about letting go of power over others.

(2) The person who lets go of such power is almost always given greater authority by the group.

Enabling Power

The third kind of power can be called 'enabling' or 'facilitating' power. It is the ability to help others,

— to understand their situation better,

— to take responsibility by making their own free choices,

— to plan and implement ways of making their choices effective.

This enabling power can be used at the interpersonal level to facilitate individuals or small groups. But it can also be employed at the 'public' level: there may be widespread participation by 'the ordinary people' in determining the policies of whole nations or of large international bodies such as Churches.

Obviously, what is in question here is the opposite of domination; it is service. But it is not sufficient to call this 'the power of service'. The word 'service' is often abused, because, under the name of 'service', authorities often dominate the people they are claiming to serve. We may find 'civil servants' who are neither civil nor of real service to the public. However, it is true that the basic *attitude* of service must characterise those who set out to facilitate others. Like other kinds of service this involves respect and sensitivity towards others — which in turn implies willingness to sacrifice one's own status or privileged position:

> Jesus called his followers together and said: 'You know that the kings of the heathen lord it over their people and dominate them. That is not the way you are to exercise authority. Any of you who wants to be great must be the servant of the others; and the one who wants to be first among you must become your slave . . . '   (Mt 20:25-27)

In cases where enabling power is exercised, the particular kind of service that is offered is not primarily that of doing something for others but rather allowing and encouraging them to do it for themselves. *Willingness* to offer this service is very important; but it is not sufficient. One needs also to learn appropriate *techniques*. For we often find a subtle collusion taking place between authoritarian leaders and passive followers: the authorities justify their holding on to power by blaming the community for lack of initiative; meanwhile the community evades responsibility by dumping the blame for everything on to the authorities. If people on both sides really want to escape this vicious circle the best way forward is to begin using a variety of facilitative techniques.

In one diocese where I worked, the bishop always chaired the various diocesan meetings. Consequently, he often became embroiled in arguments about procedural difficulties. If there had been a facilitator to conduct the meetings, the bishop would not have lost any of his real authority; in fact he would have *more* authority, since he would not have been wasting it on minor matters. Similarly, if participative planning techniques had been used, all members of the committees could have felt fully involved in decision-making; whereas in our situation the majority often felt they were being asked to rubber-stamp decisions made behind the scenes by one or two people.

Techniques of facilitation and planning are not sufficient on their own to transform such situations. They have to be used in a context of trust where there is real listening to others and sharing with them. In most of the previous chapters (and especially in chapters 3 and 4) I have written about that context and proposed exercises that may help to create it. In the second section of the present chapter I shall go on to propose various techniques or exercises that are directly related to more effective cooperation and joint planning. For what is really important in regard to 'enabling' power is not that we write or read about it in theory but that we experience and use it in practice. However, before going on to this practical material I wish to say something about the fourth type of power.

The Cross

The fourth kind of power is one that cannot be overlooked in any account of Christian spirituality. It is a mysterious reality, quite different from each of the other three kinds of power. I can only call it 'the power of the cross'. By 'the cross' here I am not referring simply to the power of the Cross of Jesus; but that is included. There were many instances of the 'power of the cross' in human history before Jesus died. But the Cross of Jesus provides us with a name for this reality — because, for the Christian, it is the clearest instance of it, and as such it has become its most powerful symbol.

What is in question here is not a human power. But it touches human life in a very intimate way. For it is an aspect of God's providential power — namely, God's ability to draw immeasurable good out of what, from a human point of view, is total failure. The primary instance of this, for the Christian, is the new life and hope that sprang from the execution of Jesus as a criminal. It is this, above all, that gives us *hope* that in situations of 'crucifixion' in our world today, we may once again see this mysterious power of God at work:

> I ask the God of Our Lord Jesus Christ . . . that your minds may be opened to know the hope to which you are called . . . and that you may understand how great is God's power working in us who believe. This is the very same power that God exercised in raising Jesus from the dead . . . (Eph 1:17-20)

As a Christian I do not have control of this fourth power. What I can do is follow the example of Jesus in relation to each of the other three kinds of power:
— nourishing my personal inner power and using it respectfully,
— relinquishing the power to dominate others,
— enabling and facilitating others to act with full responsibility.

If I do this, I can expect to go far — but no further than Jesus himself who found in the end that all this was not enough. So, in times of failure, when my best is not sufficient, I shall have to follow Jesus in the final step of entrusting myself entirely into the care of the One whom he taught me to call 'Abba'. With Jesus I can say: 'Into your hands I commit my spirit' (Lk 23:46).

Though the power of the cross is not something we can own or control, I am sure that each of us will be able to locate in our own experience some instances of this power at work. If we wish to nourish our spirituality we will treasure such experiences and allow them to strengthen our hope, our firm conviction, that there is a power operative in our lives and our world that is 'beyond anything that we could ask for or even imagine' (Eph 3:20).

It is essential that we should believe in the power of the resurrection, which is the other side of the cross — and that we should even at times experience it. For otherwise we will be tempted to take short cuts. Just as Jesus was tempted to dominate others by a display of power (Mt 4:5-6), so we will often be tempted to think that the importance of the work we are doing justifies the exercise of undue control over others. When Jesus rejected that temptation he was starting on a road that led inevitably to his death; and he was able to face death because he relied on the power of God to vindicate him. As disciples of Jesus we cannot expect things to be any different for us (Mt 10:24). So it is only wise to reflect and pray about our attitude to power of various kinds.

It is particularly important to recognise that there are limits to what can be accomplished through the use of enabling or facilitative power. Despite all the good that we can bring about by using this power, we may at times find that we are left helpless in the face of unrelenting and utterly ruthless evil. Once we acknowledge that fact, we will see the implications of renouncing the power to dominate others. Only then can we dedicate ourselves in a clear-eyed way to facilitating and enabling others — believing that if all else fails we are entitled to follow Jesus in calling on God not to forsake us (Mt 27:46). This faith can be proclaimed in the words of Job:

> I know that the one who will vindicate me is alive
> and will in the end take a stand on earth on my behalf.
> And though now my flesh is being torn from me,
> nevertheless I shall see God while still in this body.
> These eyes of mine will look on God,
> a God who no longer leaves me to stand alone.
>
> (Job 19:25-27)

SECTION TWO: TECHNIQUES AND RESOURCES

In this second section of the chapter I want to look at three practical matters that are closely related to each other: cooperation, facilitation, and joint planning. I propose first to refer to two exercises that should help people to appreciate how important it is that they cooperate with each other — and how difficult it is to do this. Then I shall go on to sketch out some of the basic elements in facilitating a discussion or planning session of any kind; linked to this I shall propose an exercise in which these skills may be tried out and reflected on. Finally, I shall say something about planning techniques — and about the context in which a group can engage fruitfully in joint planning.

Cooperation Exercises

From our earliest childhood we learn to cooperate with each other and also to compete with each other; this happens in every culture. In the Western cultures, however, competition comes to play an unduly large role as we grow older. So those who are interested in promoting genuine human development soon find that they have to spend a lot of time and energy in learning more effective ways of promoting cooperation.

The kind of sharing exercises outlined towards the end of chapter 3 can help people to develop attitudes which are more conducive to cooperation. But these are not enough. We also need to become aware of the many blind spots we have developed, which are blocks to cooperation. People working with groups have designed a wide variety of exercises in which the members are asked to cooperate together in performing certain tasks, and then have the opportunity to reflect on how well they succeeded — and on the things that hindered their cooperation. Such exercises give the members of the group a lot of insight into their own characters, particularly in relation to cooperation with others in daily life.

One very simple exercise is called 'Cooperative Squares'. It is rather like asking a group of people to do a jig-saw puzzle together. What people learn from the exercise is the need to look at the situation from the point of view of the other members of the group. It is so simple to *say* that, but to *do* it is extremely difficult. When engaged in a common task each of us tends to get absorbed in our own little part of it. Then the hardest thing to do is to stop, to look around at what others are doing, and to see if, perhaps, what we are doing is blocking them from completing their part of the task. The exercise gives people an awareness of how this happens, and enables them to learn what cooperation involves in real life. For those who would like to use this exercise I shall give full

instructions near the end of this chapter (rather than inter-
rupting the text here with instructions and diagrams).

Working with groups over the past few years, I found a
great need for another exercise of the same general kind —
but one that would be rather more advanced, suitable for
groups who have had a good deal of experience in working
cooperatively. I found just what I was looking for in an
exercise called 'Flower Power'.

The particular value of this exercise is that it enables a
group to explore in a very practical way the role of a *leader* in
promoting cooperation. It offers a group the chance to
experience different kinds of leadership — one that is
authoritarian, and one that is participative — and to explore
the effects of each of these on the members of the group.

The 'Flower Power' exercise has an added advantage: it
helps people to be more flexible in their understanding of
what it means to find the correct solution to a problem or
issue that faces a group. For it frequently happens that when
people are working together on a common task, each of them
sees only one 'right' way to do it — and is therefore trying to
persuade or compel everybody else to adopt this particular
way. Whereas in reality there may be a number of good ways to
perform the task or solve the problem; and, in these
circumstances, the 'right' approach is the one that they all
agree on.

In workshops with experienced groups in many parts of
Africa — and also in Europe — I found this a most valuable
exercise. So, at the end of this chapter, I shall give full instructions on how to prepare and run the exercise, and some
guidelines on facilitating the discussion afterwards.

Practice in Facilitation

The word 'facilitation' has become so much a part of my
everyday language that I tend to forget that I probably
hadn't even heard the word twenty years ago! It may well be
that many readers of this book consider the word to be mere
jargon, and no explanation that I could give is likely to
convince them otherwise. It requires a kind of conversion to
realise that the best way to teach people is to *facilitate* them
to discover things for themselves. For years I accepted that in
theory, while in practice I continued to give lectures. I now

realise that it was mainly my own insecurity that led me to do most of the talking when working with a group. I had to learn to trust the group, and to trust myself. But I also had to develop certain practical techniques of facilitation. These are skills which some people exercise more or less naturally while others need a lot of practice before they feel comfortable in facilitating a group.

It is dangerous to give leadership to somebody who is unable or unwilling to draw out the gifts of others and to help a group to make their own decisions. So the most crucial element in my work of leadership training in recent years was training in facilitation skills. It was a very practical kind of training, where individuals had the opportunity to use their skills in helping a group to make decisions, and then to reflect on their successes and failures. The following is one way in which this can be organised.

Invite a group of about five volunteers to form an inner circle (a 'fish bowl') for a discussion and planning session, while the rest of the group sits in an outer circle listening to what is said and noticing also the 'body language' (posture, gestures etc.) of the inner group. Propose some practical topic (e.g. an outing for the whole group) which those in the inner circle are to plan. When ten minutes are up, offer the group of volunteers a further ten minutes to come up with an agreed course of action. At the end of this period, invite the observers to comment on what they noticed during the discussion and planning; ask the observers to point out what seemed to help the group and what made it more difficult for them to come to an agreed solution. Draw up a list of the things that helped and a list of the things that hindered the group.

After a break, give a short talk in which you note some of the main ways in which a group can be helped or 'facilitated' to have a fruitful discussion and to come to a conclusion. The main point to make is that in any planning session there are really *two* important matters to be attended to:
— Firstly, it is vitally important to foster *harmony* and good relationships in the group. If this is not done, the group will become divided by rivalry, or some of the group will become apathetic; then it is unlikely that they will be able to carry out any task effectively.

115

— Secondly, there is a certain *task* to be achieved by the group at this time — some project that has to be explored and planned. If the task is not attended to, the group may become just a talking shop.

List out the different elements that contribute to each of these two aspects, as outlined in the following paragraphs. In doing so, illustrate each point, as far as possible, by referring to the list that was drawn up of things that helped and hindered the earlier discussion.

A person who wishes to help the group preserve *harmony* and good relationships can do so in two major ways — by encouraging others, and by enabling the group to deal with tension and difficulties. These can be spelled out in more detail as follows:

— *Encouraging:*

1. Acknowledging what people have said and affirming them (while not necessarily agreeing with their opinions).
2. Drawing out the silent or shy people to give their views or to express their feelings.

— *Dealing with tension and difficulties:*

3. Helping people who are in disagreement with each other to understand the other person's viewpoint.
4. Diagnosing group difficulties — especially ones that stem from fear or irritation.
5. Expressing the feelings of the group (e.g. 'It seems that we are getting bogged down so why don't we take a break.') or one's own feelings (e.g. 'I'm getting tired').
6. Encouraging others to express the strong feelings they had not noticed or have not acknowledged in the group, and which are interfering with the smooth running of the meeting.
7. Using humour to break the tension, when that is appropriate (but not joking just to avoid conflict).

A person who wishes to help a group get their *task* done can do so by engaging in any of the following operations, or by encouraging other members of the group to do so:

1. Opening up the topic.
2. Sharing ideas or relevant information.
3. Drawing out further ideas or information.
4. Clarifying what was said or inviting others to clarify what they said.

116

5. Summarizing what has already been said.
6. Suggesting some concrete action.
7. Outlining advantages and/or disadvantages of a line of action that has been proposed by somebody in the group.
8. Summarizing/clarifying various proposed courses of action.
9. Drawing out the views of others about proposed courses of action.
10. Seeking consensus on one line of action, leading to a firm decision.
11. Planning the implementation of this decision.

After this talk invite four or five volunteers to form another 'fishbowl' and give them another practical issue to discuss and plan about, asking them to try to make use of the various tips for good facilitation which you have been proposing. After some time, intervene again to remind them that they have only about five minutes in which to reach a joint decision. When the time is up, ask the observers what they noticed. Later, others may wish to volunteer to discuss the same topic or a different one.

It may be useful to organise a fish-bowl which has a revolving membership, i.e. a person from the outer circle may change places every now and then with somebody from the inner circle. Have breaks in the discussion to allow people time to reflect, in pairs or in the whole group, on the *process* of the discussion or planning as distinct from its content.

The key to good facilitation is the development of a kind of dual awareness: one is fully engaged in the *task*, but at the same time one is noticing what is going on in the group (e.g. who is being left out, who is feeling angry etc). It requires a good deal of discipline and self-sacrifice to hold back from being single-mindedly absorbed in the task in order to give attention and energy to noticing the process. The person who is able to do this, is much less likely to try to dominate the discussion. In fact many, if not most, of this person's interventions will be aimed at enabling the group to get on well with each other, rather than simply 'getting the job done' no matter what the cost in bruised feelings.

SECTION THREE:
THE CURVE OF LIFE AND DEATH[2]

In this third section of the chapter I want to say something about joint planning in a group. Obviously, such planning calls for a good deal of cooperation, and this in turn requires that at least some members of the group are fairly skilled in facilitation. But difficulties in planning do not always stem from unwillingness to cooperate or the lack of good facilitation. Another element is required: the members of the group need to be clear about their *objectives* or *goals;* and, if they are to work together effectively they must have some kind of *common vision*. When working with a group it is useful to bring this to their attention, and to ask them to work together to articulate their vision. One could give a short talk based on the following paragraphs and the accompanying diagram (Fig. 4); the talk should be followed by at least one exercise related to the early stages of planning — preferably an exercise in which the group articulate their common vision. (Make it clear that in this case the exercises are not simply 'games' or simulations done to gain practice; the group will be invited to do some *real* planning.)

Introduction

Down through history there have been many movements which aimed to bring change to the world. Some of them have lasted for many years, and a few have lasted for centuries. But very many movements are like the seed that was sown on dry ground and sprouted quickly but soon died. The life of most movements can be pictured as a curve. In some cases there is a rapid upward rise of life while in others the rising curve is much slower. What is most important to note is that it is almost impossible for a movement to stay for long at the peak of the curve. Either it rises further or it begins to curve downward again. The downward curve may be gradual or sudden. But unless it is halted it will lead eventually to the death of the movement.

What I am saying here is not intended to provide purely theoretical knowledge but to help people to look closely at the curve of life and death of the movements in which they are involved themselves, in order to see where they are situated on this curve. The exercises that follow are designed

118

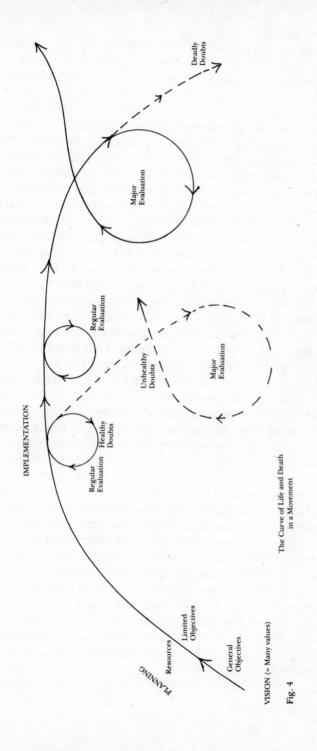

The Curve of Life and Death
in a Movement

Fig. 4

to help people to plan ways to promote new life and hope in some movement to which they are deeply committed, rather than allowing it to slide down the curve of death into oblivion.

Common Vision

Any successful movement or joint enterprise requires good organization which enables it to channel the rich gifts and resources of those who are involved in it. But its success does not depend first of all on its organization or even its resources. Prior to any organizing of resources there is something even more basic — a *common vision*. The key people involved have in common a certain way of looking at life, a particular way of understanding their world, and a common commitment to working for certain goals. They will not of course have identical views about everything; but they do have a shared outlook that is the basis for their work together.

It often happens that what brings a group of people together is just such a common vision. And for this very reason they may be inclined to take their common vision for granted. This is alright for some time; they may find no need to spell out their vision clearly for themselves and for others who come to work with them. But it is very likely that the movement will run into trouble after some time if the group never take time to articulate what they stand for. The key leaders may find themselves pulling in opposite directions. Or the leaders may retain their common vision but may discover too late that the followers do not really share it.

Such problems cannot be solved by exercising a more authoritarian style of leadership — imposing more discipline to tidy up the organization. The best way to deal with the problem is to ensure that it does not arise! That can only be done if the group are prepared to spend time on articulating their common vision at an early stage, and occasionally coming back to look again at it. Furthermore, as the movement expands, it is not enough for more recent members to be given the task of *implementing* the vision of the founding group. It is important to offer an opportunity to the newcomers to share in the articulation of the vision of the whole group, re-examining the original vision and perhaps expanding and adapting it.

120

Values

But what do we mean by a common vision and how best can we examine and articulate the vision that is our source of inspiration? The kind of common vision we are referring to is very comprehensive, something that affects our approach to almost every aspect of life. But it is possible to spell it out by focussing attention on its different aspects. Then we will see that the vision is like a cloth woven of many different *values*. A value is something that we consider good, important, worth striving for.

Instead of giving a theoretical account of different values it seems better to approach the question in a more concrete way. This can be done by dealing with the topic of a common vision in a context where members of the group have *already* spoken about their hopes, expectations, and reservations in coming together. It is fairly easy to show that each of these hopes and reservations reveals a value, something which at least some of the participants consider to be important.

By way of example, I mention here how I did this in a recent workshop (— but I stress the point that this is only an example of how the expectations can be linked to the vision; it is important to use the actual expectations given by the particular group with whom one is working.) In this case the group had asked for help in getting people to take initiatives. I pointed out that this meant they were committed to the value of personal initiative and responsibility. The group had also asked for some help in how to cope gently but firmly with obstructive people. This implied that they were committed to two further values — that of consensus in a group and that of respect for each individual even when the person is being rather 'awkward'. Another of the expectations of this group was to learn more about what Paulo Freire calls 'generative issues' and how these are related to motivating people to action.[3] This showed that they were interested in the value of respect for the goals and priorities of the people, rather than simply trying to get them to do what the leaders think is important. The participants' expectations had also included a request for a variety of exercises that they could use with grassroots groups. This implied that they believed in the value of experiential learning. It also showed that they saw variety as a value, since it would hold the interest of people, and would help the leaders to treat the group as adults, not like children being taught things by rote.

On that occasion we found that when we put together these different *values* we had articulated quite a lot of the common *vision* of the whole group. This is usually the case: taken as a whole, the different values fit together into a fairly coherent vision. The people concerned treasure these values and are trying to live by this vision — even though they may not have been using the words 'vision' and 'values'. Introducing the words 'vision' and 'values' does not mean imposing new ideas or commitments on them. It means rather giving them words to express what they have already been doing. This new language is useful, since it enables people to spell out their own commitment and the vision that inspires them.

Objectives

People who have a vision of a better world have to plan to bring it about; otherwise their vision remains an idle dream. Once the vision has been articulated the next step is to begin to make it concrete, to embody it in some *general objectives*, which are attainable. For instance, one movement to which I belonged had a vision of a just and caring world and of a Church that promoted justice and compassion. One of its general objectives was the setting up of a network of committed and trained leaders in many different countries — people who would support each other and work together to overcome oppression and exploitation, and to ensure that everybody has the opportunity to live a full human life. Another general objective of this movement was to help the Church become a community of communities and an institution that would be a living witness to justice and compassion. A group might have four or five such general objectives. Each of them would be a way of making their common vision practical in one particular sphere of life. Each of them would have to be compatible with the others — otherwise the movement would become bogged down by inconsistencies. During a particular period the group could concentrate most of its energy on attaining one of these objectives, while not totally neglecting the others.

Limited Objectives

In order to attain their general objectives a group needs to pick out particular *limited objectives* as means to achieve the over-all goal. For instance, the movement to which I belonged chose to have a series of international 'solidarity workshops' as one step towards attaining the general objective of a network of committed leaders in different countries. The group needs to have a whole succession of such limited objectives in many different areas of action in order to accomplish its general objectives.

Resources

When a group is planning how to achieve its limited objectives it has to take account of the resources that are available. It is not a question of deciding first of all on the limited objectives and then looking for resources. Neither do they begin simply by looking at the available resources and then choosing objectives to fit in with them. Rather there is a kind of circular movement by which people spin around in their minds both the limited objectives they would like to achieve and the resources that are currently available. Each is spelled out in the light of the other; and all of this is done as a means of attaining the general objectives which in turn are the concrete embodiment of the common vision.

The principal resource that is available to any movement is not money or buildings but *people*. If the movement is one that sets a high value on social justice, then its primary resource must be the people who have been marginalised or deprived in some way; its second major resource will be the trained leaders who can offer inspiration and facilitation to those who have been left on the margins of society. In addition to people, a movement also needs other resources — for instance, the use of buildings, typewriters, etc.

Programmes

A programme is a planned series of actions. The programme lays down the way in which the resources are used, in order to attain the limited objectives, which in turn are steps towards bringing about the general objectives. For instance, a group may set up a programme which consists of a series of weekly meetings over a given period.

A programme has to be carefully planned. *Who* will do *what* has to be spelled out, and the planners also have to lay down *when* and *where* these actions are to take place. Furthermore, they have to plan their *evaluation* of these actions. Only then will they be ready to begin implementing their plans in a truly organised way. In practice, of course, they may have been doing quite a lot of work prior to this. But it is only now that this work fits into a carefully planned programme, where the group can be fairly sure that the whole project will not fail through lack of organization.

Regular Evaluations

Almost as soon as a movement begins to implement a planned programme, its members are choosing to move in one of two very different directions. Either they are acting in such a way that the curve of life, hope, and expansion continues to rise, or their approach is one that causes the movement to begin to slide down the curve of death. Of course no group is likely to set out consciously to die. But the movement will almost certainly sink back into oblivion unless its members take steps to evaluate their actions on a regular basis.

If a group make fairly frequent and *regular evaluations* of the implementation of their programme they can expect to go from strength to strength. Of course certain questions and even doubts will arise from time to time. But these will be *healthy* doubts — mainly about the ways of achieving the objectives. These regular evaluations should always include an examination of two aspects:

— What is the quality of the personal relationships of the membership as a whole and especially of the organizing team?

— How effective are the group in attaining their limited and general objectives?

If the group fails to have regular evaluations then the process of decline will quickly set in. The doubts that arise will soon become *unhealthy* ones — the kind that gnaw away people's hope and inspiration. It is also likely that the interpersonal relationships in the group and the organizing team will deteriorate and this will not only cause unhappiness but will also interfere with the work.

124

Major Evaluation

Apart from these ordinary evaluations there is need for a *major evaluation* every few years. This is needed because over the years it is likely that some deeper questions and doubts will arise. For instance the group may wonder if their priorities are right, or whether they have taken sufficient account of significant changes in the situation since the programme began. The major evaluation should include a serious re-examination of the vision of the group and the values which make up the vision.

If the group has been careless about having regular evaluations then the need for a major evaluation becomes much more urgent. This is because all kinds of carelessness and disorganization will have crept in, and will have gone unchecked. Furthermore, the tensions and rivalries within the group will be giving rise to serious problems at this stage.

The effect of a careful major evaluation will almost certainly be to bring new life and inspiration to the group. The curve of life will probably rise sharply. The movement will go from strength to strength. On the other hand, if no major evaluation is carried out, then the curve will turn sharply downward. *Deadly* doubts will creep in and sap the energy of the group. Their vision will become clouded and/or there will be division in the group even about their fundamental values and their basic priorities. A movement which has reached this stage of decay may be doing more harm than good. It would be better for all concerned if it simply died out and were replaced by something new.

An Exercise

After an account of the curve of life and death of a movement it is important to have some practical exercise which will help people to internalise and use the ideas that have been presented. I shall give here an outline of an exercise which I used recently for a group who had been working together to organise a series of national conferences for lay people in the Church. After some time the members of the group found themselves at times pulling in opposite directions. It was clear that not all the members had the same priorities. Some of them were beginning to wonder to what extent they really had a common vision. So they agreed that

125

it would be worthwhile spending some time in articulating their vision and objectives.

Having displayed the diagram and talked about the curve of life and death for about fifteen minutes (concentrating mainly on the early parts of it), I invited each person to take about ten minutes to jot down the main values which she or he considered to be crucial in the movement; and also to jot down the general objectives to which they felt the movement should commit itself. The values were then read out and listed on large sheets of paper; there were twenty-nine of them! When the objectives were read out and listed they added up to thirty-five. There was a good deal of over-lapping between the values and the objectives, since some members of the group did not make a clear distinction between the two.

The lists were so long that it was necessary to do some prioritizing; and on this occasion it seemed best to concentrate on the values and on those of the objectives which were so general that they could be called values. We added these latter to the list of values. Then I asked the group to look carefully at the revised list of values. I gave one pink sheet and two blue sheets of paper to each member of the group and invited them to write on the pink sheet (in large letters) the value to which they gave the highest priority and to write on the two blue sheets the two values which came next in importance for them. When this was done we started to build up a 'mosaic' on the floor in the centre of the group — a pattern formed of the coloured sheets of paper. We began with the pink sheets on which each member had written his or her highest priority values. These formed the inner core of the mosaic. The blue sheets were grouped around the outside of the pattern. Everybody became involved in building up a coherent pattern in which sheets containing similar values were placed together, and alongside sheets with closely related values.

The result of this work was twofold:
— From the point of view of relationships within the group it had a very unifying effect; people really listened to each other and made great efforts to integrate their own values with those of the others; this created a great sense of community in the group.

— From the point of view of the task in hand the exercise was very effective. The members of the group began to 'buy into' each other's values so that the common vision which was worked out was really 'owned' by all the members. A group of two or three members volunteered to prepare a *written* statement that would express the common vision that had been visually expressed in the 'mosaic'; a first draft was discussed and amended at the next meeting and a definitive statement was accepted by all. This has been used since then by the group to explain what the movement stands for. Having worked out this vision statement the group were much more confident in establishing their general objectives and the more limited objectives required to implement them. The group then divided up into small working teams each of which undertook the detailed planning and implementation of some specific objectives.

ADDENDUM:
COOPERATION AND LEADERSHIP EXERCISES

'Cooperative Squares' is an exercise which is played in teams of five participants.[4] Divide the group into a number of five-member teams, and invite each team to sit around a table. (If the number of people in the group is not a multiple of five, you will have to invite the extra people to sit in as observers on some of the teams.) Distribute an envelope to each member of each team. Each envelope contains some pieces of light cardboard. The following are the instructions given to all:

Each person has an envelope containing pieces for forming squares.

The task of each team is to cooperate to form five squares of equal size, one square in front of each member of the team.

During the exercise nobody is allowed to speak or to give a signal to others.

Members of the team may give their pieces to other members of the team; but people are not allowed to take pieces that have not been freely given to them.

Before the exercise, the coordinators prepare the materials as follows:

Cut out a set of five six-inch by six-inch squares of light cardboard for each five-member team. Draw lines on each square according to the pattern given in Fig. 5, and write in the letters 'a' to 'j', writing lightly with a pencil. Cut up each of the squares into pieces along the lines and distribute the pieces as follows:

In the first envelope: pieces a, c, h, i.
In the second envelope: pieces a, a, a, e.
In the third envelope: piece j only.
In the fourth envelope: pieces d and f.
In the fifth envelope: pieces b, c, f, g.

Fig. 5

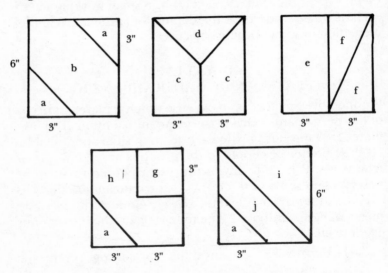

Before putting the pieces in the envelopes erase the letters which had been written on them. Make sure that each team has its own set of envelopes. (It will help if each team has its own distinctive colour which is used for its cards and envelopes.)

It may take up to thirty minutes for some teams to complete the task. After that, invite each team to discuss what happened during the exercise, with special reference to how each person *felt* at key moments. After about fifteen minutes

128

of discussion in the teams, invite all the teams to form one large circle to share their experiences. The facilitator should then lead the discussion on from the detail of the exercise to its application in real life — helping people to relate it to concrete experiences of cooperation (or the lack of it) which they have had in their work. Then the facilitator can help people to draw out such lessons as the following:

— If I concentrate single-mindedly on solving my own particular part of the problem I may be making it difficult for others to find a solution.

— At times it is necessary to give up my own neat solution in order to enable the whole group to find solutions for everybody.

Flower Power [5]

This exercise may be done some months (or even years) after the 'Cooperative Squares' exercise. It can be used with a group numbering between twelve and thirty-five. The group does not break into small working teams, as was done in 'Cooperative Squares'. Since the whole group has to act as one large working team, it is a much greater challenge to ensure coordination and cooperation in the group.

There are two distinct stages in the exercise — two 'games', each with its own rules. The first provides the participants with an instance of a situation where the leader has all the power; the second is one where the power exercised by the leader is purely facilitative. However, it is important to allow the participants to discover these things for themselves in the course of the exercise, or when reflecting on it; to explain it beforehand may deprive the exercise of its effectiveness as an experiential learning event. So it is best simply to introduce it by saying: 'We invite you to take part in a cooperative exercise which is rather like "Cooperative Squares".'

Materials and equipment:

— A large table around which the whole group can gather and on which the pattern may be built up. (If no such table is available, the floor may be used.)

— A set of forty-five pieces of cardboard in five colours made according to the specifications of the diagram in Fig. 6. These pieces are sorted into groups on a random basis and placed in envelopes: if there are fifteen participants in the exercise, then there should be fourteen envelopes; if there are twenty participants, there should be nineteen envelopes, etc.

— A forty-sixth piece which will be given to the leader. This piece is the key to the solution, since it is a reproduction in miniature of the overall shape to be made when the forty-six pieces are correctly assembled. See Fig. 7 for a full description of this piece. This 'key piece' is put into a special envelope which has the following instructions written on it:

— You are in charge, so it is your responsibility to exercise your power effectively to complete the task.

— Your own contribution, which is contained in this envelope, is the key to the whole pattern; your task is to ensure that the others follow this model.

— Get each of the different colours together first.

— Then organise the pattern from the top down.

Tell the group that this is an exercise in leadership and cooperation. Ask for a volunteer from the group to act as leader; check that the group as a whole accepts the leader. Then put up a chart on which the following is written:

TASK: To arrange the pieces in the correct order.
RULES:
— The leader is responsible for organizing the pieces.
— Participants are to hold their cards so that the leader can see them.
— Pieces may be taken up, put down, or exchanged — but only on the instructions of the leader.
— Participants are to maintain silence and are not to distract the leader by making suggestions.

As coordinator you will have to keep a close eye on what is happening during the exercise. If the leader fails to understand the significance of the key piece, try to ensure that she or he comes to realise that this is a model of the final 'correct' solution. Encourage the leader to follow the instructions written on the envelope of the leader's piece, especially as regards working from the top of the pattern downwards. If necessary, encourage the leader to ensure that the rules are not broken. Monitor what is happening among the participants. It is likely that many of them will

130

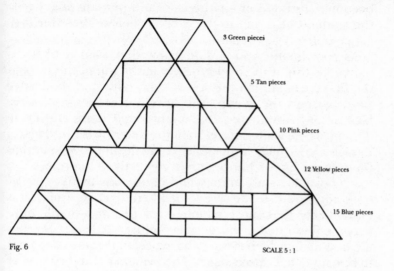

3 Green pieces

5 Tan pieces

10 Pink pieces

12 Yellow pieces

15 Blue pieces

Fig. 6

SCALE 5 : 1

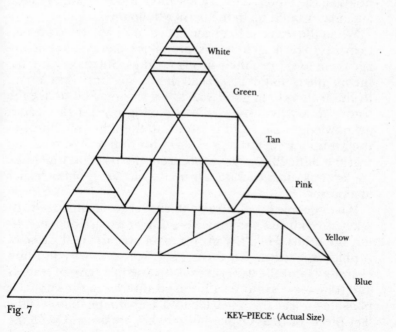

White

Green

Tan

Pink

Yellow

Blue

Fig. 7

'KEY–PIECE' (Actual Size)

become frustrated or apathetic — and perhaps angry with the leader. Call a halt to the exercise before these feelings get completely out of hand.

As coordinator you should know that what is likely to happen is this: if the leader begins at the top of the pattern the first parts will fall into place very easily and the leader (and perhaps the group) will have a great sense of satisfaction and confidence. But the task gets more and more difficult as the leader moves to fit the lower pieces into place. In fact it is virtually impossible for the leader to ensure that the bottom line is put together correctly — there are too many possible combinations, and in this case the 'key piece' does not show how they are to be fitted together. In fact it is quite likely that most members of the group will have become frustrated or bored even before the leader reaches the bottom line. So it is not to be expected that the exercise is to be completed 'successfully'. The *real* aim of this first part of the exercise is not to have the leader work out the solution successfully; rather it is to allow both leader and participants to realise how difficult it is to do a complex task if one leader holds all the power; and to allow them to see how frustration and apathy build up in the passive 'followers'.

When the exercise has been called to a halt, invite the participants to form a circle to share their experiences. Encourage them to express their strong feelings. But make sure that the members do not project all their anger or frustration on to the leader. One good way to do this may be to ask the leader to say how she or he is feeling now; if the leader acknowledges pain and frustration, the other members of the group may begin to feel sorry for him or her, realizing that the difficulties arose more from the position which the leader took on, rather than from the character of the leader as a person.

When people have had a good chance to air their feelings, ask if anybody has had somewhat similar experiences in real-life situations. Help the group to analyze the real cause of problems — the structures in which authority is often exercised, and the expectations that people have of leaders and followers. Explore with the group whether it would be possible for leaders in real life to share with the followers the 'key piece' or 'master plan' which they are using. Could the plan be one that emerges from and is 'owned' by the whole group, rather than just the leader?

Now is the time to invite the group to take a short break and then to return to take part in the second part of the exercise. Tell them that the second part of the exercise is called 'Flower Power'. Assure the group that this time they will not be 'trapped' by any ready-made plan or structures. It will be an opportunity for them to have a good experience of collaboration, putting into practice the points that have emerged in the previous discussion. The only 'rules' will be those that reflect the reality of real life, e.g. that each person controls his or her own gifts so that nobody else can force one to use those gifts. This time, the leader will be expected to play a purely facilitative role. Invite the group to choose a leader who is able and willing to exercise leadership in this way.

Material and equipment:

— Several tables, around which the participants can work in informal, *ad hoc* groupings.

— A large chart on which the following is written:

'FLOWER POWER'

TASK: To arrange the pieces in a correct and pleasing pattern.

RULES:

— Pieces may be exchanged, one for one, by agreement between those who hold them.

— Pieces may be given away.

— Pieces may be placed on the table where others can see them.

— The pieces of other players may not be moved or taken without the permission of the owner.

— Players may work in small or larger groups and may discuss how best to use all their pieces.

— The leader has no special power; but it is well to remember that the group has chosen this leader to be an over-all facilitator of the group.

—A set of forty-five pieces of cardboard, in five different colours, made according to the specifications in Fig. 8.

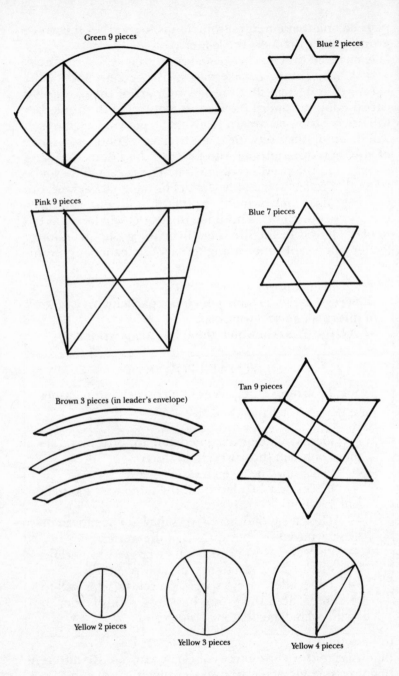

Green 9 pieces

Blue 2 pieces

Pink 9 pieces

Blue 7 pieces

Brown 3 pieces (in leader's envelope)

Tan 9 pieces

Yellow 2 pieces

Yellow 3 pieces

Yellow 4 pieces

Fig. 8

These pieces are sorted into groups on a random basis and put into envelopes. There should be one envelope for each participant, not counting the leader.

—A special envelope for the leader; this will contain four further pieces of a colour different from the other five colours. The leader's envelope has the following written on it:

Advice to the leader/facilitator of 'Flower Power':

— Your task is to help the group to work well together and to facilitate others in making a useful and satisfying contribution to the joint task.

— You will find that it is helpful if the participants form several groups, based on the different colours.

— Encourage the different working groups to work independently — but keeping an eye on how their different contributions will eventually fit together.

— Your own pieces will help to link the other groups of pieces together.

— When a certain amount of work has been done, encourage the groups to take 'time out' to gather in one large group to report on what they have done, and to reflect on where they are going, and what over-all pattern they are working towards. Propose another such break for evaluation at a later stage.

— Ask yourself, who is to decide what is a 'correct and pleasing' solution? Try also to find a suitable opportunity to put this question to the whole group.

As coordinator of the whole exercise, you will have to mon-itor what happens during it. Intervene as little as possible — and only to ensure that the group have a good experience of working together. If necessary, encourage the chosen leader to re-read the advice given on the leader's envelope. If the leader is becoming too authoritarian you may find it necessary to say quietly that the task is to facilitate the group. (But it would be better if such a challenge came from the participants themselves.) You may find it necessary to help the leader to realise that a 'correct' solution is one that is acceptable to the whole group; but again it is better that this insight should emerge from within the group.

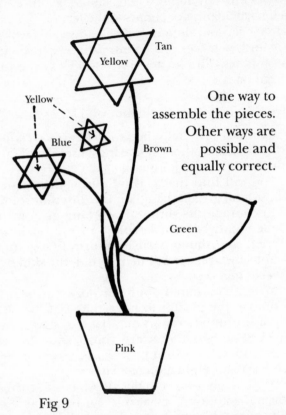

One way to
assemble the pieces.
Other ways are
possible and
equally correct.

Fig 9

If the group comes up with what they consider to be 'a correct and pleasing pattern' there will probably be little need for a long reflection on the exercise itself: the lessons will be obvious. However, it may be well to allow a little time for people to share how they felt at key moments, or to mention some insights they got during the exercise. If the solution arrived at by the group happens to be different from the one shown in Fig. 9, you may find it useful to show them Fig. 9 as another, *equally correct*, solution; this may help them to see that there can be more than one correct answer. However, if the solution which the group came up with was different from that shown in Fig. 9, it is very important not to give the impression that theirs was a *wrong* answer, or even a less perfect one.

136

Now move the discussion on to real-life situations. Ask if any members of the group have had similar good experiences of collaboration; if so, help them to analyze such situations, locating the elements that contributed to effective collaboration. Help them to appreciate the fact that there may be a number of different ways of resolving a problem — all equally correct. Draw the sharing to a close by asking for suggestions about how the present group can promote truly facilitative leadership within the group itself and with others.

NOTES

1. I am referring here to Rudolf Otto's well-known phrase '*mysterium tremendum et fascinans*'; see his book, *The Idea of the Holy*, Oxford, London, New York (OUP: 1958).

2. The ideas presented here were developed by the Cincinnati-based institute 'Management Design Inc.' These were used, with permission, by Anne Hope and Sally Timmel first in their *Delta Handbook* and then in *Training for Transformation*; there the subject is called 'the parabola'. I used this material on many occasions in West Africa and Europe. The groups I worked with found the general ideas very helpful; but they frequently became confused by the use of the different terms 'dream', 'vision', 'goals', and 'objectives'; and also by the account of different kinds of doubt; furthermore, most of the ordinary people with whom we were working were not familiar with the word 'parabola'. So, two years ago, I took the liberty of revising and adapting the presentation, with a view to making the language more simple and clear; I also adapted the accompanying diagram. It is this adapted version which I give here.

3. See especially Paulo Freire, *Education for Critical Consciousness*, New York (Continuum/Seabury: 1974) 2nd, revised ed., London (Sheed and Ward: 1985).

4. I have used, with permission, an adapted version of the 'game' as given in *Winners All: Cooperative Games for All Ages,* London (Pax Christi: 1980), 24-26; in this booklet there is a note which says: 'In its basic format, this exercise was first published in the N.E.A. Journal, U.S.A., October 1969.'

5. This is an adapted version of an exercise which was prepared by Frank Dorr for the Social and Health Education Programme in Cork, Ireland, in 1980. It has not been previously published.

6

Justice, Culture, and Economic Development

In the last chapter I looked at participative community-building, a place where the public and the interpersonal aspects of spirituality converge. I propose in this chapter to move on to look more closely at the central element in the 'public' aspect, namely, structural justice. People who are interested in spirituality tend to get switched off very quickly when confronted by material about structural justice and economic development. Some feel helpless in the face of statistics, and hopeless in the face of intractable problems. Others feel guilty because of their own complicity in the injustice of society. The result is that many people leave social justice on the margins of their spirituality. I would like to bring it back into the mainstream. In an attempt to do so I propose in this chapter to make extensive use of pictures, reflection on texts from Scripture, and exercises, rather than statistics and theoretical analysis. I shall also attempt to integrate what I have to say about economic development with a consideration of the role of culture in society. This is partly to make the treatment of economics somewhat lighter and more interesting: but it is mainly because economic development can be understood only in the light of culture — a point that is often neglected by economists and planners. In the final section of the chapter I shall go on to deal with the issue of justice for women.

SECTION ONE:
IMAGES OF STRUCTURAL INJUSTICE

I begin this chapter with a simple exercise. It is just a matter of looking at a series of six pictures. They illustrate different words used to describe the situation of the 'underdogs' in a society. Taken together, they can give one some sense of what structural injustice means in practice.

Topham Picture Library

(1) A group or an individual may be OPPRESSED — crushed under a heavy load imposed unfairly by those who have power. The picture suggests this by showing a grossly over-burdened worker who has few of the basic rights that workers ought to have; such a person is oppressed both economically and politically.

Topham Picture Library

(2) A group or an individual may be DISCRIMINATED against. This means they are denied the basic equality before the law that should be part of any just society; and this is done because they are black, or female, or live in the 'wrong' part of town, etc. In the picture we see one aspect of apartheid in South Africa.

Barnaby's Picture Library

(3) People may be EXPLOITED. Unfair advantage is taken of them, perhaps because they are not in a good bargaining position, or because they are not aware of their rights. The picture shows young children being exploited by having to work long hours.

Barnaby's Picture Library

(4) The climber in the picture is utterly dependent on the partner who holds the rope. Similarly, groups or whole nations are often left in a position of DEPENDENCY; for instance, the Zambian economy depends very much on copper and the people there have become very poor because the price of copper has been kept low on the world market.

Barnaby's Picture Library

(5) Some categories of people are left in a MARGINALISED
position in their society. Those who have power don't take
any account of the interests or opinions of the ones who are
left on the fringes while the important decisions are being
made. The picture illustrates this by showing shanty-dwellers
near a prosperous city.

Barnaby's Picture Library

(6) Whole segments of the population of some countries are left VOICELESS and powerless. For instance, the workers who will lose their jobs as a result of 'rationalization' may have no voice in the decision taken thousands of miles away in the board-room of a big company.

These pictures and examples may perhaps stimulate people into looking at their own experience in order to locate instances of structural injustice. Take a little time to 'sit with' these words ('exploited', 'voiceless', 'marginalised' etc), and see whether they find echoes in your own life:

— Call you recall situations where you were the *victim* of such structural injustice? Which of the above words (or other words) are most appropriate to describe the injustice? How did you feel at the time? How do you feel about it now? (In each case try to find words that describe your feelings as accurately as possible; note that you may have a mixture of rather different feelings, e.g. anger and sadness; explore also where in your body you hold these feelings and how they are affecting your body.)

— Looking back on your life, do you now see situations where you *perpetrated* structural injustice — or at least *colluded* in it by not stopping it or protesting against it? To what extent were you aware *at the time* that the situation was unjust? How do you feel about it now? (Try to locate your feelings — not just your thoughts.)

144

(If you are working with a group, suggest that some of these reflections be shared in sub-groups of about five people, making sure that everybody gets heard, and that nobody is 'probed'. Then there can be some sharing in the whole group. After a break, the group leader or an 'input' person may respond to what has been shared in the large group, by gathering together some of the fruits of the sharing and noting the different spheres of life where structural injustice commonly occurs.) It is helpful to recall some of the *feelings* that were experienced and look at their effects; for instance, a feeling of being worthless is likely to leave a person unable to take effective action, while a feeling of anger may strengthen the person to act courageously.

A Stratified Society

A theoretical understanding of social injustice is not very helpful in moving one to action. This is because people are moved more by feelings than by ideas. (It is interesting to explore the different usages of the word 'moved' — e.g. 'I was moved by what you said' and 'she was moved to action'.) Over the past ten years I have been involved in perhaps a hundred different workshops where justice was an important theme. In these, the most powerful learning experiences for most of the participants came through taking part in a 'simulation' exercise — a kind of game which mirrors, in a simplified and perhaps exaggerated way, certain key aspects of real life. The most powerful simulation for most of the groups I worked with was 'Star Power'.[1] It is a trading 'game' in which the participants presume at first that everybody has an equal chance to do well; but it turns out that, as in real life, the cards are stacked against some and in favour of others. The players begin to experience frustration and anger, or, on the other hand, smugness and self-righteousness. Participation in this 'game' gives people the opportunity to feel what it is like to be exploited and marginalised, or to be comfortable and insensitive. 'Star Power' has changed the lives of a lot of people whom I know — far more than lectures and books could ever do.

In our workshops we found it important to allow a significant break after 'Star Power' (or any such major simulation) before any resource-person gave 'input' on social justice. For the real lessons of the simulation are drawn out by the participants themselves in the hours (or days) after it. But once participants had drawn their own lessons they welcomed a talk which offered a framework within which these lessons could be situated. In my book *Spirituality and Justice* I offered such a framework by describing how most societies tend to become stratified. Four different kinds of power (economic, political, cultural, and religious/ecclesiastical) are concentrated in the hands of small groups of people who sit on top of four 'pyramids of power'.[2] What I said there was worked out very largely in the context of responding to groups who had taken part in the 'Star Power' exercise.

Big Fish and Little Fish

Within the past three years I have been searching for ways to express the same general insights in more vivid and concrete ways. I worked out two approaches, both of which use pictures rather than diagrams. The first is an expansion of an idea and picture used by the well-known economist and theologian Charles Elliott.[3] He used a picture of a stack of three fish bowls as an image of our stratified society. Recently I expanded this so that there are now four sets of the smaller fish bowls on top of the one large fish-bowl at the bottom (see the accompanying diagram).

The large bowl is filled with very many small undernourished fish, representing the millions of people in the world who are disadvantaged and largely 'voiceless' in decision-making, and many of whom are exploited and oppressed in some degree. Some of these little fish lie exhausted on the bottom, but most of them are still struggling to get into one of the narrow funnels that lead up to the second layer of fish bowls. The fish in these middle bowls are struggling to get into the top bowls where the really fat fish live. These privileged 'top' fish represent the groups who hold power in the *economic* sphere, the *political* sphere, the *cultural* sphere and the *ecclesiastical/religious* sphere. (So these are the people who, in the other image of the world which I mentioned above, sat at the top of the four 'pillars of power'.)

The fish in the four middle bowls represent 'the service people', in each of the four spheres where power is exercised:

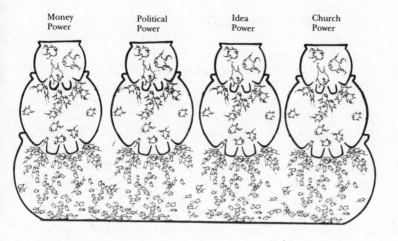

| Money
Power | Political
Power | Idea
Power | Church
Power |

— in the economic sphere: lower management people in industry, agri-business, banking, catering, etc; and health workers;

— in the political sphere: police, prison officers, and civil servants, and various other officials (except the top management people in these services); and ordinary members of political parties;

— in the cultural sphere: teachers, journalists, entertainers, etc.

— in the ecclesiastical sphere: all full-time Church workers (priests, pastors, ministers, deacons, catechists, religious sisters and brothers) except those in the top positions (e.g. bishops and high ecclesiastical officials).

These 'service people' keep the various systems in operation, and they benefit to some extent from them. But the major policies and decisions are handed down to them by the small group of people in the four top fish bowls.

In this situation the dialogue is not vertical but horizontal. By this I mean that those in each of the four top bowls are in a position to trade off certain privileges to people in the other top bowls; they can bargain with each other from a certain position of strength. Vertical dialogue — between those at the top and those in the lower bowls — is very restricted, because of the absence of the kind of equality that is required for real dialogue.

One of the best insights of Charles Elliott was his idea of including in the picture a number of cones or funnels which connect the lower bowls to those above them. These funnels are wide at the bottom but narrow at the top. They give the illusion that it is relatively easy for the fish in the lower bowls to swim up into the higher ones. And so they 'con' the smaller fish — leading them to spend their energy in *competing with each other* to move upwards in the system, rather than in trying to change the whole system. Elliott calls these funnels 'confidence-mechanisms' or 'con-mechs' because they trick people, giving them the impression that there is far more social mobility in the system than in fact there is.

There are a number of mechanisms of this kind in our stratified society. The most obvious one is the educational system which seems to promise advancement to anybody who is intelligent and hard-working; in practice, of course, the poorer classes and countries are at a great disadvantage. Other such mechanisms operate in each of the four 'pyramids' or 'bowls' where power is exercised. Some examples: a small number of business people succeed in moving from rags to riches; an occasional politician comes up from 'the masses'; some artists or entertainers rise up from below to positions of real influence; and, even in the highly stratified power-structures of the Churches, there is room for some mobility.

At the bottom of the picture there is only *one* large fish-bowl — not four. This brings out the point that to a large extent it is the same mass of people who are disadvantaged, voiceless, and powerless in every sphere. The person who is poor is also very likely to lack political power, to have no power in shaping the prevailing climate of ideas, and to carry little weight in Church policy-making.

The picture of the fishbowls gives an insight into certain aspects of society; but, inevitably, it is rather like a caricature because it is an attempt to express a complex reality in a simplified and one-sided manner. It focuses attention almost exclusively on the divisions between *classes* in society, while by-passing other aspects of social injustice. The same applies to the account of the four pyramids of power; it is not untrue but it is incomplete. Furthermore, this line of analysis seems to me to come out of a particular European tradition of thought, in which Marx is the dominant influence.

SECTION TWO: CULTURE AND DEVELOPMENT

Working in Africa in recent years I tried to find an approach to the issue of structural injustice that was less abstract, less dependent on European thinking, and — above all — more obviously related to the immediate experience of ordinary people there. We were using the handbook *Training for Transformation* which proposes an approach to social analysis which calls for an examination of the *economic, political, and cultural* structures of society.[4] It occurred to me that we might provide a set of pictures that would illustrate the traditional pattern of life under these three headings. I was fortunate that my co-worker and friend, Steve 'Lani Adeleye, was a gifted artist; he was eager to prepare posters of the kind of scenes I had in mind — and he added in all the detail that made them true to life.

We ended up with a set of nine pictures — three to illustrate different aspects of the *economy* of a traditional society, another three to illustrate different aspects of *politics* and community decision-making in such a society, and the final three to cover different aspects of the *culture and religion*. Taken together, the nine pictures helped people to understand the over-all pattern of traditional society. They also helped people to appreciate the strengths of such a culture, and to be proud of their tradition. And of course they sparked off a lot of very animated discussion about the value of such things as the traditional methods of healing and of resolving disputes.

Having used the pictures first of all to promote understanding and appreciation of the traditional way of life, we then went through them again with participants in our workshops. This second time round the participants were asked to consider the changes that have taken place — and, particularly, the ways in which structural injustice has increased. When doing this we generally used scripture texts to spark off discussion on the different kinds of injustice; I shall refer to some of these texts a little further on.

149

Some hours or days later in the workshop we generally returned for a third time to the pictures, looking at them this time in the light of what the Bible has to say about the values that believers should seek to embody in society. This led on to an exploration of 'alternatives', that is, the kind of structures that would take what is best in both the traditional and the 'modern' ways of life, then shape and adapt them to provide the basis for a society that is truly just — and one that is ecologically sensitive and sustainable.

I propose to follow roughly the same pattern in the following pages. However, in order to help readers appreciate the wider relevance of this material, I now have a somewhat different set of pictures — mainly photographs of real situations in different parts of the world.[5] (If you are working with a group, and if you have large-size copies of the pictures, it is helpful to display them one by one, so that eventually all nine of them form a large circle, with the first three at the bottom, the next three on the left and the last three on the right. Generally each picture can be used simply as a visual aid for what you want to say. But you may find it helpful to use at least one or two of the pictures as what Paulo Freire calls a 'code'; that means using it, not to give *answers* but to evoke *questions* and discussion for the participants, about what they see in the picture and about how that relates to the reality of their daily lives.)[6]

Economic Structures

The first picture shows farmers at work, producing food mainly for their own families and for the town or village market. In traditional societies each area is generally self-sufficient in the production of food. Not merely each area, but even most families can manage to meet their own needs as regard staple foods; though some local crafts-people may serve the local community by specializing in their own work — and, in return, getting food from other members of the community. In general, the members of a traditional community do not depend for their basic needs on some outside agency or on people whom they do not know personally. This is a great strength, since it means that the problem of 'dependency' seldom arises.

150

Barnaby's Picture Library

The second picture shows traditional craft-workers, producing goods mainly for use in the local community. Housing, clothes, footwear, cooking utensils, pottery, soap, farming implements — all these are provided by local workers. Much of the work is done by hand, since the demand is limited and the items are not mass produced.

The third picture shows a traditional market. Almost all the goods bought and sold there are locally produced. Only a few luxury items come from outside. Consequently, the fluctuations in world trade will have only a peripheral effect on this market and this community. Prices of foodstuffs will fluctuate according to the season; but neither the sellers nor the buyers are vulnerable to the unpredictable collapses or escalations of price that begin to occur once the local market gets tied in to a world market. In traditional society, money is just a means by which local people can more conveniently exchange goods with each other. So the local currency is not likely to lose all its value — as so frequently happens nowadays in poor countries, because they are the weak members in the international system of trade.

Vivant Afrique

Taken together, the first three pictures bring out some significant features of the economic life of traditional societies:
— for the most part, what is produced locally is consumed locally;

152

Topham Picture Library

— again, for the most part, what is consumed locally is produced locally;

— consequently, production is on a small scale;

— most of the materials and sources of energy used are renewable.

There are some disadvantages in this economic pattern. For instance, it is not so easy to standardize the quality of what is produced; and highly specialised goods, or ones that involve a high level of technology, cannot easily be produced locally. Furthermore, it is commonly assumed that mass production lowers the cost of goods. This is obviously true in the case of certain items — for instance, computer chips and printed circuits. But we cannot take it for granted that it applies in general.

Mass production undoubtedly lowers costs if the costing is done according to the current economic models. But if one takes account of the full social and environmental costs of mass production, the answer is more doubtful. Consider first the *environmental* costs:

— Mass production generally uses up large amounts of non-renewable energy sources (e.g. oil), and minerals; so, from an ecological point of view it is far more costly.

153

— When goods are produced for a world market there can be enormous waste due to over-production, because the demand cannot easily be predicted.

The *social* costs of mass production are also significant:

— Producers are at the mercy of a world market controlled by countries, or individuals, or forces that have no concern for them; so they can easily be put out of business, even though they may have an excellent product and be working very hard.

— In traditional societies unemployment is unknown. The change from craft-work to mass production generally gives rise to chronic unemployment. The hidden economic costs, and the not-so-hidden social costs, of long-term unemployment are extremely high — for instance, a great increase in crime and vandalism, as well as the loss to the community of the productive capacity of so many people.

— Craft-work is personally fulfilling, and there is generally a certain variety in the work so boredom can be avoided; mass production, on the other hand, causes workers to feel bored and unfulfilled.

— Finally, mass production causes the worker to be 'alienated' from the product and the consumer — it puts a wide gap between the worker and the person who uses the final product. This is in sharp contrast to the situation where a small farmer or craft worker knows the person who is to eat or use what is being produced, so that the product creates a personal link between the producer and consumer.

Political or Decision-Making Structures

In the fourth picture we move on to the subject of how authority is exercised in a traditional village community in order to ensure the harmony and welfare of the local people. The picture reminds us that decisions are usually taken by some kind of local council. (In tribal societies this council will probably consist of elders, with a chief who presides over the meeting; interesting questions arise about whether the interests of women are adequately represented — they often have their own separate organizations). Two significant points to note are that decisions are usually taken on a consensus basis and that they are made by local people who themselves have immediate experience of the problems they are confronting.

154

Vivant Afrique

The fifth picture indicates how authority is exercised on a regional level. The ceremonial and regalia associated with the King/Queen or 'Clan Head' symbolise the unity of a whole people or clan. The person who presides in this way is expected to foster harmony between the different village communities. The 'higher' authority does not supplant that of the local authorities, or reduce them to being its agents. In fact, far from being that of an absolute ruler, the authority of the King or Queen comes more from the respect of the people than from the use of force.

In every society there has to be some way of adjudicating disputes and ensuring enforcement of the laws or customs of the place. The sixth picture shows a traditional African 'diviner'. Such people can resolve disputes by administering an oath to the parties who are in conflict with each other. People believe that this oath will reveal who is telling the truth, or that anybody who swears it falsely will die. Their belief in the mysterious power of the oath helps to resolve disputes and restore order to the community.

Taken together, the fourth, fifth, and sixth pictures bring out important differences between traditional societies and 'modern' ones:

155

The African Missionary

— One of the more obvious differences is that in the former there is little need for a large bureaucracy of civil servants. The reason is that authority is exercised locally, each community being largely self-sufficient and therefore not very dependent on a centralised authority.

— For the same reason there is no need for a large police force. Law enforcement takes place at a local level. The cohesion of the traditional society is greatly strengthened by the cultural traditions which emphasize community solidarity and respect for the wisdom of the older people. Religious beliefs (for instance belief in the power of the oath) also foster cohesion and law enforcement.

Vivant Universe

— A major weakness of the traditional society is that it is vulnerable to aggression from outside; it is not well organised to resist such interference.

— The 'modern' notion of equality before the law does not arise very much in traditional societies; in fact older people are given more respect than those who are young; and frequently women have less rights than men. (In practice, of

157

course, women may be better protected there than in some 'modern' societies which only give notional allegiance to equal rights for women.)

Barnaby' Picture Library

— Perhaps the most significant difference of all is that in 'modern' societies decisions are often taken by authorities or bureaucrats who have no real links with the people affected by their decisions. This is already a major structural injustice, and it gives rise to many other injustices. The nature of traditional society is such that decisions are normally taken by those who have to live with their effects.

Beliefs, Values, and Celebrations

The seventh picture brings us into the area of people's deepest beliefs about the meaning of life. One such matter is their understanding of sickness and death. In traditional societies, healing is not seen as merely a matter of getting the body in working order; it also has to do with the state of a person's spirit, and with how the person is relating to the family and the community — and even to those who have died, and to the spirit world in general. Therefore health is not a private matter but very much a social issue. The most important first step in traditional healing is diagnosis of the source of the evil. Does it perhaps arise as a result of the animosity of a family member or neighbour? Or could it be a curse brought on by some social misdemeanor?

Irish Folklore Commission

Education is a central part of any society. The traditional form of education had a strong practical dimension:

159

children learned farming or trade, crafts or child-care by working alongside the adults. This knowledge was set in the context of a body of traditional wisdom — which included folklore and specialised education for new stages in life (adulthood, marriage, becoming an elder, etc). This picture of a traditional Irish storyteller indicates that such education is usually less cut off from daily living than school is in 'modern' society.

Barnaby's Picture Library

The final picture is of a traditional celebration. It combines what we would now call 'secular' and 'sacred' elements. It gives expression to some aspect of what the community sees as the basic meaning and purpose of human life. In traditional dances, processions, or other ceremonies the people re-enact the story of their origins, and of the other great events in their history. The community becomes more united and stronger in spirit through the celebration. The harmony of the members is fostered and restored — harmony with each other, with those who have gone before them, and with the spiritual powers that govern their lives.

Is the cultural/religious aspect of life more fundamental than the others? In one sense it is, since it provides people with a meaning and purpose for their lives; if that is lost, the society deteriorates very rapidly — for instance, many of its people may become alcoholic. But from another point of view the economic aspect of life is fundamental; for survival is impossible if a people's basic needs (shelter, water, food, clothing) are not met. Then again, from another point of view, the political aspect of life is most fundamental: people cannot survive without a measure of security, some means of resolving disputes, and a way of allocating resources and responsibilities.

Disrupting the Pattern

The traditional society forms a coherent whole, a unified pattern. Each aspect is linked to the others and supported by them. This fabric is strong. It enables a people to survive most natural calamities, and to put up some resistance to interference from outside. It is at the same time flexible enough to allow for changes and growth. When the economic and political aspects of life are running smoothly there is often a great flowering at the cultural level. On the other hand, if life becomes a hand-to-mouth struggle for survival then the traditional beliefs and values may help to sustain the people.

It would be sheer romanticism to suggest that every traditional society is a model of social justice. But the notion that justice is a foundation for peace is not just an abstract ideal; it is a fact that is verified in history — though rather imperfectly. Most societies that survive over many generations have certain 'checks and balances' built into them, thereby ensuring some measure of equity.

Things can go seriously wrong and gross structural injustice can arise in two different ways:

(1) Some outside power becomes very powerful, and begins to interfere — politically (often in a military way), economically, and even in the cultural/religious sphere. One example from the Bible is the change that took place in the situation of the Jews as an immigrant people in Egypt shortly before the birth of Moses:

> The new king . . . said: 'These Israelites are so numerous and strong that they are a threat to us. . . .' So the Egyptians put slave-drivers over them to crush their spirits

with hard labour. The Israelites built the cities of Pithom and Rameses to serve as supply centres for the king.

(Ex 1:8-11)

In this case the king used his political power to divert the economic activity of the Jews from meeting their own needs — they now had to build cities for the king; and there was a further purpose in this — to crush their spirits. The colonial powers in the last century acted just as ruthlessly. They disrupted the political systems of many nations in what is now called the Third World, and they undermined their belief-systems and values. The aim of the colonisers was partly strategic and partly economic:

— strategic: it enabled the colonial power to secure its interests vis-à-vis its rivals;

— economic: the colonisers re-shaped the economies of the colonies to provide raw materials and markets for the colonial powers.

(2) Structural injustice can also arise from *within* the society itself. There will always be individuals and groups willing to take advantage of others; but in a smoothly functioning society the greed of such people is held in check by curbs on their power. However, in a rapidly changing society the curbs and checks often become less effective; and so there are more opportunities for exploitation and oppression. It is then that social injustice starts to grow out of control. The fabric of the society begins to be torn apart, because the increased power of some sectors is no longer balanced out by the power of other sectors. As a result, there is no longer an equitable or balanced distribution of resources and responsibilities. Some groups or classes get most of the privileges while others have to carry most of the burdens. This is what is meant by structural injustice.

Structural injustice tends to be most severe when there is a combination of outside and inside causes. This frequently happens when the foreign imperial power 'coopts' some local power group, giving them an unfair advantage over others. For instance, the representatives of the European colonial powers often did a deal with local chiefs, making them their agents in return for trading privileges. Sometimes, even whole ethnic groups colluded with the imperial powers for their mutual benefit — but at enormous cost to the region as a whole (for example, in the slave trade). What is happening today in much of the Third World is quite similar — but now it is a privileged *class* of local people who collude in the exploitation of the mass of their own people. Their access to arms from abroad, their links with foreign governments, and the fact that they have been coopted as local agents of transnational companies — all this gives them the power to take advantage of their own people, making the 'independence' of their countries a sham.

The Bible gives many examples of such abuses of power. Time and again the prophets protest — e.g. 'The wealthy cheat and rob; they mistreat the poor and take advantage of foreigners.' (Ez 22:29). One striking instance occurred after the Israelites returned from the Exile. Some of them ran into debt and found they were being exploited by those of their neighbours who were more fortunate or more unscrupulous. They went to their leader Nehemiah to complain:

> Some said, 'We have had to mortgage our fields, our gardens, and our homes, just to get enough food to avoid starvation. . . . Are we not of the same race as the other Jews? Are not our children of as much value as theirs? Why then should we have to sell our children into slavery? Why should these people be in a position to take sexual advantage of our daughters? We are powerless because they have taken away our farms and gardens.' When I heard their complaints I was angry and decided to take action. I denounced the top people and the officials, saying: 'You are oppressing your own brothers and sisters'.
>
> (Neh 5:3-5)

Such exploitation is common today. It occurs on every level, from that of the local moneylender to that of the loans given, or refused, by the International Monetary Fund (IMF). Those who have economic power use it to take advantage of those who are poor. One of the clearest examples is the way in which the IMF itself is used shamelessly to promote the economic interests of its major shareholders, namely, the leading Western powers.

It is not just economic power that is abused; political power can also be used to oppress others. Security forces

163

(police or army), politicians, and officials of all kinds from judges to civil servants can take advantage of people who have no protection. There are very strong condemnations of such abuses in the Bible (e.g. Amos 5:12: 'You take bribes and prevent the poor from getting justice in the courts'; cf I Sam 8:11-18; Zeph 3:3; Jn 18:22).

Power in the religious and cultural spheres may also be abused. It is not uncommon today to hear of people being sacrificed because they are seen as a threat to the power of the opinion-formers or of those who hold religious power. I myself know a number of people who were squeezed out of their teaching positions in colleges — and even in seminaries — for reasons of this kind. It is perhaps some consolation for them to realise that the biblical writers were familiar with such abuses of power. The prophet Jeremiah clashed many times with the Temple priests and the false prophets. In order to serve their own selfish interests, these religious leaders colluded in the misguided policies of the King and gave them religious sanction (e.g. Jer 26:11; 37:19). A major theme of the preaching of Jesus was his condemnation of those who misused their religious power to put heavy burdens on the common people (Mt 23:2-4). And John's Gospel shows the chief priests condemning Jesus because they perceived him as a threat to their interests (Jn 11:47-50).

'Development'

I have been suggesting that rapid change often leaves an opening for the emergence of structural injustice. The changes brought about by modern 'development' have had a very damaging effect on many societies in the Third World. The reason is rather shocking. It is that a basic element in the gaining of 'independence' by the colonies was their adoption of a model of 'development', which in some respects was simply a new and more sophisticated way of continuing the process begun by colonization. This was the process of becoming tied in to a single world economic order dominated by the powerful nations of 'the North'.[7]

As I have already pointed out, this process allowed a fairly small group of people in most of the former colonies to gain a monopoly of power in the economic and political spheres.

This is itself a structural injustice, and it is the cause of further structural injustice. But there is a deeper underlying cause of injustice in these societies; it is the effect which modern 'development' has in the *cultural* sphere.

The problem stems from the fact that 'development' is basically a Western notion. Economic, political, and social 'development' all presuppose a cultural underpinning which is not indigenous to Third World countries. For instance, a certain 'professional ethics' is required for the effective functioning of a 'modern' health service, or an agricultural advisory service, or an educational system — or even a civil service. Such a professional ethics is largely taken for granted in the Western world and in countries where Western cultural values have become part of the way of life of the people. But in many Third World countries the Western value system was only grafted on rather superficially in colonial times; and since then it has been largely eroded.

In this situation major question marks lie over the whole effort to promote development. Many development projects fail because they presuppose a willingness to follow a particular pattern of behaviour, while the people concerned have no inclination or incentive to 'play by the rules'. This does not mean that the people concerned are immoral, or that they are incapable of understanding the rules that would make development succeed. It is simply that they are playing according to a *different* set of rules — ones that are more in line with their own cultural traditions.

A major element in any culture is a whole series of codes of behaviour, governing the conduct of the different aspects of living. For instance:
— farmers do not normally steal each others' crops;
— sick or old people are not normally thrown out to fend for themselves;
— local leaders aim to serve the community;
— those who conduct examinations seek to treat all candidates equally. Such norms of behaviour develop over centuries and are inculcated and imposed by the community in a whole variety of ways.

Cultures change and adapt to new inventions and new circumstances; and the accepted norms of each profession

165

change to take account of the new situation. In the Western world such changes have taken place very rapidly in recent times; and many would say that the ethics of some of the professions have not adapted quickly enough. But, in the Western world, there is at least some continuity between the present and the past. This is because the technological innovations that have led to major social changes have for the most part come out of the Western tradition and culture itself. Consequently there are solid roots from which the new codes of behaviour and systems of professional ethics can grow.

In much of the Third World the new technology and economics are quite alien to the local culture. So too are the new systems of education, health care, political organization, civil administration, social services, and Church life. These new systems have all been laid down on top of a totally different culture; in fact many of these new systems were imposed by force in colonial times. It is hardly surprising, then, if 'development' runs into difficulties that are almost unheard of in the Western world.

For better or worse the new Western-style systems are now widely established in 'the developing countries'; and the presupposition of the whole machinery of government — and of international aid — is that they can and should be made to work. People have little difficulty in learning the practical and technical aspects of the new systems. Africans or Filipinos can operate tractors or computers just as effectively as people from Western countries. But what remains absent for the most part is any effective way of inculcating or enforcing the codes of behaviour that are appropriate to the new professions and are necessary if the new systems are to function effectively.

Local and expatriate experts on 'development' think almost exclusively in terms of technical advancement; for instance, farmers are taught how to use fertilizers to increase the yield of crops. But the development planners often fail to take account of the cultural aspects — and their ethical implications. The new style of agriculture may be so different from what has gone before that the traditional ethics of farming seem quite irrelevant. In the past, crops were not normally stolen. They were protected by a kind of

166

social balance in the village, reinforced by the authority of local chiefs, and by certain religious or protective-magic practices. Again, the traditional norms ensured an ecological balance through crop rotation. The new styles of agriculture often undermine the credibility and effectiveness of this traditional 'professional ethics'.

The problem is not simply that the older norms are made to seem obsolete. It is that, when this happens, no effective alternative is put in their place. Consequently, the people who are growing rich through Western-style agricultural 'development' soon find that they have to make use of new and costly forms of security in order to protect themselves and their property from alienated neighbours or outsiders. Frequently, the kind of 'security' that is introduced is brutal and repressive.

I have used the example of agricultural 'development' to illustrate the point I am making. But I could just as easily have chosen examples from other spheres of life. For instance, Western-style schooling has undermined the traditional forms of education; and the obtaining of certificates has become more important then genuine and relevant education. Again, the traditional holistic approach to health-care has been partly undermined; many Third World people now oscillate over and back between Western medicine and the traditional approach to healing — sometimes ending up with the worst of both worlds.

There are similar problems in regard to the whole area of ritual. The traditional celebrations gave expression to the deep hopes and fears, joys and sorrows of the people. They gave people a sense of the purpose of life; and they nourished the beliefs and values which held the society together. Modern 'development' tends to undermine the credibility of the traditional rituals. The new imported forms of religious and secular celebration do not always strike the same deep chords in the hearts of the people. As a result, their culture becomes impoverished. The cohesion of the community is weakened. And many are left without any clear sense of the purpose of their lives.

It would appear, then, that Western-style development is a very mixed blessing indeed for many Third World countries. It is supposed to bring progress and prosperity. But it often

167

plays a major role in disrupting the cultural underpinning of the society. No wonder then that the social fabric begins to unravel.

A Way Forward

My conclusion from all this is not that Third World countries should give up the idea of development. Rather it is that there is need for a more authentic development. It must be realised that the cultural aspect of development is the primary one, since it determines the success or failure of any technological changes. Consequently, planners must look very hard at the cultural effects of the technical changes that are to be introduced

That is not enough. In my opinion real development must give priority to helping people to understand and appreciate their own cultural heritage and tradition. Of course this should not be a totally uncritical acceptance of the past. But people need to find ways of living that are in continuity with their own tradition. (Perhaps Japan might be taken as an example — though some serious questions can be raised about that.) Individuals or groups need also to understand what has gone wrong in their society and to explore ways of correcting it. Only in this way can people begin again to live in a world where values and codes of professional ethics are experienced as credible and relevant to everyday living. Without this, opportunism will become the only practical rule of life for most people.

Since the present model of 'development' has seriously undermined the trust that existed in local communities, authentic development in the Third World must pay special attention to activities that promote personal and communal responsibility. I mean activities that encourage individuals, families, and communities to trust each other, to share responsibility in decision-making, to share their resources with each other, and to work cooperatively, using a technology that is appropriate to the economic, social, cultural, and ecological situation.

Such cooperative activity should make use, as far as possible, of traditional values and structures, adapting them where necessary to take account of modern conditions of life. Examples would include:

168

— styles of decision-making that seek consensus from all participants rather than relying on authoritarian or majority decisions,

— forms of credit union that are in continuity with those used in the past,

— patterns of agriculture and of land distribution that retain some of the traditional values.

Economic Science

Some of the critical remarks I have been making about the process of 'development' in Third World countries apply also to Western countries. The problem in the West is not that the whole concept of 'development' is a totally alien import. Rather it is that a misguided model of development has been adopted. For this, the blame must be laid on planners who have given undue weight to the pronouncements of certain economists.

The science of economics is quite abstract: it generally takes account only of items that are easily measurable. Economists bridge the gap between their science and the real world by making a whole lot of assumptions. Unfortunately, we often find out too late that the assumptions were unjustified because some key factor had been overlooked. The most obvious examples can be found in the Third World and in sheltered parts of Western countries where there is a sudden boom in 'development'. Crucially important factors, with major economic implications, were ignored or played down. For instance, as I mentioned above, little account was taken of how the local culture would affect policies for economic development. To this we may add other items that were scarcely taken into account:

— the economic effects of the serious social disruption that arises as a result of the extremely rapid growth of the cities;

— the economic cost of major problems of 'security';

— the fact that in many African countries the agricultural workers are mainly women rather than men;

— above all, the (Western) economic advisors to Third World countries seem to have overlooked the fact that the poorest countries cannot hope to 'develop' in the way the Western countries did, since they have no other set of

169

countries below them to colonize and exploit. The 'experts' have tacitly ignored the fact that there simply aren't enough resources to enable all countries to be 'developed', and that the rich countries are determined not to give up their disproportionate share of the cake.

However, it is not only in the Third World that ordinary people have had to pay a high price for the unwarranted omissions or assumptions of economists. There are many debt-ridden farmers in the USA and Europe today who bitterly regret the advice to expand given them by economic 'experts'. And the crippling international debt that has skewed the economies of both Ireland and the USA is the result of a scandalous collusion between politicians and certain economic 'experts'.

More recently, some economists have once again abused their position by lending so-called 'scientific' backing to what are called 'monetarist' economics. The theories these economists are propounding are little more than an ideological justification for policies which favour the rich and make the poor carry the burden of national economic 'recovery'.

Probably the most dangerous assumption made by many economists is that we need set no limit to 'economic growth' and to what they call 'production'. They fail to advert to the fact that the 'growth' and 'production' of which they speak are in fact largely a matter of *consumption* — the using up of precious resources of energy and raw materials, and frequently the pollution of the environment as well. It is only in very recent years that economics has begun to take seriously the whole ecological question. A few of the more radical staff in the universities are at last emphasizing the limits of 'growth' and the need for ecological balance. But what about the economic planners in government service — people who were trained in an earlier age? Have they kept up to date? Have they allowed themselves to undergo the major conversion that is involved in shifting from an uncritical growth-oriented model of economics to one that is more realistic from an ecological point of view? If so, how far have they been willing to go in fighting the rhetoric of growth so glibly trotted out by politicians?

Those who are interested in a spirituality of justice need to know something about economics. Not primarily for the knowledge it can give about what is happening, and what will happen, in the world. Rather it is mainly to recognise just how uncertain, incomplete, and tentative is the knowledge provided by economic science; and to be able to challenge the assumptions and oversights made by economists.

We can help to make economics into a more realistic science by pinpointing the questions that are not being asked and the values that are being taken for granted. When dealing with the topic of 'ecological wisdom' in an earlier chapter I pointed out the need for a revised kind of economic science — one that recognises the true economic value of such resources as clean air and water. I now add that we need to insist that economists work in close partnership not only with ecologists, but also with anthropologists, psychologists, and ethicians to search for answers to questions that have as yet been scarcely posed in a serious way.

Among the questions I would like to see studied are the following:

— What are the full long-term costs to the community, of unemployment, especially chronic 'structural' unemployment?

— What mechanisms are needed to ensure that those who introduce new labour-saving technology will have to pay the full social cost of putting people out of work and the full ecological costs of high technology?

— How are the economic values of efficiency and quality control to be integrated with other human values such as personal involvement and creativity in work?

— What is a realistic price to pay for the consumption of scarce resources of energy, metals, forest, clean water, etc — and to whom and in what form should it be paid?

— How can we calculate a fair balance between present and future needs?

— On what basis should the spare resources of some be made available to others as grants or loans?

— When is it acceptable to charge interest on a loan and at what point is it right from a moral and pragmatic point of view to say 'enough is enough' and simply to write-off massive international debts?

Alternatives

Reading about economics and the problems of development one can begin to feel helpless and even guilty. The person who has become dispirited in this way is almost incapable of bringing about effective changes. So it is important to move on from the problems to look at alternatives, with a shrewd mixture of idealism and realism. When my friends and I were running workshops about justice issues we found it helpful to look once more at the set of pictures that illustrate the economic, political and cultural/religious spheres of traditional life, and to match them with Scriptural texts. This time we chose texts that would suggest *alternatives* to the present unjust economic, political, and cultural structures — texts that would inspire us to take effective action.

As regards *economic* life, a key text is the one that proposed that the Israelites have a 'Jubilee year' every fifty years — a year when the gap that has opened up between rich and poor is closed again:

> In this year all property that has been sold shall be restored to its original owner . . . Your land must not be sold on a permanent basis, because you do not own it; it belongs to God, and you are like foreigners who are allowed to use it. When land is sold the right of the original owner to buy it back must be recognised . . . If an Israelite becomes poor and is forced to sell land . . . and does not have enough money to buy it back . . . it will be returned to its original owner in the next Year of Restoration.
>
> (Lev 25: 13-28)

This text evokes interesting questions about how ownership is organized in different societies. It certainly raises doubts about the way in which, in Western societies, those who have money and power are allowed to use them to amass more and more. People may wish to explore the value of other systems and the feasibility of returning to them — for instance, common ownership by a whole clan or village, or the wider use of 'commonage'. The whole question of the use of taxes to redistribute wealth also comes in here.

In the New Testament there are some particularly interesting texts about the economic life of a community.

The more obvious ones are those that show the early Christian community sharing their belongings with each other, distributing them according to the need of each person, and making sure that nobody was left in poverty (Acts 2:44,45; 4:32-35). This approach was in line with the story of Jesus about the eleventh-hour labourer; this suggests that a worker should not be penalised for failing to find employment (Mt 20:1-16). More radical still is the teaching of Jesus that those who are materially poor are especially privileged — they are 'blessed' or 'happy' because they share in the new Realm of God (Lk 6:20). The poor are the primary beneficiaries of the new order inaugurated by Jesus. This is not because they are morally better than others; it is because the liberating activity of Jesus and his followers is already taking place, changing oppressive structures into liberating ones, and making sure that the marginalized are brought back into the heart of society.[8]

Groups or individuals — and, particularly, those who are trying to set up basic communities — can ponder on such biblical texts and explore how they can be made credible in today's world. I recall one 'faith-sharing' session with very poor people in a slum on the fringes of a great African city. The text was the story of the multiplication of the loaves and fishes (Jn 6:1-13). A man who lived with his whole family in one small room told us that, a few days previously, a number of his relatives from 'up country' had arrived unexpectedly to stay with him. He was very short of both sleeping space and food. But by a great act of faith he decided to share what he had — and found to his astonishment that there was enough for all. He had no doubt that this was another miracle of the loaves and fishes . . .

Moving on to look again at the pictures about the *political* life of a community, one can set alongside them two Gospel texts on the use of power. The first of these is the insistence by Jesus that for him power means service:

You know that the rulers of the nations lord it over their subjects; and their leading people make their power felt. With you it is not to be like that. Any one of you who wants to be great must minister to the others; and any one of you who would like to have the first place must be your servant

— like the Human One, who did not come to be served but to serve and to give up his life on behalf of many people.[9]

(Mt 20:25-28)

This message is echoed in the action of Jesus: the night before he died he became the servant of his followers by washing their feet (Jn 13:15).

When participants in our workshops reflected on these texts they went on to explore what it would mean today to replace the oppressive use of authority with genuine service. It became clear that a change of *attitude* on the part of authorities is not enough; there must also be *structures* and *procedures* that ensure participative decision-making.

The pictures about the *beliefs* and *values* of a people can also be matched with interesting texts from Scripture. The Gospels present Jesus as one who challenged radically many of the accepted norms of his time. He flouted convention by mixing freely with women (Jn 4:27). He spoke intimately with one of the despised Samaritans (Jn 4:9). And he showed special affection for people regarded as public sinners (Lk 7:36-50). In the strictly religious sphere, John's Gospel puts words in the mouth of Jesus that call in question any attempt by ecclesiastical leaders to control access to God:

The time is coming when the worship of God will be centred neither on this mountain nor on the Mount of Jerusalem . . . God is Spirit, so those who worship God properly must do so in the Spirit and in truth.

(Jn 4:21-24)

Reflection in small groups on these and similar texts can be both challenging and inspiring. People begin to realise that Jesus is calling them to witness to, and work for, the Realm of God. This is a new world where no privileged 'elite' will have the right to impose their values on others, and where God is present and active in the hearts of the ordinary people — and is with them as they struggle to create this better world.

SECTION THREE:
GROUP EXERCISES ON STRUCTURAL INJUSTICE

At workshops in Africa and Ireland I sometimes used a short video-film called 'For People or Power' to spark off discussion.[10] The film is about how the local poorer people were affected by the building of a large hydro-electric scheme in a remote part of the Philippines. When we tried to show the video in one workshop the electricity supply let us down on three occasions. So we decided to present the same general ideas in the form of a story.[11] For our purposes, the story turned out to be more effective than the film. So, since then, I have used several different versions of this story in various places. (On one occasion we even wrote and staged a short play on the same theme.) The variations in the story were designed to make it more relevant to local conditions; where the notion of a hydro-electric scheme was not appropriate we changed it to a scheme for mining, or for tourism, or for some cash crop. The roles of the people in the story could also be adapted so as to make them relevant to the particular audience. What follows is an African version of the story; but it could be changed to apply to a remote 'undeveloped' place in any part of the world:

Development in Mulu

In the remote village of Mulu in Central Africa the people lived according to the traditional way of life. The people were not wealthy, but nobody went hungry. The local chief was called Pata. Living nearby were his daughter Elizabeth and her husband James, both of whom had been to school for a number of years.

Meanwhile a very large company called 'The International Mining Corporation' whose head office was in New York had set up a subsidiary company based in the capital city of this little African country; they appointed a local accountant called Sabastian as manager of this subsidiary company. The company employed experts to do a mineral survey of the whole country and they discovered that there was a large deposit of uranium deep in the earth all around the village of Mulu.

When he heard this good news, the manager Sabastian went at once to his good friend Mr Thomas, the Minister for Mining in the government of the country. He asked

175

that his company be given exclusive mining rights for this uranium. In return he promised that the government would get five per cent of the profits; he also guaranteed that the company would employ local labour as far as possible, and would even train some of the more promising workers as mining engineers.

The Minister wanted the government to set up a company to do the mining; but he discovered that the cost would be fifty million dollars and the Minister for Finance told him the government could not get a loan of such a large sum from the IMF or World Bank. He then said he would allow the company to do the mining provided they paid a tax of forty per cent on the profits. After some hard bargaining between Sabastian and Mr Thomas it was agreed that the company would pay twenty per cent tax on the profits — provided there was no trouble in the village of Mulu.

Sabastian, the manager, then went down to the village of Mulu and told Chief Pata and his council about the great opportunity that was opening up for the village — an opportunity to move into the twentieth century. When the mining began the village would have a modern school and a small hospital; many of the local people would find employment at the mine. The local community would have to move away from their homes and land; they could settle instead on a hillside about five kilometers away; there the company would build new houses for them.

Chief Pata was not very pleased with this proposal, but he said he would discuss it thoroughly with his full council, and it would also be put before the Women's Committee. The discussion went on for two full days. Only one or two of the younger men and women were in favour of the proposal. They were over-ruled by the senior members who held very strongly that they could not leave the land in which their ancestors were buried. Finally, Sabastian was informed that both the Chief's Council and the Women's Committee rejected his proposal.

Sabastian reported this difficulty back to the New York Headquarters of his parent company, 'The International Mining Corporation'. Within a few hours he received an urgent personal message from the President of the Corporation: 'The international market in uranium is very precarious at present. So we are expecting that you will get agreement immediately *at all costs.* I am allocating to you a Special Contingency Fund of $100,000 to help you persuade the village people to change their minds. If you succeed you may expect advancement in our company; but if you fail, we may have to look for a more effective local manager.'

Sabastian want back to Chief Pata, and this time he insisted on meeting him alone. He told him that he, the Chief, would be given $50,000 to distribute as he saw fit in persuading the local community to agree to be re-located. But Chief Pata only got angry and stubbornly refused the offer. While in the village Sabastian had been staying in the home of Elizabeth, the daughter of the Chief, and her husband James. After the Chief turned down his offer he stayed on with Elizabeth and James for a couple of days and made friends with them. He found that they, as educated people, were in favour of bringing progress to the village. So Sabastian offered to make $50,000 available to them quietly, to use in any way they wished for the welfare of the community, provided they could persuade the younger people and some of the older ones to agree to move.

Elizabeth and James got working on the younger people and on the more progressive of the elders. Eventually Chief Pata was forced to call a meeting of all the village people. Elizabeth and James spoke so persuasively of the advantages of progress that eventually almost everybody agreed to move; only Chief Pata and a few of the elders refused to agree.

Sabastian went back to the capital and spoke to Mr Thomas the Minister for Mining, who in turn asked his friend the Minister for Internal Security to send a detachment of military police to the area in case of trouble. Trouble erupted quickly enough. Some of the younger people demanded the resignation of Chief Pata. He refused. When the day came for the re-location of the village the Chief and about twenty of the villagers refused to move. A squad of the military policy came in to force them out. There was a brawl. One policeman was struck in the face. Then some of the police opened fire and six of the village people were left dead — two women, three men, and one child. At that point the rest of the villagers turned on the police and beat one of them to death. Reinforcements were called in, all the houses were demolished, and twenty villagers were beaten up and arrested. Three of them were tried for murder and hanged. The others are still in jail.

Chief Pata was deposed by the government and his son-in-law James was made chief in his place; his wife became head of the Women's Committee. The villagers were resettled on a barren hillside on poor land infested with tsetse fly. Farming was difficult there, and in any case the people seemed to have no heart for farming any more. The uranium mine opened and some of the men got work there as security guards; but they later lost their jobs because it was thought they were allowing some pilfering by local people. Many of the younger men and women drifted off to the capital city to look for work.

The new chief James and his wife Elizabeth used the money given them by Sabastian to build a large bar and supermarket. The mining corporation ran electricity cables up to the new village, so Elizabeth got a television set and a video installed in the bar.

The new clinic led to a decrease in the death rate of young children. The older people also had better medical care; but, on the other hand, some new problems arose — especially a great increase in alcoholism and a rapid spread of AIDS.

The young people attended the new school. But as they grew older they found it hard to get work. So most of them left the village for the cities. Life in the village of Mulu was very different from what it had been in the past.

* * *

If you are working with a group, ask them to divide into mixed sub-groups of about five people and discuss the following questions for about twenty minutes:

1. What struck you most in the story? How do you feel about the end result?

2. Would you have acted differently if you were Chief Pata? If you were Elizabeth or James? If you were Mr Thomas, Minister for Mining?

178

At that point gather the groups together into one large group to share their answers to the second question. Then ask the group to sub-divide again — this time into *local* groups. Put up the following questions for discussion and ask the groups to return with reports written up on large sheets of paper in about forty-five minutes (— propose forty-five minutes, but be aware that if the discussion is animated and fruitful you may have to allow some extra time):

3. Do you know of any situations in real life where something like this has happened? What were the good effects and the bad effects at the *local* level?

4. How can the good effects be increased and the bad effects diminished?

5. What are the effects at the *national* level of this kind of development? How can the good effects be increased and the bad effects diminished?

6. Is there anything that *we* as a group or as individuals undertake to do about these issues?

When the whole group re-convenes, ask each sub-group in turn to display and clarify their reports. Then invite some general discussion.

In some of the more advanced workshops which we organised we explored the issue of development much more fully in later sessions. We usually went on to some other topic for about a day, in order to allow time for people to 'digest' the ideas about development that had emerged in the above discussion. When we returned to the topic we did so at both the theoretical and the practical levels. We began by forming mixed groups and asking them to discuss and report on the following two questions:

— What are the good elements in the traditional pattern of life that you would like to preserve or restore? Are there some elements you would like to get rid of?

— What are the good elements in the 'modern' pattern of life that you would like to foster? Are there elements you would want to avoid?

Role Play on Development

In a workshop in Sierra Leone about three years ago I found the discussion on development so interesting that I was inspired to design a Role Play which would carry it a stage further. My aim was to help people face up to the kind of difficult choices that have to be made in relation to development — the need to prioritise, to balance the local good and the national good, to make compromises. I wanted the participants to be realistic — and to have sympathy for the kind of predicament in which governments find themselves when trying to promote genuine development. I have used this Role Play in some other workshops since. Each time the outcome was different; but the process was always very educational.

Having heard the reports on what the participants wanted to preserve from traditional life, and what new elements they wanted to foster, I recalled very briefly the main outlines of the story of Mulu village. I then explained that the present group could now have the opportunity to change the history and ensure that there is a more successful outcome — incorporating the various values of traditional and modern life that they had already emphasised. This could be done if they were willing to take part in a Role Play based closely on the story of the village of Mulu. I checked out to make sure that they were willing to take part in the proposed Role Play.

In outlining the Role Play I shall assume that there are twenty-four people in the group; if there are more than twenty-four participants then the number of the characters in the Role Play can easily be increased; if there are less than twenty-four, the characters can be decreased. This Role Play needs plenty of time and the organisers have to be flexible about the time allowed. It will probably take at least three hours, and it may run even longer. The time to finish is when the group agrees that they have done what they can; it is not essential to have an agreed 'solution'. Occasionally during the Role Play it may be necessary for the organisers to remind the participants that there are other values involved besides the economic ones: they should be encouraged, if necessary, to use a respectful approach and participative techniques to reach consensus.

Explain that there are four groups of six people in the Role Play. On each of the four walls of the room put up a large sheet of paper on which you have written out the roles of one of the following teams.

I.   The Village Group:
   1. The Head Person of the village.
   2. The Wife/Husband of the Head Person.
   3. The daughter of the Head Person (who has spent years in school).
   4. The son-in-law of the Head Person (who has spent years in school).
   5. A member of the local Council.
   6. A young person in the village.

II.   The Mining Company Group:
   1. The Manager.
   2. A Mining Engineer.
   3. The Company accountant.
   4. An employee who will lose her or her job if the mine is not opened.
   5. A former employee who hopes to get a job in the new mine.
   6. A representative of the parent company in New York.

III.   The Government Group:
   1. The President.
   2. The Minister for Mining.
   3. The Minister for Finance.
   4. A government economist.
   5. A government mining expert.
   6. The Minister for Trade who depends for electoral support on the villagers in whose area the mine may be opened.

IV.   Representatives of Other Parts of the Country:
   1. A representative from the President's village, which needs a clinic.
   2. A representative from the port city which will flourish if the mine is opened.
   3. A representative from the home village of the Minister for Finance, a village which has no proper road in to it.
   4. A representative from a village near the proposed mining village, who hopes there may be employment in the mine for some of its people.
   5. A representative from the opposite end of the country who wants to have a new road and clinic provided by the government.

181

Invite the participants to choose the group they wish to belong to, dividing themselves out evenly; ask them to go and sit under the sheet of paper which lists the roles of the group they have chosen. Then ask each group to decide which of its members will play each of the different roles. Emphasize the point that everybody is expected to play his or her own part in good faith — sincerely responding to the pressures that come from the role, but *not* acting for *personal* gain. There should be no bribery. The task given to the whole group is: *To work for a common agreement about whether or not a uranium mine should be opened at the village; and, if so, under what conditions.*

Tell the whole group that the Company manager and the representative from New York will have their own private specialised information about the concessions they can afford to offer; and they can share this information as they see fit. Similarly, the Minister for Finance and the government economist will be given some specialised private information about income and costs; they can share this information with other members of government — and with anybody else if they wish to do so. Give a typed sheet containing the following information to the following people:

— *To the Manager and the New York Company Representative:*

The head office in New York has decided that you should make an initial offer of fifteen per cent of the profits to the government and five per cent to the local community. If you are pushed very hard you may agree to give up not more than a *total* of thirty per cent of the profits, divided between the government and the local community in any way they agree on. If you agree to give away more than a total of thirty per cent of the profits then the extra money will have to come from your own salaries and those of the mine-workers; you can work out the details with them.

If you can settle for a total of twenty-five per cent or less, you will both be promoted, and have a share in the profits of the company.

Company experts inform you that eight per cent of the profits, over a ten-year period, would meet the cost of new housing for the villagers and a new clinic, a new school, and some scholarships.

182

— To the Minister for Finance and the Government economist:

If the Minister for Mining can ensure that the government gets forty per cent of the profits of the company, then you can meet the cost of building a clinic in one of the areas that are demanding it. You can also begin to build a new road to the village of the Minister for Finance, and have it completed over three years.

If the government only get twenty-five per cent of the mining profits you will need all of that money to pay interest on the present loan from the International Monetary Fund, so the road project will have to wait for two years.

If the government has to pay for the resettlement of the villagers, this will cost the government five per cent of the profits over four years.

As I already mentioned, it is not essential that full agreement be reached; but it is important that the group end up with some sense of satisfaction that they have at least explored the issues carefully and have also taken account of each others' views. The organisers of the Role Play need to be sensitive to how the different members are feeling, and not prolong the exercise to a point where people get bored or exhausted.

When the exercise has been completed and people have had time to rest, ask the members of the group to take some time for personal reflection on the following questions:

1. What did I learn from this exercise about human development?
2. What did I learn about dialogue, communication, and negotiation?
3. What did I learn about myself?

Ask the participants to share some of their answers in groups of three. Then spend some time in general sharing in the whole group. It may be a good idea to take the answers to the third question first; it will give a personal tone to the sharing and may also provide some light relief.

Gandhi

I have found that one of the most powerful instruments to help people explore the whole issue of human liberation and development is the film 'Gandhi'.[12] This is the way in

183

which we used it. We showed the video in the evening, more or less as a recreational film. Next morning we showed again some key passage from it — for instance a ten-minute segment beginning with the negotiation between Gandhi and the British governor (during which Gandhi is asked, 'Do you think we will walk out?' and he says, 'Yes'), leading on to the speech by Gandhi's wife and then on to Gandhi's own speech which culminates in the burning of the cloth from Manchester. (This passage shows clearly the links between the political, economic, cultural, and spiritual aspects of liberation.)

After a few moments of reflection ask participants to share in groups of four or five on these questions:
— What touched you most in this part of the film?
— What were the basic problems Gandhi was tackling?
— How did he tackle them?

Take brief verbal reports from the groups and then ask them some further questions:
— Do you see any similarities between this passage of the film and your own situation?
— What lessons can we learn from Gandhi in working for liberation and genuine human development in our situation?
— What practical action can we now undertake?

There are two other passages from the film which can be 'processed' in a similar way. The first is when Gandhi returns to India and goes on a long journey to experience for himself the situation of the ordinary people — and then returns to challenge the would-be leaders for failing to be in solidarity with the ordinary people. The second is the Salt March, where Gandhi chooses what Paulo Freire would call 'a generative issue' and finds a non-violent way of building up a swelling protest, culminating in a solemn and symbolic ritual as he makes his own salt on the beach. If you choose these segments from the film to stimulate discussion, make sure to design the questions carefully: concentrate first on what people *felt* while looking at it, and then on the basic *issues* addressed in this segment of the film; thirdly, move on to a *comparison* with the present situation of the participants, and finally to some practical *action* which can be undertaken here and now.

Earlier in this chapter I mentioned the simulation 'Star Power' which was devised by R. Gary Shirts to promote awareness of how exploitation and oppression operate in our world. The same author has also devised another remarkable simulation called 'Bafa Bafa'. This one helps people understand the differences between different cultures — and in particular between the more traditional types of culture (still found widely in the Third World) and the more competitive 'trading culture' that has developed in the Western world in recent centuries. It would be very appropriate to use this simulation *prior* to giving 'input' based on the material in this chapter about the pattern of traditional society. (However, if you plan to use both 'Star Power' and 'Bafa Bafa' then it is not a good idea to have them too close to each other; allow several days to elapse between them so that people can derive full benefit from each; it would be even better to use them in different workshops, separated by an interval of some months.)

The film 'Man Friday' can be used to stimulate discussion about the relationship between Western culture and other cultures — and to evoke questions about the assumption of superiority which affects many First World people. It tells the story of Robinson Crusoe from the point of view of the local man who became Crusoe's 'Man Friday'. The film stars Peter O'Toole.

SECTION FOUR: JUSTICE FOR WOMEN

In the previous three sections of this chapter I have concentrated on the issue of justice in relation to economic development. In this final section I want to focus attention on another crucial issue, namely, that of justice for women. I do not propose to write anything on the *theory* of the matter — mainly because this is one of those issues that have to be resolved more by a 'conversion' than by rational discussion. This kind of 'conversion' has more to do with the heart than with the head. As a way of appealing to the heart I shall include in this section two simple exercises and two poems.

The following are some quotations from a book about motherhood written by a Catholic priest and published in 1986:

> Leadership belongs to the man. Authority is essential to a happy home; mothers must realise this fact and be ready not only to respect the authority of the man but also to cooperate with it for the efficient running of the home.[13]

> The wise mother and wife takes long steps towards recognizing her husband's needs and accepting him for what he is — a man by nature always wants to express himself forcefully and authoritatively. The man who is the embodiment of strength, industry, ability and inventiveness; the deputy of God in your home. He is the voice of authority.[14]

Read these passages a couple of times and see what feelings they evoke in you. How do you feel about the fact that these ideas are being proposed by a priest?

Contrast the above statements with the following excerpts from the Apostolic Letter 'On the Dignity of Women' written in 1988 by Pope John Paul II:

> . . . man and woman are called from the beginning . . . to exist mutually 'one for the other'. This . . . explains the meaning of the 'help' spoken of in Genesis 2:18-25 'I will make him a helper fit for him.' — . . . it is a question of a 'help' on the part of both . . .

> Gen 3:16 . . . implies . . . that the woman's 'sincere gift of self' is responded to and matched by a corresponding 'gift' on the part of the husband . . .

> Christ's attitude toward women . . . revealed . . . the dignity belonging to women from the very 'beginning' on an equal footing with man.

> . . . in the relationship between husband and wife the 'subjection' is not one-sided but mutual . . . However, the awareness that in marriage there is a mutual 'subjection of the spouses out of reverence for Christ' and not just that of the wife to the husband must gradually establish itself in hearts, consciences, behaviors and customs. This is a call . . . which people have to accept ever anew.[15]

(7, 10, 25, 24)

What feelings are evoked in you by these statements? Do they represent a significant change in the spirituality of marriage and sexuality proposed by the Catholic Church? Can you suggest ways in which the notion of 'mutual subjection' can 'establish itself in hearts, consciences, behaviour and customs', as the Pope proposes?

Two Circles

The second exercise is one that can be done in a mixed group of men and women. Ask the women to sit in an inner circle while the men sit in an outer circle around them.[16] The men are asked to remain silent and to listen attentively to what the women have to say. Ask the women to reflect silently for a few moments on the question: 'What is it like to be a woman?' Then ask them to share with each other on the topic, in the presence of the listening men. (The facilitator should intervene as little as possible, except to make sure that people are not interrupted; if possible try to evoke an atmosphere where there is no discussion but rather a sharing of feelings or experiences, followed by a few moments of respectful silence before anybody else speaks.)

After a break, ask the participants to reverse the roles: this time the men sit in the inner circle and share their experiences of being men, while the women listen. (If you wish to have a little variety, you might ask the men to answer two slightly different questions — 'What I like about being a man' and 'What I find hard about being a man.') It is probably better not to have a general sharing at the end of this exercise, as it might degenerate into an argument; it is better to allow people time to reflect on what they have heard.

If you are looking for a video/film which can be used to stimulate discussion about the role of women in society then I can strongly recommend 'The Color Purple'.[17] One good way to use it would be to show it some evening as 'entertainment'; next morning you could show again some short passage from it, and ask the same kind of questions as those I proposed in the case of the film 'Gandhi'.

Another very interesting film to use as a basis for discussion is a documentary made for Swedish television. It is called 'Our God is a Woman' and is about life on the island of Kanjabao, off the West African coast.[18] This is a place where the usual gender roles are reversed, and men have to put up with the kind of second-class treatment to which women are subjected almost everywhere else. So it can give rise to lively discussion and can help people to question many of the attitudes which are taken for granted in the patriarchal societies in which most of us live.

Poems

I end this chapter with two poems. The first is one I wrote some time ago to try to express my attempt to cross the great divide between the experience of a man and that of a woman.

To Enter
I

I shuffled through the desert sand each day
And lost all sense of progress or direction.
The measured manna kept me half alive
And never let me feel the living pain
Of hunger or of gluttony.
The landscape and horizon were reduced
To fifty shades of brown,
And this brown land had come to be my home.
Through senses shaped by forty desert years
How can I now project a promised land?
Did Moses really want to take the risk?
Or did he climb his lonely hill
Relieved to know he was not called to enter in?

II

These forty years of desert may not quite be waste
If I have come to glimpse what 'enter' really means.
Not Rahab's route of conquest, scream and spoil.
Not crossing Jordan dry-shod to the other shore.
Not even plunging boldly in
To swim across with power.
But timid paddling, groping on the shelving sand,
Then slipping, sinking, gasping, losing every hold . . .
Convulsive mindless hopeless struggle to maintain
The breath of life. But fail.

Then endless vivid instant of reprise,
Playback/erase the spool of life
Then yield, allow the lens to slip,
The focal point to fade, identity to merge
Into the dim green light of primal water.
. . . .and thence emerge reborn
To occupy another person's world
By being occupied myself.
And so I find that 'enter' is a verb
That contradicts its deepest human sense
so long as it retains an active voice.

III

Now having strangely entered on your land
I gingerly explore the woman I've become.
And first of all I feel reluctant to accept
That *I* could be a promised land
Where milk and honey flow.
My milk is sour, my honey scarce
For I am still an exile in the wild,
A pilgrim lured by fading hope,
Another searcher for a promised land.

IV

I've entered by being entered
and no longer feel it strange
To welcome life in woman's way,
To know that I am life, and life is love,
And love is pain, and it endures
Because it welcomes life, and can receive.
I now define myself as she who waits
To open up my body and my soul
To one who comes to tell me not to fear
The shadow of the power of God
A God who stirs the spark of life
That waited for that touch of power
And now begins to grow within — Emmanuel.

V

This understanding of myself and of my sex
Is desecrated by the world in which I live.
Like all my sisters for five hundred thousand years
I walk each day and sleep each night
Beneath a threatening sky —
The background fear of every woman's world,
A fear that never fully fades.
This fear now forces me to live
Within a zone marked out by hidden wires
That trip alarms when men come close
And trespass on my fear-full space.
This fear now feeds on every effort that I make
To arm myself against attack.
What kind of human liberation
Could ever set me truly free,
When sin pervades the culture — and pollutes the love
That is the only way
In which that sexist culture could be changed?
And even if the culture were transformed
The new age will arrive too late for me
Who carry in my spirit and my nerves
The wound of half a million years. . . .

Vl

For many months I've waited now
For words to bring these verses to a close
A nice catharsis, or a note of hope
Which integrates the pain and says that all is well.
But nothing came — and so at last I see
How very male that notion is.
(For even Christ who died and rose
 — he did it as a man.)
And so I fear that you will think
That my fine effort to explore
What 'entry' really means
Was just a nice poetical disguise to hide
Another kind of rape.[19]

The second poem is by Frances Croake Frank. It expresses
the pain that many women feel about the refusal of some
Churches to allow women to be ordained as priests.

Did the Woman Say

Did the woman say,
When she held him for the first time in the dark
    dank of a stable,
After the pain and the bleeding and the crying,
    'This is my body; this is my blood'?

Did the woman say,
When she held him for the last time in the dark
    rain on a hilltop,
After the pain and the bleeding and the dying,
    'This is my body; this is my blood'?

Well that she said it to him then.
For dry old men,
Brocaded robes belying barrenness,
    Ordain that she not say it for him now.[20]

NOTES

1. Devised by Gary Shirts.
2. Donal Dorr, *Spirituality and Justice*, Dublin (Gill and Macmillan: 1985) and Maryknoll (Orbis: 1985), 55-61.
3. Charles Elliott (assisted by Françoise de Morsier), *Patterns of Poverty in the Third World: a Study of Social and Economic Stratification*, New York (Praeger: 1975). The same material is presented in a more popular form in David Millwood, *The Poverty Makers*, Geneva (World Council of Churches: 1977).
4. Anne Hope and Sally Timmel, *Training for Transformation: A Handbook for Community Workers*, Gweru, Zimbabwe (Mambo Press: 1984), Vol 3 20-3. The headings given are: (1) Survival — the Economic and Social Level; (2) Organization — the Political Level; (3) Values and Beliefs — the Cultural Level.
5. For those who are interested, I hope to have sets of Steve 'Lani Adeleye's posters of African scenes included as part of the resource materials which will be available to accompany this book.
6. See especially, Paulo Freire, *Education for Critical Consciousness*, Continuum/Seabury 1974,; 2nd, revised ed London (Sheed & Ward: 1985); this is perhaps the most readable of Freire's books.
7. 'The North' is a term that in recent years has come to be used instead of the term 'the developed countries'; so 'the North' is the equivalent of 'the First World' (i.e. the Western countries, including, oddly, Japan, Australia and New Zealand) plus 'the Second World' (i.e. the Eastern block countries — but not China). Meanwhile, 'the South' is used instead of the terms 'the developing countries' or 'the less developed countries', or 'the Third World'.

8. Cf. Segundo Galilea, *The Beatitudes: To Evangelize as Jesus Did*, Maryknoll (Orbis: 1984) and Dublin (Gill and Macmillan: 1984), 14-15.

9. It has always been difficult to find a phrase which conveys the real meaning of the term that is commonly translated as 'the Son of Man'; the phrase 'the Human One' is the nearest I can come to conveying in simple language the rich theological significance of the term as used in the Gospel (with its Old Testament echoes from Eziechiel 2:1 and Daniel 7:13). This translation has the further advantage of avoiding any flavour of sexism.

10. Made about 1980 by the Irish film-making team 'Radharc'. Radharc was started by a group of priests from the Archdiocese of Dublin. Many of their video/films about situations in Latin America, Asia, Africa, Oceania, and Australia are very helpful for sparking off discussion in groups on topics related to culture and justice.

11. Berne Eyewan Okure and Teresa Mee (of the Centre for Renewal, Jos), Yusufu Turaki (of the Ekwa Church), and myself all helped to put the story together; and Yusufu was our story-teller.

12. Richard Attenborough's 'Gandhi' Columbia Pictures, 1982; RCA/Columbia video.

13. John Mary Anojulu, *Motherhood: Vocation and Full-time Job*, Milbourne Port, Sherbourne, Dorset, England (Dorset Publishing Co: 1986), 18.

14. *Ibid.*, 68.

15. *Dignitatem Mulieris* — Vatican English-language text taken from *Origins*, Vol. 18, No. 17 (October 6, 1988).

16. The term 'fishbowl' is commonly used to describe this kind of exercise where some of the participants in a group are asked to sit in an inner circle and share their experiences while the remainder of the group sit in an outer circle observing what is going on. However, in order to avoid confusion, I am not using the term 'fishbowl' here because earlier in this chapter I have had occasion to write about 'fishbowls' in a more literal sense.

17. Steven Spielberg's 'The Color Purple', 1985, Warner Home Video.

18. 'Var Gud ar en Kvinna', available from Swedish Television SVT1, S-105 10 Stockholm, Sweden.

19. The following notes may help to clarify some obscure points in the poem:

In referring to Rahab in the third line of the second stanza I have in mind the biblical story of the capture of Jericho (Jos 2:1-24). Rahab was the prostitute who betrayed her city to the invaders. So, when I speak of 'Rahab's route' I am suggesting a devious and violent manner of entry.

Also in the second stanza there is a line 'playback/erase the spool of life'. I am thinking here of the accounts given by many people, of 'near death' experiences in which the events of their lives seem to be replayed for them.

The final line of the second stanza speaks of the verb 'enter' being used in the active voice. This is what I have in mind: to enter a room or a city is an action I perform (active voice); but the only authentic way in which I can enter the consciousness of another person is to allow the other into my consciousness; so in this case the verb 'enter' has to be understood as being more in the passive voice than in the active voice.

20. This poem was first published in *The National Catholic Reporter.*

7

A Spirituality of Peace

SECTION ONE:
BLESSED ARE THE PEACE-MAKERS

Peace lies at the heart of a holistic spirituality — and it should permeate every part of it. We need to be at peace within ourselves; we need peace in our relationships with others; we need peace in the 'public' sphere; and we need it in our relationship with Nature and the cosmos. Our spirituality will be distorted if we concentrate our efforts exclusively on looking for an inner peace, or if we focus all our attention on any one of the other aspects. Because peace is so all-embracing, I cannot hope to deal with every aspect of it in one chapter. I hope that the reflections and exercises of the previous chapters will help people to work for peace within themselves, in their interpersonal relationships, and in their relationship with the cosmos. In this chapter I shall deal mainly with the the 'public' or political dimension of peace; so what I have to say here follows on from the treatment of justice in the previous chapter. However, though I am concerned with political activity, my focus is on *spirituality* rather than politics; so I deal mainly with the *attitude* of the peace-maker.

The development of an authentically Christian spirituality of peace involves a real conversion. This means a change of heart, since spirituality is centred more in the heart than in the head. The heart is the centre of our affectivity — our feelings; and a conversion of heart means a transformation of our feelings, our spontaneous reactions to the situations in which we find ourselves. This transformation may take place quite suddenly, or it may be more gradual. It is not important to fit into a particular pattern, for there is not a single ideal pattern; there are as many patterns as there are people. But whether the change be sudden or slow it has to include certain crucial elements. I propose first to look at some examples of 'conversion of heart' using them to focus on the key elements in a Christian spirituality of peace.

Conversion

Prior to the conversion of affectivity of which I am speaking, the person is living in a state of insensitivity and complacency. There may be theoretical awareness that suffering and injustice and violence are widespread; but the person has not allowed that awareness to touch the heart, has not been moved to radical action by it.

Let's take the case of Andrei Sakharov, the scientist who played a key role in the development of nuclear weapons in the Soviet Union. At first he committed himself single-mindedly to his work. But gradually he began to allow himself to let in its implications — to imagine what would happen if the bombs were actually used. This was the beginning of his 'conversion' into a peace-campaigner, a man who sacrificed his career and dedicated his life to working for disarmament. Similar conversions marked the lives of many others who had been involved with nuclear weapons — for instance, Group-Captain Leonard Cheshire, and the pilot of the plane that dropped the atomic bomb on Hiroshima.

Suppose I am a soldier, trained to kill the enemy, toughened by a training designed to ensure that no squeamishness interferes with my efficiency as a killer. One day the conditioning cracks and I begin to experience 'the enemy' as real people like myself. That is an obvious instance of the beginning of conversion. Not so obvious but equally important is the conversion required of good people who have been caught up in a system that does violence to people by failing to respect their human dignity. Not long ago I was with a group of people who were searching for a more authentic spirituality. As we listened to a homeless battered wife tell her story, I watched a member of the group quietly weeping. He was a civil servant working in our government Department of Social Welfare. Clearly this was no longer a statistic for him, or a face behind a grill, but a human being who spoke to his heart. He had begun to let in her pain — and with it a sense of the inadequacy and

194

heartlessness of the social security system which violated her dignity as a human being.

In the case of both the soldier and the civil servant, conversion of heart takes place when they allow themselves to reverberate affectively with the violence that is inflicted on people either by war, or by the insensitivity of our society. Then the scales fall from their eyes and they begin to see the world in a new light. That is an essential first step; but of course it is not sufficient on its own. If their conversion is to be *effective* as well as *affective* they must go on to take action to change the situation.

So far I have been describing the conversion of people who may have been in some way responsible for *inflicting* violence on others. But there is a corresponding conversion which has to take place in the *victims* of such violence. People who have been brutally oppressed for a long time — perhaps for generations — tend to live in what is called a culture of silence. They live in a state of partial numbness, enduring their suffering but scarcely adverting to the injustice and violence which has brought it about. The effort to survive absorbs all their energies, so they have little energy to spare for anger or for planning change.

People in this situation, too, may undergo an affective conversion. Suddenly or gradually the 'culture of silence' is broken; the oppressed wake up to the realization that they do not have to be victims for ever, but can look for ways to change the situation.

There seem to be two crucial elements in the affective conversion that leads to becoming a peacemaker. The first of these is a keen sense of the suffering that is unjustly inflicted on so many people and groups in our world. The second element is a vivid awareness that violent attempts to overcome these injustices are likely to make the situation worse rather than better. Both elements are essential, but there is a strong tension between the two, and it is very difficult to hold them together. Without the sense of unjust suffering, our commitment to peace will be marred by complacency and triviality. Without the awareness of the dangers of violence, our commitment to peace will become corrupted by arrogance and domination of others. In the following pages I hope to show how easy it is to develop

195

attitudes and ideologies which give undue emphasis to either one of these elements at the expense of the other.

A Need for Security

It is risky to allow myself to become sensitive to the violence and unjust suffering that are all around me. My initial reaction is likely to be shock; for the comfortable securities of my life are now called into question. There is a strong unconscious urge to escape; and two escape routes open up before me. The first is *retreat* — closing myself off again from this shocking reality. The second is *lashing out* in destructive violence against what has shocked me. I shall look at each of these reactions in turn, beginning with the reaction of 'retreat'.

Many individuals and groups — and sometimes whole societies — have such a deep sense of insecurity that they cannot allow themselves to face the full reality of the violence and injustice that is going on around them. They prefer to retreat into some comforting illusion rather than acknowledge the pain, the injustice, the fragility of people and of society — and the guilt they feel about being partly responsible for some or all of this.

The most common escape is to *blame the victims:* we imagine that they are 'responsible' for making us feel upset and guilty. This 'blaming the victims' approach is rarely thought out in a logical way, so there may be elements that are quite irrational in it. For instance, at one level I may know very well that there are not enough jobs to give employment to everybody; but I may still 'feel' that the unemployed are lazy and shiftless — perhaps even untrustworthy and dangerous.

Frequently linked to this attitude is the 'law-and-order' mentality. It assumes that social problems are best dealt with by a strong and resolute government which makes full use of the security forces to maintain order and deter unrest. The social sciences provide convincing evidence that this is a grave over-simplification. Furthermore, history indicates that, where security forces are used in this way, they become more and more oppressive. So, the security forces themselves become one of the main sources of violence and injustice, rather than eliminating them. But such rational arguments

196

make little impression on people who are moved by neurotic fear.

The law-and-order mentality can easily lead on to the ideology of 'National Security'. This makes the State the supreme value, and it justifies all kinds of repression on the grounds that the State must be defended at all costs. That is idolatry. And what is most frightening is that those who adopt the ideology of 'National Security' frequently justify it by claiming that they are defending 'Christian values' or the 'Christian heritage' against 'subversives'!

To seek security by violent means gets one into a spiral of force. More and more resources are spent on providing security. Therefore less and less is available to overcome the deprivation which is a major source of the threat to security. I have lived in Third Wold countries where the only two 'growth industries' were armed robbery and security firms, one living off the other. Some time ago I stayed for some days at the cathedral of an African capital city; I felt rather uncomfortable when each evening I saw a private army of night-watchmen gathering in the cathedral grounds; they used it as a marshalling yard before marching off with their guard-dogs and weapons to protect the homes of the wealthy. From the point of view of the individuals involved it seems reasonable to protect their property and themselves even if it involves spending large amounts of money on security. But looking at it from a wider point of view it is clear that the society as a whole has become 'hooked' on security; it is like a drug addiction which eats up the resources of individuals and whole societies.

At the international level, the search for security has given rise to the extraordinarily costly arms race between the super-powers. Equally serious, at present, is the arms race between small neighbouring countries which are often beggaring themselves just to ensure that they are not left behind in modern weaponry.

Those who cling on to the 'law-and-order' mentality and the 'National Security' ideology have closed themselves off from part of the reality around them. So, even at best, they are only tackling the symptoms rather than the causes of the problems; at worst, their approach adds enormously to the problems.

The Violent Response

The second way of trying to escape from the shock of seeing all the violence and injustice around us is to *lash out* in destructive violence against whatever is perceived as its cause. It is a natural and healthy reaction to experience a sense of outrage in the face of unjust suffering. The unhealthy escapism arises when one gives in to the illusion that social evils can be overcome by lashing out in anger without weighing the consequences. We can see this in a story from the life of Moses:

> When Moses was put out of his home the daughter of the king [of Egypt] adopted him and brought him up as her own son. He was taught all the wisdom of the Egyptians and became a great man in words and deeds.
>
> When Moses was forty years old, he decided to find out how his fellow-Israelites were being treated. He saw one of them being ill-treated by an Egyptian, so he went to his help and took revenge on the Egyptian by killing him. (He thought that his own people would understand that God was going to use him to set them free, but they did not understand.) The next day he saw two Israelites fighting, and he tried to make peace between them. 'Listen, men,' he said, 'you are fellow-Israelites; why are you fighting like this?' But the one who was ill-treating the other pushed Moses aside. 'Who made you ruler and judge over us?' he asked. 'Do you want to kill me, just as you killed that Egyptian yesterday?' When Moses heard this, he fled from Egypt and went to live in the land of Midian.
>
> (Acts 7:21-29)

Moses learned the hard way that there is no instant solution to violence and oppression. His impetuous action was of no help to the Jews; and Moses himself was forced to become a refugee as a result of it. He had to live in exile for many years before God showed him how to channel his righteous anger into constructive and truly liberating action. For each of us, too, there is no short cut. Our spirituality of peace must have at its heart a keen awareness of suffering and injustice; otherwise we remain smug and insensitive. But, like Moses, we have to learn to combine indignation against injustice with patience and sensitivity. Otherwise we shall do more harm than good.

The violent response to violence and other social evils may be just a spontaneous reaction. But it may also be expanded to become a settled attitude, and even at times an ideology. Some sincere and dedicated people think of violence as a cleansing force, a liberating power that will sweep away evil and allow a new and better world to emerge. That is the kind of ideology proposed by Frantz Fanon.[1]

Of course Christians cannot accept such an approach. But we should not be too glib in our rejection of it. First of all, we must remember that Fanon was from the Third World, and he was reacting on behalf of millions of oppressed people against centuries of Western domination in the political, economic, and cultural spheres. Secondly, we have to admit that there are strands in the Judeo-Christian tradition that could provide a certain basis for an ideology of violence. Some of the prophetic-apocalyptic passages in the Bible seem to glorify violence — at least when it is attributed to God. They suggest that God is about to 'wipe the slate clean' in a violent conflagration; and that this will usher in a new age of justice and peace. 'The axe is laid to the root of the tree . . . the winnowing fan is in God's hand . . .' (Mt 3:10-12; cf Jer 4:23-27; 6:11-12; Ez 14:13; Hos 13:3). This tradition has sometimes led Christians to justify a violent and destructive 'solution' to what they perceived as evil; one example that springs to mind is the ferocity with which the Albigensian heresy was attacked during the Middle Ages. Committed Christians may now accept that to try to extirpate evil through violence is to 'tempt God' — usurping the divine prerogative of deciding when and how evil is to be overcome; but, unfortunately, Christians have not always been content to wait for God's time to come.

Furthermore, it has to be admitted that lurking deep within the tradition of many Western peoples there are tales and myths that romanticise and glorify violence, presenting it as a mark of heroism and a source of life and justice. A major challenge for Western Christians today is to exorcise these violent demons. We need to adopt new models of courage, replacing the violent heroes and heroines with people like Martin Luther King, the Greenham Common women, Gandhi, Franz Jägerstatter, the women of the Plaza del Mayo in Buenos Aires, the Ploughshare group, those who are involved in the 'sanctuary' movement, and the peacemakers of Corrymeela in Northern Ireland.

Shalom

If we wish to develop an authentic spirituality of peace we need to explore the biblical understanding of 'shalom'.[2] It is a word that is very rich in meaning. At its heart lies the notion of well-being or human flourishing and fulfillment. Fundamentally, this is the gift of God rather than something that can be brought about by mere human effort; it is God who gives peace to the people. One of the most beautiful passages in the whole Bible is in Psalm 85, which celebrates the links between peace, justice, and the bounty of God:

> I listen to what God is saying,
> a voice that speaks of peace,
> peace for God's people and friends,
> and those who turn their hearts to Yahweh.
> Those who respect God will surely be rescued
> and the saving presence of God will abide in our land.
> Unwavering love and fidelity now meet,
> justice and peace embrace.
> Human steadfastness stretches up from the Earth
> while divine graciousness reaches down from God's abode.
> Yahweh will enable us to flourish
> and our soil will yield rich harvests.
> Yahweh comes, with justice marching in front
> and the gift of peace following behind.
>
> (Ps 85:8-13)

Although Shalom comes as a gift from God, yet human agents are chosen by God to bring about this peace. In the Old Testament the specially chosen instrument of God in bringing peace is the King. He is the one whose task it is to promote justice in society; and justice is the basis for true peace. Precisely because God's gift of peace is so closely linked with social justice, it is particularly outrageous if the king practices or condones injustice. The prophets spoke God's word of condemnation on kings and ruling elites whose injustices disrupt the peace, e.g.:

200

Jerusalem is doomed, that corrupt, rebellious city that oppresses its own people . . . Its officials are like roaring lions; its judges are like hungry wolves, too greedy to leave a bone until morning.

(Zeph 3:1-3)

Despite the warnings and threats of the prophets, Israelite society continued to be marred by social injustice. When it seemed unlikely that true peace built on justice could come about immediately, the later prophets began to direct people's hopes towards a future true 'Kingdom' or 'Reign of God'. The marks of this realm would be justice and peace. So the hope of the people for liberation from oppression began to have an eschatological tone: the true 'Kingdom' or reign of God would come about *within* human history, but it would also be the *culmination* of history. In it, God's power and love would be demonstrated for all to see: evil would be wiped out and God's faithful people would at last be able to flourish:

Yahweh says: 'I am making a new Earth and new heavens. The events of the past will be completely forgotten. Be glad and rejoice for ever in what I create. The new Jerusalem I make will be full of joy, and its people will be happy. I myself will be filled with joy because of Jerusalem and its people. There will be no weeping there, no calling for help. Babies will no longer die in infancy, and all people will live out their full span of life. Those who live to be a hundred will be considered young . . . People will not be forced to build houses for others while remaining homeless themselves; they will build homes in which they themselves can live. When they plant vineyards and make wine they will not have to give it up to others; they will be able to enjoy their own wine. My people will live as long as trees. They will fully enjoy the things they have worked for. The work they do will be crowned with success. Their children will not meet with disaster. I will bless them and their descendants for all time to come. Even before they finish praying to me, their prayer will be answered. The wolf will eat side by side with the lamb. The lions will eat straw as the cattle do; and the snake will be content to eat dust. On all of my holy mountain there will be nothing to do hurt or cause damage.

(Is 65:17-25)

But how was this new world of justice and peace to come about? A high point in the Old Testament was reached in the search for an answer to that question. One of the great prophets had a vision of a specially chosen instrument of God — one who would come, like Moses, as a true 'Servant of God'. This new 'Servant' would not exercise power in the traditional way; his would be a strength that was gentle and delicate:

Here is my servant, to whom I have given my strength
this is my chosen one, in whom I delight.
I have given him my own spirit,
so that he may bring justice to the nations.
He does not shout out or raise his voice
or roar in anger on the city streets.
He does not break the reed that is crushed,
and does not snuff out the light that burns dim.
He does not falter or hesitate
as he brings true justice to the nations,
and carries this message of peace to distant shores.
This now is the word of Yahweh,
who created the heavens and gave them their shape,
who moulded the Earth and all that lives on it,
who gave the breath of life to all its peoples:
'I, Yahweh, have called you to serve the truth,
I have taken you in my hand and shaped you for my
    purpose.
I have chosen you to be my pledge to the people,
a ray of light to all nations,
to open the eyes of the blind,
to set free the prisoners who are locked in jails.
My name is Yahweh, the One Who Is.
Do not dare give allegiance to any false god,
forsaking the true God for a worthless idol.
My former prophecies are already fulfilled.
A new prophecy I give you now,
announcing the promised future before it takes place.
(Is 42:1-9)

We hear more of this second Moses, the dedicated Servant of God, in the second of the 'Servant Songs' of the second part of the Book of Isaiah (Is 49:1-6). The Servant knows

202

that he has been called by God before ever he was born, called not merely 'to bring back the scattered people of Israel' but also 'to be a light to the nations, so that God's salvation may reach out to the whole world.' Despite this conviction, the Servant has to struggle against self-doubt and a sense of failure: 'I was thinking, "I have laboured in vain, used up my energy to no avail; I have nothing to show for all my efforts." But all this time Yahweh was there, waiting to repay me for what I endured.'

In the third 'Servant Song' (Is 50:4-9), the Servant is presented not as one who imposes his will on people but as a person who is willing to suffer:

> Yahweh God has opened my understanding,
> so I do not shirk or turn aside.
> I offer my back to those who torture me.
> I do not resist them
> when they pull the hairs from my beard
> and spit in my face.
> Yahweh stands by me, so I endure their insults.
> I set my face like flint, determined not to give in,
> for I know that God is here,
> ready to vindicate me in the end.

The fourth of the 'Servant Songs' (Is 52:13-53:12) goes even further. The pain and degradation of the Servant are presented in vivid detail. The writer then suggests that these sufferings are *salvific*. The Servant is so utterly self-sacrificing that he is willing to suffer on behalf of others. So the way the Servant brings healing and hope to others is by enduring pain and humiliation:

> He no longer had any beauty or dignity,
> nothing to make him look attractive.
> He was a shocking sight, a repulsive thing,
> broken by suffering, twisted by pain,
> a thing you could scarcely look at,
> a despicable, worthless creature.
> Yet it was our sufferings that he endured.
> the pain he bore was our pain.
> When we saw his misery we smugly assumed
> that this was a well-deserved punishment from God.
> But it was for our sin that he was pierced,

for the wrongs we did that he was crushed.
The punishment he endured made us whole,
the pain he bore brought healing to us . . .

Jesus: The Suffering Servant

The presence and witness and words of Jesus can only be understood in the context of the hope of the Old Testament:
— hope for the coming at last of a reign of justice and peace;
— and hope for a Servant who would be God's chosen agent in overcoming evil and bringing healing and peace.

The Gospels present Jesus as one who claimed to be the fulfillment of such hope:

> He stood up to read the Scriptures and was handed the book of the prophet Isaiah. He unrolled the scroll and found the place where it is written: 'The Spirit of the Sovereign God is upon me and has chosen me to bring good news to the poor, to proclaim release to captives, and the restoration of sight to the blind, to set free those who are oppressed, and to announce that God's promised time has come.' Jesus rolled up the scroll, gave it back to the attendant, and sat down. Every eye in the synagogue was fixed on him. Then he spoke: 'Today, in your very hearing, this text is coming true.'
>
> (Lk 4:16-21)

Though he had come to establish God's reign of peace, Jesus soon came to be seen as a trouble-maker. This paradox arises from the fact that the 'Shalom' of God is very different from the false peace of 'a culture of silence', where people have been cowed into accepting an unjust social order. The peace brought by Jesus is not the peace that 'the world' gives (Jn 14:27). He did not offer the peace of a quiet, undisturbed complacency; in that sense, what he offers is 'not peace but a sword' (Mt 10:34). Like the prophets before him, Jesus challenged injustice and oppression. His most severe condemnation was for those who, in the name of God's law, laid heavy burdens on the backs of the common people. He set out to bring true peace to these oppressed people by enabling them to live in the freedom of God's children (e.g. Mt 17:26 — 'the children go free').

Jesus' way of bringing peace was not that of a crusader but that of the beloved Servant of God. Love and personal integrity seem to have been the two dominant values in his life as presented in the Gospels. His love was practical and specific: he spent his time and energy in healing and teaching all who were willing to heed him. His commitment to personal integrity is articulated in the Gospels as total dedication to the will of God (Jn 4:34 — 'My food is to do the will of the One who sent me'; Lk 22:42 — 'not my will but your will be done'). This commitment determined the pattern of his life, leading him from obscurity to popular fame, then into harassment by the religious establishment, and finally to his execution as a criminal. He lived his life according to his faith, and he was willing to suffer for his convictions.

When people began to realise the implications of the message and life-style of Jesus, opposition built up to all that he stood for. In the last period of his life he was subjected to a mindless hatred from the very people who exercised authority in the name of God. How could he make sense of that? What was it that enabled him to bear the pain of total rejection by those whom he had been taught to respect? He must have turned more and more to the 'Servant Songs'. There can be no doubt that in the end he came to see his suffering as part of his God-given task; in other words, he saw himself as a 'Suffering Servant' of God. Conscious of that calling he remained true to the end. It enabled him — and, later, his followers — to understand his suffering and death as God's way of bringing healing and hope to his own people and to the nations.

There was nothing 'soft' about Jesus, no compromise with evil; he was a fearless champion of the common folk who were so weighed down by disease, poverty, and the arrogance of those who thought they were holy. Jesus had to be strong to face down the lawyers and the people who had taken it on themselves to interpret the word and will of God, to stand silent before Herod, and with dignity before the Roman governor. But his was a gentle strength. He challenged others but never imposed on them. He refused to use force — even in the desperate moments of his arrest (Mt 26:52). The attitude of Jesus can be summed up in the words of the Irish patriot, Terence MacSweeney: 'victory goes not to those who can inflict the most suffering but to those who can endure the most.'

The Christian Peace-Maker

To be a Christian peace-maker today is to live in the midst of the paradoxes that characterised the life of Jesus. To work for *peace* is to engage in a *struggle*. So, those who hunger for true peace must endure the pain of being branded as trouble-makers, and 'disturbers of the peace'. They believe in the promise that a time will come when poor people will have their own homes, when the children of the poor will not die young, when peasants will no longer be compelled to sell food to others while they go hungry themselves, when wives will no longer be beaten by their husbands, when there will be no more battered babies, when women will be able to walk the streets without fear. But meanwhile they may have to give up their own comfortable homes, to go short of food, perhaps even to put their lives 'on the line' in the struggle for peace.

Those who try to be peacemakers have to cling on to hope in situations that, humanly speaking, seem hopeless. Above all, they have to endure — as Jesus did — the utter incomprehension and rejection of many of those who should be most open to what they stand for. In the face of a bitter hostility which seems at times to be quite perverse, they have to cling on to the belief that God can draw good out of evil. In rare moments of special grace they may perhaps feel a sense of solidarity with Jesus in his agony; they may even dare to think that they too have been called to share in some degree the call of the 'Suffering Servant'.

The greatest obstacle that confronts those who work for peace in situations of political tension is the fact that those who hold power almost always give precedence to *stability* over *justice*. In places such as the Middle East, Cyprus, or Northern Ireland, governments and international agencies almost invariably prefer to hang on to the *status quo*, no matter how unjust it may be. Those who hold power in society are seldom prepared to risk that power to bring about the justice which is essential to genuine peace. Concern for justice or human rights is given a poor second place; and when changes are introduced it is more likely to be because the outcry has become so great that the stability of the society is now under threat.

In the Christian understanding of peace the priorities are reversed. Stability is important — but more as a means than as an end or value in its own right. For instance, in Old Testament times the King had the task of ensuring a measure of stability in society — but this was in order that the people could flourish. A stable society is not necessarily a good one. Too much stability is bad. It encourages complacency in the face of the injustices that are built into every social, economic, and political system. It stifles human growth. Worst of all, it quenches our hope for something radically new and different — for the promised reign of God, a reign of justice and true peace. Moses was sent as a disturber of the stability of the Egyptian empire, sent to lead his people into the insecurity of the desert in the hope of coming into a Promised Land. Jesus, too, came as a disturber. He came to lead people out of the life they had become used to, and into the risk of living in the freedom and love and integrity of the children of God.

The Christian peace-maker is one who thirsts for Shalom. And Shalom is not to be reduced either to a *social* system or to a *personal* state of mind. It means human flourishing in all its dimensions. It is possible to list some of these in a purely schematic way:

— Shalom will certainly include socio-cultural and political-economic elements, such as social justice, respect for human dignity and rights, and a participative mode of exercising authority.

— It must also include community aspects, such as openness to others and mutual support.

— There will also be deeply personal elements in it: the peace of heart and spirit that comes from integrity and 'transparency'.

— The ecological and cosmic dimensions are not to be ignored either — a sensitivity to the Earth and partnership with the rest of nature.

— And there is a deeply religious element, in so far as all of the above are experienced as the gracious gift of God.

The fact that an account of the 'content' of Shalom has to be so schematic reminds us that it is not really possible to spell out the concrete details. For Shalom is the *Future* that awaits us and that we hope and strive for. Does it not exist, then, in reality? The answer has to be both 'yes' and 'no'. 'Yes', to the extent that it is realised partly — and in varying degrees — in any particular society of today. 'No', in the

207

sense that it is not fully present in any society, no matter how perfect we may imagine it to be. Another way of expressing this 'yes' and 'no' is to say that Shalom belongs to a future that is both eschatological and historical:

— Eschatological, because it always remains beyond us, a goal to be striven for, an ultimate that serves to relativise our commitment to what has already been achieved.

— Historical, because it is not some abstract and unreal ideal; rather it provides us with a set of values which we can work to incorporate in the society we are building together. Furthermore, it calls us to make 'a historical commitment'. This means that we are not entitled to stand back from all human societies, judging them all from outside. We have to make a concrete option, to choose whether or not we will work *within* a particular system. For instance, the Christian in South Africa today has to choose whether or not to recognise the legitimacy of the regime, whether to work for its *reform* or for its *replacement*. And if the choice is for replacing the system, then this too must be a concrete choice. That means giving one's allegiance not just to some better system in the abstract, but to a particular movement that is working to replace the corrupt system. It does not, of course, involve approval of all the policies of such a movement; one may work within it to change the policies.[3]

Does Shalom add something to all the values noted above? It does not have some *separate content* of its own, over and above the various elements that I have indicated above and illustrated (in the introduction to this book) by three interlocking circles. What is most important in Shalom, from the point of view of its content, is the way it *integrates* the various values — the fact that genuine peace includes them all. That is why, in the diagram, Shalom is located at the centre, where all three circles overlap.

What is most distinctive about Shalom, however, is not its content but the manner in which it comes. It is the gift of God. But surely everything we have is the gift of God, so why lay such emphasis on peace as *gift*? Because there is a more obvious gap in this case between what we are promised and what we can achieve. To work for peace is to throw ourselves more obviously into the loving hands of God. Perhaps we could pray in these words:

'You call us to follow in the way of the Suffering Servant, the way of Jesus, a way of love and integrity, of willingness to endure — even to suffer on behalf of others. And you promise that if our steadfastness reaches up from the Earth, then your divine graciousness will reach down to touch us with its power. So, here we are, doing what we can, but apparently in vain. Our efforts to bring peace seem only to provoke people to hate us, to label us as trouble-makers. We are sorely tempted to cut corners, to fight violence with violence, to force people into doing what we consider right. Be with us in this hour of trial. Remember your promise. Strengthen us to be faithful to our convictions, to what we believe to be your will, as Jesus was. Stand by us now; vindicate us by giving your gift of peace to us, to the people for whom and with whom we work, and to the whole world.'

I do not propose here to go into a discussion of whether the Christian is ever entitled to employ force, to fight, to wage war. My concern here is not with the detailed (and necessary) casuistry that comes into moral theology, but rather with the basic attitudes of a truly Christian spirituality. And there is no doubt that a fundamental attitude of non-violence is central for anybody who wishes to follow Jesus and develop a holistic spirituality.

The Five-Hundred Year War
It often happens that people who are interested in issues of global justice — especially if they are from the Third World — find a tension between themselves and activists from Europe or North America who are concerned about peace and ecology issues. The 'justice people' are irritated by the intensity with which the others focus on peace and ecology, while apparently willing to give a much lower priority to the injustice of the economic and political domination exercised by 'the West' over poorer countries. The peace and ecology activists often feel the same kind of irritation with those who focus almost exclusively on the justice issue. It is important that both sides broaden their perspectives and realise that the issues are convergent rather than opposed to each other. I want here to make a few comments which may help those committed to peace to extend their horizons.

If we are really serious about renouncing violence we should be ready to renounce the *fruits* of violence. What then about the fruits of what I have to call 'the five-hundred year war'? I mean the centuries of political, economic, and cultural conquest which have left our world divided into present or former imperial powers on the one hand, and, on the other, the victims of this imperialism.

The original aggressors in the 'five-hundred year war' were the ruling elites of several European nations. Their first victims were the weaker sectors of the population in their own countries; and this exploitation continued while the appetite of the oppressors increased. Next they reached out to swallow up as far as possible the groups which might now be called the little peoples of Europe, e.g. the Celts, the Basques and some of the Slavs; and this too continued while they looked further afield. The full thrust of imperial aggression came with the expansion of the imperial powers into what we now call 'the Third World'. They ruthlessly destroyed the economic and social structures of the peoples living there. They adapted the political structures to make them pliant instruments of the invaders. They refashioned the economies of their colonies to serve the economies of the colonial powers.

The aggression and exploitation has changed over the years; it is now more indirect, more subtle; and for these reasons it is often more effective. More use is now made of local ruling elites. One effect of these changes is that Western nations that had little or no involvement in the old-style colonial expansion now benefit enormously from the way the power and resources of the world are divided.

While living in Africa in recent years I came to realise that the most accurate way to describe the plight of the people there was to say that they are *war victims*. This is obviously true, of course, of the people of Mozambique. But it applies in a more general sense to the people of the former colonies. They are the losers in a relentless political and economic war that has been going on for the past five hundred years.

Ordinary people in 'the West' can no longer disclaim responsibility for the victims of this long-drawn-out war. For we are benefitting from the fruits of victory. They are unjust fruits. We cannot in good conscience say: 'Let us forget the past and begin now together to work for peace.' We must rather remember the past and try to undo some of the harm — replacing the unjust structures with a more justly ordered world. And we must renounce the *fruits* of the present unjust situation. Otherwise we are not true peace-makers, but are like those condemned by the prophet Jeremiah: 'They gloss over the wounds of my people, saying "peace, peace", where there is no genuine peace.' (Jer 6:14).

Of course this seems unrealistic. But committed peace-makers have heard that phrase often before and have not been deterred. The spirituality of peace is one that gives us hope in tackling apparently hopeless causes. If we set out to be peace-makers it is well to do so with our eyes open to the full dimensions of the challenge facing us. Hope does not come from narrowing our vision. It springs from deep within us and from all around us where the Spirit of God is at work. The exercises in the second section of this chapter may help people to get in touch with that hope.

SECTION TWO: EXERCISES AND RESOURCES

A Christian peace-maker needs to develop the ability to mediate between people or groups who are at loggerheads with each other. This will, at times, call for the use of various skills and techniques in working with groups — for instance, helping people who are on opposite sides in a dispute to really *listen* to each other's point of view, or helping them to find more participative ways of making *decisions*; the exercises I suggested in chapters 3 and 5 should help in the development of these skills. In fact the peace-maker is likely to be helped, on one occasion or another, by almost all of the practical exercises which I give in different parts of this book. (This illustrates the point that peace is an *integration* of all the other values.) So I do not need to add here a whole lot of further exercises of this kind. What I offer in this section are some exercises that are particularly relevant for 'peace activists', i.e. those who commit a lot of time and energy to challenging the militarism that has come to pervade many countries today.

211

Despair and Empowerment

One of the biggest problems which confront peace-workers and other social activists is that they tend to use up all their physical, psychological, and spiritual energies. They do not take the time and space they need to nourish the spirit — and indeed they may never have learned how to get such nourishment; they may not even advert to the need for it! The result is that they 'run down' and eventually they may become victims of 'burnout' — a sense of emptiness and futility in the face of the intractability of the problems they are facing.

A few years ago, on both sides of the Atlantic, there emerged a network of people and groups who set out to address this problem. They called themselves 'Interhelp'. They developed a remarkable approach to helping people come to grips with the major threats to the life of the planet — especially the nuclear and ecological threats. A leading member and theorist of this network is Joanna Rogers Macy. She has written a very helpful book, entitled *Despair and Personal Power in the Nuclear Age*.[4] In it she offers various exercises which help people to acknowledge the urgency of these problems, without becoming paralysed by fear or guilt or a sense of futility and helplessness.

There are two main stages in the process. The first stage is to 'let in' in the pain — the threat of nuclear annihilation and of ecological disaster for our world, and the sense of futility which hits us when we see how feeble and ineffective are even our best efforts to confront the mighty powers that are responsible. This 'letting in' of the pain helps people to realise how the *objective* threat to our planet links in with personal, *subjective* pain and futility deep within each of us. We then can see that our sense of futility and hopelessness comes from the conjunction of the 'out there' threat with the deep primal pain that each of us carries within.

By giving expression to fear, pain, and a sense of hope-lessness, people already begin to feel more free of it; they are no longer paralysed by nameless dread. However, Inter-help and Macy carry this process on to a second stage which they call 'empowerment'. This consists of a variety of exercises which enable people to get in touch with the deep sources of life, energy, and hope which are available to them.

For instance, the mediation on 'The Web', which I have given in a previous chapter, can give people a sense of being sustained and nourished by the whole community of life on this planet, and by the Earth itself.

About three years ago I was introduced to this approach through a workshop conducted in Ireland by two members of the U.K. Interhelp network. It was a very powerful experience for me personally, and it added significantly to my repertoire of exercises for use in my work with groups. I introduced some of the exercises into the leadership workshops in which I was involved in Africa and Ireland, adapting them to suit the local culture and situation. They were remarkably effective. I recall one occasion during a bilingual workshop where, after much hesitation, I led a guided meditation in English, and had it translated, more or less simultaneously, into Hausa; at the end I was astonished to find the interpreter in tears!

A Death Meditation

I propose to share here two 'meditations' and a meditation/exercise which I have borrowed (with the publishers' kind permission) from Joanna Macy's book. The first is a short 'Death Meditation', which can be done in a group setting where there has already been some sharing about the threat of nuclear war.[5] Each member of the group is asked to pick a partner. (The 'meditation' can work equally well whether the partner is a friend or a person who is scarcely known, provided there is a lot of trust in the group.) The pairs sit in a comfortable position and follow the 'meditation' which is given out very slowly by the leader:

Look at this person before you . . . Let the realization arise in you that this person may die in a nuclear war . . . Keep breathing . . . Observe that face, unique, vulnerable . . . those eyes can still see, they are not empty sockets . . . the skin is still intact . . . Become aware of your desire, as it arises, that this person be spared such suffering and horror . . . feel the strength of that desire . . . Keep breathing . . . Let the possibility arise in your consciousness that this may be the person you happen to be with when you die . . . This face may be the last that you see . . . that hand the last that you touch . . . It might

213

reach out to help you then, to comfort, to give you a drink of water . . . Open to the feelings that come to you with the awareness of this possibility . . . Open to the levels of caring and connection it reveals in you.

After this meditation, allow people a little time to be alone or perhaps to share quietly with their partners. It may be more appropriate *not* to have any large-group sharing after this meditation.

A Meditation on the Future

The second 'meditation' is entitled 'Thirty Years Hençe'.[6] It is one that can empower us by putting us in touch with the future we hope for and believe in. It also allows us to make contact with 'the child' that is in each of us and that is a deep source of life-energy, hope, and simple joy. When the group has relaxed, the leader reads out the meditation fairly slowly (but without long pauses until near the end). When all of the meditation has been read out, allow the participants at least twenty minutes to find their answers to the questions it contains:

Put yourself forward in time. It is a day just like this, but thirty years from now. The year on the calendar has a different number, but you are still you, same name, same gestures and feelings and skin, same action of heart and lungs. Some of us may be pretty ancient by then, but let's assume you are still around and in one of your favourite places. Don't worry about figuring out all the changes that have taken place in the world; just know that there is one key difference. It is that all weapons have been dismantled — the nuclear rockets that are on submarines, the ones that lie deep in their silos under the earth, the weapons on satellites in space, the chemical and bacteriological weapons, and even the conventional weapons; all are now gone and the world is disarmed. It may have happened back in the early nineteen-nineties; by now everybody is so accustomed to the idea that you all take it for granted.

Now a child approaches you, about eight or nine years old. She has heard, perhaps from the songs and stories about those times, what you and your co-workers did back then to save the world from disaster. She approaches you timidly, but with great curiosity. 'Were there *really* bombs that could blow up the whole world?' Listen to her questions and hear how you would answer them . . . 'Were there *really* millions and millions of people who were sick and hungry?' . . . 'What was it like to be alive in a time like that? Were you not frightened?' . . . And lastly she asks, 'What did you do to get through that scary time, and not be discouraged? . . . What helped you to stay strong, so you could know what to do?' . . . And listen now to your own answers . . .

Cradling

The third excerpt from Joanna Macy's book is several pages long.[7] It contains her explanation of the meditation/exercise which she calls 'The Cradling', and then gives the text of it. She suggests that it be used at a fairly early stage in a workshop for people interested in peace issues. But in fact it is equally effective at a later stage. The only thing that really matters is that the atmosphere be right — that there is a fair measure of trust in the group and that people have already begun to express some of the pain and despair which they feel.

The Cradling

A form of guided meditation on the body, the cradling exercise, serves several purposes: It permits deep relaxation, which is all the more welcome after dealing straight on with frightening issues. It builds trust, and a kind of respectful intimacy between participants. It widens awareness of what is at stake as we face the dangers of the nuclear age. At the same time it taps deeper levels of knowing, breeding respect for life and recognition of the powers that are innate in us.

It does all this by focusing on the body — which is appropriate enough since our nuclear anxieties and fears for our collective future have ultimately to do with that. Dangers of fall-out and famine, of environmental collapse and genetic mutation, of nuclear blast, burn and radiation — all come down, after all, to their effects on the physical embodiment that we are and that we share. Usually, in contemplating these danger, we try to get our *minds* around them; we deal with them on the infor-

215

mational level, as if we were brains on the end of a stick. The cradling exercise offers us the occasion to still our chattering, defensive minds and to listen to the wisdom of our physicality. For many participants it is the most memorable part of the workshop.

Depending on the time and space available, it can take two forms: the shorter one takes from 10 to 20 minutes; the fuller version, lasting about 45 to 60 minutes, is described here in the way I usually conduct it.

The participants work in pairs, Partners A and Partners B. Partners A, removing shoes and glasses, loosening ties and belts, lie down on the floor, close their eyes and relax. I help them do so by offering a brief guided relaxation (stretching, lying heavy, feeling the breath, relaxing toes, feet, legs, etc., moving awareness gently up through the whole body to release all tensions). I also model how Partners B will attend to them: lifting and cradling legs, arms and head in turn. B will do this in accordance with the verbal cues I then proceed to give. Soft nonmelodic background music, like flute sound, is helpful, but not necessary; carpet is nice, too; but even when done on a hard linoleum classroom floor, in the midst of a busy conference, this exercise can be profoundly effective.

Two key dimensions of the experience are these:
(1) On the sensory level, the participants experience being physically supported and cared for. After having acknowledged and shared their pain for the world, they can now let it and themselves be held, as in the vaster web of life. 'To the same extent they have in turn the experience of giving support, of ministering to the other.
(2) On the psychological level, the exercise enhances awareness — indeed permits rediscovery — of certain qualities of life, as it takes form in us. Here the verbal cues of the facilitator are important, quietly calling attention to the uniqueness of the human body, its long evolutionary history, its organic complexity and beauty, its vulnerability . . .

A matter-of-fact tone is appropriate. Few participants have opened themselves to such an experience; respect them for their trust and stay ordinary, avoiding a charged, portentious or sugary tone. Allowing appropriate pauses of

216

silence, remain casual and reflective, as if observing some constellation in the heavens or a conch shell on the beach.

Lift gently your partner's arm and hand . . . Cradle it, feel the weight of it . . . flexing the elbow and wrist, note how the joints are hinged to permit variety of movement . . . Look, look as if you had never seen it before, as if you were a visitor from another world . . . Observe the articulation of bone and muscle . . . Turning the palm and fingers, note the extraordinary intricacy of their inner structure . . . What you now hold is an object unique in our cosmos: it is a human hand of planet Earth . . . In the primordial seas where once we swam, that hand was a fin — as it was again in its mother's womb . . . Feel the energy and intelligence in that hand — that fruit of a long evolutionary journey, of efforts to swim, to push, to climb, to grasp . . . Note the opposable thumb, how clever and adept it is . . . good for grasping a tool, a pen, a gun . . . Open your awareness to the journey it has made in this lifetime . . . how it opened like a flower when it emerged from the birth canal . . . how it reached out to explore and to do . . . That hand learned to hold a spoon . . . to tie shoelaces . . . to throw a ball . . . to write its name . . . to give pleasure . . . to wipe tears . . . There is nothing like it in all the universe.

Gently laying down that hand, move now to your partner's leg and slowly lift it . . . Feel its weight, its sturdiness . . . This species stands upright . . . Bend the knee, the ankle, note the articulation of bone and muscle. It allows this being to walk, run, climb . . . Holding the foot, feel the sole, no hoof or heavy padding . . . It is this being's contact with the Earth . . . Feel that heel; when it kicked in the womb, that was what the parents first felt through the wall of the belly . . . "See: there's its heel" . . . And such journeys that leg has been on since then . . . learning to take a step and then another . . . walking and falling and getting up again . . . then running, climbing, kicking a ball, pedaling a bike . . . a lot of adventures in that leg . . . and a lot of places it has taken your partner . . . into work places and sanctuaries, mountainsides and city streets . . . gotten tired . . . sore . . . still kept going . . . Gently putting it down now, move around to the other leg and cradle that one, too.

Observe this companion leg and foot . . . which shared those journeys . . . and many yet to come . . . For all its weight and sturdiness, it can be broken, crushed . . . no armor . . . just skin that can tear and burn, bones that can fracture . . . As you hold that leg, open your thought to all the places it will take your partner in the future . . . into places of suffering perhaps . . . of conflict and challenge . . . on missions that your partner doesn't even know about yet . . . to serve, to guide . . . As you lay it back down, let your hands express your wishes for its strength and wholeness, that it may serve your partner faithfully.

Lift now your partner's other hand and arm . . . Observe the subtle differences from its twin on the other side . . . This hand is unique, different from all other human hands . . . Turning it in yours, feel the life in it . . . And note also its vulnerability . . . no shell encases it, for those fingertips, that palm, are instruments for sensing and knowing our world, as well as for doing . . . Flexible, fragile hand, so easy to crush or burn . . . Be aware of how much you want it to stay whole, intact, in the time that is coming . . . It has tasks to do, that your partner can't even guess at . . . reaching out to people in confusion and distress, helping, comforting, showing the way . . . This hand may be the one that holds you in the moments of your own dying, giving you water or a last touch of reassurance . . . With gratitude for its existence, put it gently down; move now around behind your partner's head . . .

Placing a hand under the neck and another beneath the skull, slowly, gently lift your partner's head . . . (Partner A keep your neck relaxed, let your head be taken, heavy, loose) . . . Lift that head carefully, cradle it with reverence, for what you now hold in your two hands is the most intricate, complex object in the universe . . . a human head of planet Earth . . . a hundred billion neurons firing in there . . . vast potential for intelligence . . . only a portion has been tapped of that capacity to see, to know, to vision, create . . .

Your hands holding your partner's head — that is the first touch he or she knew in this life, coming out of the birthcanal into hands, like yours, of a doctor or midwife . . . Now within that skull is a whole world of experience, learning, thought, memories, scenes and songs, beloved faces . . . some are gone now, but they live still in the mansions of that mind . . . It is a world of experience that is totally unique and that can never be fully shared . . . In that head too are dreams of what could be, visions that could shape our world and guide us . . .

Closing your eyes for a moment, feel the weight of that head in your hands. It could be the head of a Russian soldier or an

Indian farmer, of an American general or a Chinese doctor . . . It is each of us . . .

Looking down at it now, open your awareness to what this head may have to behold in the times that come . . . to the choices it will make . . . to the courage and endurance it will need . . . Let your hands, of their own intelligence, express their desire that all be well with that head . . . Perhaps there is something that you want your partner to keep in mind — something you want them not to forget in times of stress or anguish . . . If there is, you can quietly tell them now, as you lay their head back down . . .

Allow time for the recumbent partner to stretch, look around, slowly sit up. Then A and B reverse roles, and the verbal cues are offered again with new variations. At the conclusion of the whole process, time to re-orient is important — for the participants have journeyed into reaches of experience far from ordinary modes of inter-action and need a quiet interval for return. It is useful then for the pairs to gather in foursomes to reflect together, sharing what emerged for them from this experience.

The example of verbal guiding that I wrote out here is not offered to be followed verbatim, only to illustrate the kinds of cues that are evocative and appropriate to the work. Each facilitator has their own style in leading this exercise, their own knowings to draw from. But whatever the language or images used, it is wise to touch on certain themes. Interweaving through the spoken words, these motifs renew and sharpen awareness of what it means to be a living person. They include:

1) the uniqueness of the human species in the cosmos.
2) its long evolutionary journey.
3) the uniqueness of each individual, and of each personal history.
4) the intricacy and beauty of the human organism.
5) its universality, linking us to other humans around the globe.
6) and its vulnerability.

In the context woven by these themes, the act of holding and observing is as potent as being cradled. Indeed the two halves of the process are complementary, letting us experience in both the active and passive mode the wonder and fragility of life as it takes form in us.

Note that if the number of workshop participants is uneven, it is best for the guide to pair up with the extra person, so that no one is left out. Then lead the exercise while acting as Partner B, simultaneously speaking and doing the cradling — but then not reversing roles.

When participants lie down remember to have them so place themselves that there is adequate room for their partners to move around them to cradle arms, legs and head.

If there is not enough floorspace for half the participants to lie down, a brief version of the exercise can be conducted as they sit facing each other. This also can be done if time is insufficient for the longer form. In that case, the exercise focuses on the hands, arms, shoulders, neck and head. Since the head, in the sitting position, cannot be really cradled, have the partners direct their attention and touch to the shoulders and neck (with awareness of the stress they hold, the kinds of burdens and tensions they carry, etc.), and then gently hold and rock that head in their hands. For that, if space permits, they can move around to hold the head from the rear. If this is impossible or too awkward, don't worry. So long as there is touch and attention, even the briefest form of this exercise is evocative and powerful.

In the crowded auditorium of a conference on the hazards of nuclear war, I asked members of the audience to take the hand of the person next to them, to hold it for a moment, and look at it. Then, as above, I offered reflections on what they held and saw. It took three minutes, yet out of a whole day's worth of speeches, panels and films, that is what many people remembered most vividly; for some it was a turning point. In this time of abstractions and information overload, the simple reality of touch, of embodiment, can break through our numbed defenses.

Win-Lose Exercise

The final exercise in this chapter is of a very different kind. It is an interesting and exciting 'game' called 'Win-Lose', which is really a simulation of situations in which we can find ourselves in real life. Reflection on the 'game' can help people to see how difficult it is to build up trust

220

between different groups, and how easy it is to get locked into competition and aggression. One lesson which many people learn from the exercise is how important it is to ensure that we avoid having 'winners' and 'losers'; instead we have to look for ways which will enable *all* the people involved in any decision or activity to experience themselves as 'winners'. I give here the formal rules of the simulation[8] but I note that in my experience a certain flexibility and creativity on the part of the organiser may be required; some groups need more time than others to develop a co-operative approach. (On one occasion I found it necessary to play the whole exercise over again *after* the 'de-briefing', in order to enable the participants to internalise the lessons of their failure to cooperate the first time round — and in order to develop a good sense of trust in the group.)

Steps:

1. Explain to the group that the purpose of the exercise is for each team **to get a positive score.** This must be stressed and written on newsprint for all to see.
2. Two teams are formed and named Red and Blue. The teams are seated at opposite ends of a large room. They are instructed not to communicate with the other team in any way, verbally or non-verbally, except when told to do so by the organiser.
3. The Red Team is given a card marked 'A' and one marked 'B'. The Blue Team is given a card marked 'X' and one marked 'Y'.
4. Score Sheets are distributed to all participants. They are given time to study the directions. The organiser then asks if there are any questions concerning the scoring.
5. Round One is begun. The organiser tells the teams that they will have three minutes to make a team decision.
6. The two teams are asked to hold up at the same moment the cards they have chosen. The scoring for that round is agreed upon and is entered on the scorecards and on newsprint.
7. Rounds 2 and 3 are conducted in the same way as Round 1.
8. **First negotiation:** Round 4 is announced as a special round, for which the payoff points are doubled. Each team is instructed to send one representative to the

221

chairs in the centre of the room. After representatives have conferred for three minutes, they return to their teams. Teams then have three minutes, as before, in which to make their decisions. When recording their scores, they should be reminded that points indicated by the payoff schedule are doubled for this round only.

9. Rounds 5 through 8 are conducted in the same manner as the first three rounds.

10. **Second negotiation:** Round 9 is announced as a special round, in which the payoff points are 'squared' (multiplied by themselves, e.g. a score of 4 would be $4 \times 4 = 16$). A minus sign should be retained, e.g. $-3 \times -3 = -9$.

   Team representatives meet for three minutes, then the teams meet for five minutes. At the organiser's signal, the teams write their choices, then the two choices are announced.

11. Round 10 is handled exactly as Round 9 was. Payoff points are squared.

12. The entire group meets and the total for each team is announced.

Discussion Questions
1. Did you feel frustrated or angry? Why?
2. What increased the competitive spirit?
3. What encouraged co-operation?
4. What did we learn from this game?
5. How is this related to real life? Give examples.
6. How is it possible to change the win/lose situation in life, into a win/win situation?

Score Sheet for 'Win–Lose'

Instructions: For ten successive rounds, the Red team will choose either an 'A' or a 'B' and the Blue Team will choose either an 'X' or a 'Y'. The score each team receives in a round is determined by the pattern made by the choices of both teams, according to the schedule below.

Scoring Schedule

AX — Both teams win 3 points

AY — Red Team loses 6 points; Blue Team wins 6 points.

BX — Red Team wins 6 points; Blue Team loses 6 points.

BY — Both teams lose 3 points.

Round	Minutes	CHOICE		CUMULATIVE POINTS	
		Red Team	Blue Team	Red Team	Blue Team
1	3				
2	3				
3	3				
4*	3(reps) 3(teams)				
5	3				
6	3				
7	3				
8	3				
9**	3(reps) 5(teams)				
10**	3(reps) 5(teams)				

* Payoff points are doubled for this round only.
** Payoff points are squared for these rounds (keep the minus sign.)

Songs

I conclude this chapter with four songs. The first is a hymn used some years ago at the New York Riverside Church Disarmament Conference:

We'll build a land where we bind up the broken
We'll build a land where the captives go free,
Where the oil of gladness dissolves all mourning
oh, we'll build a promised land that can be.

Chorus
Come build a land where sisters and brothers
anointed by God then create peace
where justice shall roll down like waters
and peace like an ever-flowing stream.

We'll build a land where we bring good tidings
to all the afflicted and those who mourn,
We'll then give them garlands instead of ashes
oh, we'll build a land where peace is born.

We'll be a land building up ancient cities,
Raising up devastations from old,
Restoring ruins of generations
oh, we'll be a land of people so bold.

Come build a land where mantles of praises
resound from spirits once faint and once weak,
Where like oaks of righteousness stand her people
oh, come build the land, my sisters, we seek.[9]

The words and music of the second song were written some months ago in Ireland by my friend Pádraig Ó Fátharta, who has since returned to his work as a missionary in Central Africa. The song has never been published, so I hope to make a recording available as part of the resource materials which are to be prepared to supplement this book.

Light in my Night
The fruit in the orchard falls,
there's a breach in the crumbling walls,
the blossom is blown, the swallow is flown,
all life is on hold, in a world that's grown old.

224

Then,
    Out of my night you shine, Bright Light;
    Wait for the dawn,
    wait until dawn.

O where is the dew of May?
And where are the garlands gay?
Where is the dream, the clear mountain stream?
And where is the child, who saw worlds in the sky?
And,
    Out of my night you shine . . .

The city's a house of cards,
the vase now but broken shards.
The word out of rhyme, the song out of chime,
The hearth is grown cold, and the story untold,
But,
    Out of my night you shine . . .

So wait through the Winter snow,
and wait while the tempests blow.
Wait through the night and watch for the light,
wait for the sun, and a new day begun,
For,
    Out of my night you shine . . .

The final two songs are simple choruses sung by the women who played a prominent role in the peace protests on the occasion of the visit of President Reagan to Ireland:

You can't kill the Spirit
She is like a mountain, old and strong,
She goes on and on, on and on.
You can't kill the Spirit . . .

Building bridges between our divisions,
I reach out to you and you reach out to me,
With all of our voices and all of our visions
Friends we can make such a sweet harmony.[10]

NOTES

1. Frantz Fanon, *The Wretched of the Earth*, Harmondsworth (Penguin: 1963).

2. See the articles on 'peace', 'being at peace', and 'peacemaker' by Von Rad and Foerster, in Gerhard Kittel (ed), *Theological Dictionary of the New Testament* (translated into English and edited by Geoffrey W. Bromeley), Vol. 2, Grand Rapids (Eerdmans: 1964) 400-420.

3. What of a situation where some Christians were convinced that they could in conscience give allegiance neither to the existing regime nor to any of the existing alternatives? In that case they would be bound to take concrete steps to form an alternative movement, one that would cooperate realistically with others in building a new society.

4. Philadelphia, PA. (New Society Publishers: 1983).

5. *Ibid.*, 155 (slightly adapted).

6. *Ibid.*, 141 (slightly adapted).

7. *Ibid.*, 101-5.

8. Reprinted from 'Prisoner's Dilemmas' in John W. Pfeiffer and John E. Jones, *A Handbook of Structured Experiences for Human Relations Training, Vol. 111,* San Diego, CA: University Associates, Inc. 1974.

9. Words by Barbara Zinorri and music by Carolyn McDade. Despite my best efforts I have been unable to make contact with the authors to request permission to print this hymn.

10. I have been unable to trace the authorship of these two little songs.

8

Introducing and Using the Enneagram

SECTION ONE: NINE TYPES

The Enneagram is a very ancient wisdom, a tradition that was handed down orally for hundreds of years among certain groups of Sufi mystics before it came to be widely known in the West. In recent years it has become popular among Church people in English-speaking countries. Enneagram courses or workshops are now very common; and it is used as a foundational element in some major programmes of spiritual renewal or development.[1]

I am including in this book an introduction to the Enneagram because it fits in very well with the material I have covered in the previous seven chapters, and offers those who are interested a chance to go deeper. I see it as 'the honours course' for people who have benefitted from the kind of personal exploration and community sharing which I have been proposing in previous chapters.

The word 'enneagram' derives from the Greek and it may be translated as 'a diagram of nine'. The 'nine' are typical kinds of compulsive behaviour, which form the basis of nine different types of personality, e.g. 'the compulsive worker' or 'the compulsive helper'.

From my own experience I know that the Enneagram can give a great deal of insight into one's own character and that of others. This means that it is a valuable instrument both for *personal* spiritual growth and for improving the quality of *community* life. It also throws light on the manner in which people engage in *political* activity. Because it relates to personal, community, and political life it is bound to have important *religious* implications as well.

227

But there are some difficulties. One of them is that a course or workshop on the Enneagram may do more harm than good if the person taking part in it is not in touch with his or her own personality. In other words, it is helpful only to those who already have a good knowledge of themselves; otherwise it can be misleading. A second difficulty is that even the introductory courses or workshops are generally too long and confusing; participants often flounder around for quite some time in a welter of ideas and information before being able to identify their own particular pattern.

Despite these difficulties, the Enneagram is such a valuable instrument that I would like to see it made available more widely — and to ordinary people rather than just to those who can afford the time and money required to take part in the usual introductory courses. Apart from the insight which it provides into people's behaviour, there is a further great advantage in doing some study of the Enneagram in a group: it offers people the opportunity to share with each other in considerable depth about very personal material and in a way that is not experienced as threatening.

For these reasons I have been trying over the past three years to work out ways of lessening the difficulties and making the Enneagram more accessible to ordinary or poorer people. After some experimentation I now believe that it is possible to give a useful introduction to the Enneagram in the space of three two-hour sessions — rather than in the six to ten such sessions which are commonly used. This can be done by presenting an illustrated thumbnail account of each of the typical compulsive patterns of behaviour and combining this with a set of questions which can help people to narrow down the rather formidable range of choice presented to them.

What I am offering here is material for such a three-session introduction to the Enneagram, followed by a fourth session in which participants will have the opportunity to explore its political and religious implications. (In all of this I pre-suppose that time has already been given to clarifying with the participants what they are really looking for in this study of the Enneagram, and whether or not they are willing to share openly with each other; without such prior clarifications the sessions are likely to run into difficulties.)

The sessions are designed in such a way that only about half of the total time is devoted to 'input'; the remaining time is given to sharing by the participants in small groups, since, from my point of view, this is at least as important as any input. Obviously, this is *only* an introduction. But I believe that it is sufficient to give people a fair indication of whether they will find it useful to do further study on the topic. And in the meantime it provides interesting material for some helpful personal sharing by those who take part.

The material given here could be used simply by reading through it. But it will be much more helpful and exciting if it is presented to a group by somebody who is familiar with the Enneagram system. Such a person will feel fairly comfortable in facilitating the group in exchanging their experiences in order to get a better insight into the different patterns of behaviour. The resource person does not have to be an expert on all aspects of the Enneagram. Indeed it is quite important to avoid the temptation to present oneself as knowing all the answers. But it is useful if the presenter knows enough to respond comfortably but modestly to the kind of questions that arise when people begin to reflect, perhaps for the first time, on compulsive behaviour patterns.

Before presenting basic information on the nine different types, I want to make some comments on the accompanying pictures. They are the result of some rather odd cross-breeding! Twelve years ago when I was in Kenya, learning to work with community development groups, one of the exercises we learned was called 'animal behaviour'. It was an effective, light-hearted, and non-threatening way of helping people to identify and avoid uncooperative behaviour in a group. Unduly aggressive behaviour was described as being like that of 'the lion'; the person who always ran for cover was seen as acting like 'the mouse'; 'the chameleon' was the person who changed views to suit the occasion; and so on. Later, in West Africa, this exercise proved so popular that some members of our team developed it further. As well as the *negative* aspects they also noted the *positive* aspects of different styles of animal behaviour; and this provided the basis for much worth-while sharing, especially with youth groups. I was able to draw on this experience when I began, three years ago, to incorporate material from the Enneagram into our psycho-social workshops. I found it quite challenging and exciting to have to rethink the traditional Enneagram animal symbols in the light of different African cultures. For instance, many Africans consider the tortoise to be the supremely wise animal; most Western people, by contrast, think of the tortoise as slow. Again, Western people see the owl as wise, while in most African countries the owl is irrevocably associated with witchcraft and evil. So I have replaced some of the animal symbols that are usually chosen to represent the nine types of compulsion; the ones given here are the nearest I can get to cross-cultural symbols for this material; and I have found that they work fairly well in both African and European cultures.

If you intend to be the coordinator and resource person for these four two-hour sessions on the Enneagram then I suggest that you begin with a short introduction (about seven minutes) based on the first eight paragraphs of what I have said above. Then move on to give a short account of each of the nine types. Spend about eight minutes on each of the nine compulsions, illustrating what you have to say with a picture of the appropriate animal and with a sheet on which are written a few key words about that type. The pictures and headings should be displayed in such a way that you gradually build up a circle of the nine types. Prepare beforehand a chart with a circle drawn on it, and the numbers 1 to 9 marked out(see Fig. 10). After you have finished presenting the nine types (and only then) you should display the chart, in the centre of all the other pictures and sheets of paper, in such a way that the numbers on the circle coincide with the corresponding pictures and headings.

Pick out what you consider to be the key points on each type from the notes given below (or from other sources, if you prefer). Do not try to cover too much ground at this stage; speak slowly — and repeat the key points until you sense that the others have grasped them. Allow a few moments for clarifications after you present each of the nine types; but try not to get drawn into discussion at that point. Having presented four or five of the types have a short break, so that people will not become too swamped with

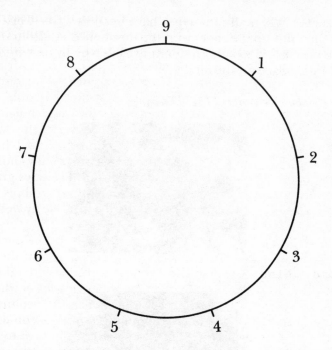

Fig. 10

material. Plan the session in such a way that you will have covered all nine types within the two-hour period (including the short break in the middle).

In the following pages I shall present the nine types in an order different from the one that is commonly used; the reason for this will become clear in the third session when I go on to deal with what are called the 'arrows'. Do not bother explaining the order in which the types are presented. In fact, I suggest that it is better at first not even to mention the number given to each type; just call them 'the Worker', 'the Helper', 'the Perfectionist', etc; then the question will not arise as to why the strict numerical order is not being followed. (However, for the convenience of those who are already familiar with the numbers, when I come to outline the characteristics of each particular compulsion I shall write down the appropriate number, inside square brackets.) When all nine types have been described briefly you then put up the sheet with the numbers on it; from that time onwards it is better to identify each type by its number and by its place on the circle.

The Compulsive Worker [The 'Three']

J. Allan Cash Ltd.

Topham Picture Library

The picture of the ant suggests the pattern of this compulsion: this is somebody who finds it hard to stop working. The 'worker' feels that the way to be appreciated by others is to be successful. These people are rather insecure, and to overcome this they identify themselves with their work and their role. So titles and job descriptions are important to them. But above all, they are achievers. They are anxious to impress others. They do this mainly by 'getting the job done'. In order to be successful they sometimes allow the end to justify the means. So they may cut corners in a way that others consider to be rather unscrupulous.

This pattern of compulsive behaviour leads one to try to earn the respect and love of others by what one does; normally this is through *work;* but another way of impressing

232

others may be by one's *appearance,* so this type of person is frequently quite dress-conscious. That is why there is a second picture in this case — that of the peacock who puts on such an impressive display. At first sight one may not see much connection between being very well dressed and working hard. But the crucial link is that both are a way of impressing others by what the person is doing, rather than by what the person is. Think of a salesperson setting out to impress a potential customer — by the image projected and the product that is being displayed. This kind of person is often a good salesperson, able to 'push' and 'sell' the product — and at the same time promoting herself or himself.

The compulsive worker has an instinctive sense of whether a project is likely to succeed or fail — and will make sure to avoid the failures. On the other hand he or she is enthusiastic and willing to commit enormous amounts of time and energy to make a project succeed, even against great odds. This person is frequently a good organiser, and if in charge of a project can be something of a slave-driver. He or she is also very 'responsible' in a rather compulsive way — for instance, in doing the work neglected by others — but often with some resentment about having to pick up the pieces dropped by others.

Compulsive workers see themselves as honest, friendly, caring, and sincere. But to others they often give the impression of being rather heartless, uncaring, and glib. The trouble is that they are not very much in touch with their feelings, and find great difficulty in exploring their own inner world. They are oriented outward, to the world of action and appearances; and they are reluctant to concede the importance of the inner world. They have a deep unconscious fear of expressing their own needs and weaknesses; for this would undermine their self-image and their sense of security which is founded on a feeling of being competent and in control.

The Compulsively Loyal Person [The 'Six']

This is an insecure person who is searching for security through being loyal to the group. Like the deer in the picture, this person is fearful, and allays the fear by being part of the herd, where it feels somewhat safer. Obedience to the law, to

Topham Picture Library

tradition, and to authorities is a very high value for the 'loyal' person. Anxiety is the driving force of this compulsion. It can drive them from one extreme to the other, e.g. from being rather distant towards others to being very friendly towards them; this happens because the person is suspicious of others but then becomes fearful about this suspicion and over-compensates for it. The insecurity and anxiety also make it difficult for the person to take decisions — or to act on decisions that have been taken.

On the other hand these people are ready to meet challenges and at times take on tasks that are beyond them. This is because they find life a great challenge and they feel the need to be brave and to push their own limits. This can give rise to difficulties: because of their obedience and loyalty they may be appointed to positions of middle-management authority, and they feel they must rise to the challenge of accepting such positions even though they may realise they are not very suitable.

To others, these 'loyal' people come across as very dog-matic. They may be quite prejudiced in their opinions — and also in their reactions to those whom they perceive as being disloyal to the group or institution. When given authority they tend to be very authoritarian. The motto seems to be: 'obey unquestioningly those above you and demand unquestioning obedience from those below you'. Yet this authoritarian ten-

234

dency cannot hide the fact that people of this type are really fearful and insecure — a fact that is frequently evident in voice and gesture. They also find it hard to confront others — unless they feel they have the firm backing of those 'above them'.

These people are very fearful and it does not take much to make them feel threatened. When they feel under threat they can be rather vicious. But in general they try to avoid feeling cornered. So they try to appear smiling and friendly towards others. And at their best they can be very endearing, seeming to know instinctively how to make themselves attractive to those around them; it may have something to do with their implicit offer of loyalty and fidelity.

The Compulsive Peace-Seeker [The 'Nine']

Topham Picture Library

The picture of the hippopotamus tells us much about this type of personality. It is somebody who sets a very high value on being undisturbed and avoiding conflict. There is a strong tendency to be rather passive, not to take initiatives or decisions, and to let others make the running in most relationships.

People who suffer from this compulsion frequently have the sense of being rather dead inside. To compensate for this sense of lifelessness they may become involved in some very active sport which involves using considerable amounts of energy and perhaps the taking of risks; such activities give them a great sense of being fully alive and 'switched on'; when the game is over, however, they slip back into the sense of lifelessness.

The reason why they feel only half alive for much of the time is that they are cutting themselves off from part of their inner life, a part that puts them in contact with the real world. Their need to avoid conflict leads them to crush down most of their strong emotions — especially feelings of aggression. Their search for peace makes them want to be in perfect harmony and at one with the world and with other people. So, without realizing it, they edit out of their experience anything that might lessen this harmony. The result is that they do not assert themselves; they may not even develop a strong sense of personal identity. This means that they attain a kind of peace — but it is flat and colourless; everything is equal — all equally grey! For them, time runs very evenly — but rather monotonously.

Other people find these 'peace-seekers' easy to get on with. They have a gift of accepting others as they are, without trying to change them. At their best they have a great capacity for love — and they can nourish this love by their patience and tolerance. Furthermore, they seem to be in harmony with nature and this brings peace into their own lives and their relationships. But they are not very inspiring companions. And to have a discussion with them can be exasperating because they tend to run away from any kind of confrontation; so to argue with them can be like hitting a sponge! When some difficulty crops up they can bury their heads in the sand as ostriches are said to do.

There is one thing that really stirs such people to action — some serious threat to their own security and stability. Here is where they act like a hippopotamus: we are told that this animal may be lying in perfect peace near the banks of a river; but, if somebody comes between the hippo and the water, then all of a sudden the hippo charges back to the river, mowing down anybody that comes in the way. That is how the compulsive peace-seeker acts when personal survival or security seem to be threatened.

The Compulsive Helper [The 'Two']

Topham Picture Library

This person is a 'giver', a person who is endlessly looking after others, frequently 'mothering' people even when they would prefer to be left alone. The picture suggests part of this pattern of behaviour — an over-friendly dog who wants to help by bringing back a stick again and again, without stopping to think whether you really want this sign of affection! It is easy to see that, under the guise of helping you, the dog is really meeting its own need for attention. Similarly, the compulsive helper is trying to meet his or her own need for love by 'earning' the love of others. It is as though the helper had made an unacknowledged bargain: 'I will look after you and in return you will appreciate and love me'.

'Helpers' are really quite needy people. They want to be appreciated, needed, and loved by others. But they are unwilling to acknowledge this deep need and are not even very much in touch with it. In fact they often imagine that they need very little — and they are quite reluctant to ask others to do them a favour. They may even feel guilty about acknowledging their own needs — they see that as being selfish. The ideal situation for a compulsive 'helper' would be if other people cared for him or her, even fussed over them, *without their asking for it!* Unfortunately, 'helpers' are often somewhat taken for granted by others. One reason for this is that they put themselves so much in the role of the 'giver' that people forget that they have needs of their own. Another reason is that they don't ask openly for help; their half-conscious hope is that others will anticipate their wishes — but that seldom happens. As a result, the 'helper' can develop a grievance against others for being thoughtless or selfish. Or the 'helper' becomes jealous of others who seem to be getting all the attention.

These grievances are not allowed fully into consciousness, so they cause personal and social difficulties. The person may develop psychosomatic illnesses — and we may guess that these are a way in which the person is unconsciously begging for the care of others. Among family or friends the person may become irritable and develop a vague air of being a martyr. Occasionally the grievances become so dominant that the 'helper' shocks everybody by becoming openly resentful and extremely angry and demanding.

The Compulsively 'Special' Person [The 'Four']
The picture of a somewhat supercilious cat conveys an impression of this compulsive pattern. It is that of somebody who feels 'different', more refined, more sensitive than others. These people are very sensitive to beauty and art and

Barnaby's Picture Library

often have great artistic or creative gifts. They have very good taste and carefully cultivated manners. They appreciate the beauty of nature — and are inclined to feel that others do not appreciate the beauty that surrounds them. Though they like to be surrounded by beauty and refinement their primary interest is their own inner world of feelings. In fact they are inclined to identify themselves with their feelings, which means that they are often moody and find it hard to rise above their present emotional state.

To others, these people often seem gifted and artistic, but also aloof and distant, as though they felt they were 'above it all'. At times they seem to be 'on stage', as though they were acting a part — especially the part of the tragic heroine or hero. They may be seen as being something of a *prima donna*. Others often consider them to be rather self-indulgent. For instance, once they find a sympathetic listener they are inclined to go on and on about themselves; they find their own emotional life intensely interesting and tend to assume that it should be of equal interest to others. They can also be rather demanding, expecting others to meet their special needs, while they themselves are rather insensitive to the needs of others. And they tend to be jealous of others, while at the same time feeling ashamed that they have 'let themselves down' if they find themselves competing with others for somebody's attention.

These people see themselves as suffering a lot — and they tend to wallow in it, so that they can become melancholic. They tend to feel that they are noble in their suffering. But they are often painfully aware that they are playing a part for much of the time. They would love to be able to experience life in a natural, simple, normal way. But the more they long for this the more it evades them. They develop a studied naturalness, a kind of false simplicity, which is quite the opposite of the spontaneity which they long for. They feel unreal — and they often seem unreal also. But they are always looking for some new special experience which will give them a sense of being truly 'real'.

The Compulsive Observer [The 'Five']

For people of Western cultures the picture of the owl conveys a sense of this personality type — a person who is rather obsessed with knowledge — seeking always to understand, to become wise by soaking up knowledge. But, as I noted already, the picture of a tortoise is more appropriate in an African context, since the tortoise is seen as very wise; and the tortoise is also like this type of human personality insofar as it feels the need at times to retreat into its own private space or shell.

This personality type is more at home with thinking than with doing. These people feel rather insecure, and their way of coping with this is to think more. Their surroundings seem rather unpredictable and pose a threat; they try to defend themselves by understanding what is going on around them. Oddly enough they often fail to understand.

240

Barnaby's Picture Library

Barnaby's Picture Library

They get things wrong because they mistake their own theories for reality. So their obsession with objectivity is self-defeating.

These people tend to be parsimonious; they store things up, and find it hard to give anything away. What they are hoarding most of all is ideas, but they can also be stingy with money or possessions. And they really find it hard to give up their *time* to others — because they feel they need this time to reflect on the world and understand it better. They are very much afraid of emptiness — especially lack of knowledge, but also emptiness in the sense of lack of money or whatever they need to feel safe.

Their need for private space is related to their need for time. They want to be able to think their own private thoughts without being disturbed. They are often people who had a lonely childhood; and they compensated for this sense of isolation by constructing their own inner world.

In a group they are often silent and may seem to be uninvolved in what is going on. It is true that at times they escape into their own thoughts while sitting in the group. But at other times when they are quiet they may in fact be more present than others realise; they may be listening silently and carefully in order to understand. The main reason they do not contribute much to the discussion is that they feel they have little to contribute; they feel their understanding is inadequate. There may also at times be an element of disdain in their silence — they despise the glibness of many of the remarks made by others.

The Compulsive Optimist [The 'Seven']

The picture here is of a monkey enjoying life. This suggests the compulsion of this type of personality: an avoidance of pain and a refusal to face up seriously to the unpleasant aspects of reality. These are people who have plenty of energy and enthusiasm — and who use them to gain as much pleasure as possible. They are greedy for enjoyment.

The compulsively optimistic person has a cheery manner and can scarcely stop smiling. This is a friendly person who enjoys entertaining others and telling amusing stories. They want everything to be pleasant and good fun; and they like to keep things lighthearted. Hurts, worries, and failures are not allowed to intrude much on their consciousness: they

Barnaby's Picture Library

are ignored or played down. And if pain and failure cannot be totally denied the optimist is consoled by the thought that things are bound to be better tomorrow.

Others find them open, playful, amusing, and friendly — but rather superficial. If the conversation turns to some painful topic the 'optimist' tries hard to change the subject. And work is done in fits and starts, depending on how enjoyable the 'optimist' finds it at any given time. People also find them somewhat naive and credulous — they are so trusting of others that they can be 'taken in' rather easily. People get annoyed with them at times because of their brashness and because they lack self-control and tend to overdo things; they often pursue their own desires single-mindedly, in a manner

243

that is insensitive to the needs of others. At their worst they are experienced as hyperactive, greedy, wasteful, and dissipated in a rather infantile way; and they may become addicted to drugs both to keep their spirits up and to enable them to relax. But at their best they are seen as highly gifted and versatile people who help others to apprehend life and everything in it as a gift and a source of happiness.

These people tend to live more in the past and the future than in the present. They look back with nostalgia on their childhood, which was probably a happy one (though the happiness may have come to an abrupt end). And they look forward eagerly to the future. In fact they spend a lot of time making plans for the future — rather unrealistic ones. They often have great schemes for changing everything for the better. But they lack the sustained commitment needed to implement them. So they tend to substitute plans for reality.

The Compulsively Aggressive Person [The 'Eight']

The picture of the lion indicates that this is someone who is assertive, authoritative, and forceful — but who can be domineering and aggressive. At best this person is a strong leader, able to inspire and command; but, when the compulsive side takes over, this same person becomes a ruthless bully.

Power is the key issue for these people. They have an instinctive or 'gut' feel for where power resides in a group — and they want a good share of that power. So one finds them jockeying for power either openly or in less obvious ways. They are self-confident, courageous, forceful in expression, and quite ready to confront or challenge other people. They are direct in their manner of speech and set out to show up any sham they find in others.

These people are very sensitive to any infringement of their rights, and can get very angry about it. They can also be great champions of the rights of others — but mainly of people for whom they feel responsible (e.g. 'how dare they insult *my* family, *my* protégés, etc.') At their best they empower others in the struggle for justice. But at their worst they think only of their own rights and trample on the rights of others.

244

Topham Picture Library

The aggressive person directs a good deal of the aggression on himself or herself, feeling blameworthy for not fighting sufficiently for justice. The compulsion leads such people to think that what they need is to be more assertive — while their friends may feel that a little less assertiveness would be more appropriate at times!

This kind of person has a great deal of life and energy. However, this energy is used mainly in the areas of work, sport, or power-struggles; and people of this type find it difficult to get in touch with the more tender emotions. They tend to crush down any softer feeling that arises, in order to ensure that they will not appear weak or vulnerable.

They seldom allow themselves to feel the need for apologising to others; they assume (quite wrongly) that others are well able to look after their own interests.

Others may find these people rather domineering and demanding, but they appreciate their leadership qualities and the inspiration and life they can give to those who follow them. If they make respectful use of the power they have and are given, then they become noble and magnanimous — and they can contribute enormously to the welfare of the community. But if they abuse their power they can do a great deal of damage.

The Compulsive Perfectionist [The 'One']

Barnaby's Picture Library

The picture here is of a spider spinning an elaborate and beautiful web; and the emphasis should be laid mainly on the web, rather than on the spider, since people might not like spiders. The picture suggests somebody who goes to infinite pains to build a perfect creation, and — like the spider working on the web — is constantly scurrying here and there to mend the damage or make things still more perfect. At first sight one might confuse this person with the compulsive worker. But it soon becomes clear that the driving force of this compulsion is different; this person is not primarily trying to impress others but simply 'to get things right'.

The perfectionist is a restless person — and, at worst, a *driven* person — not content with anything the way it is but always wanting to correct and improve people, things, and the world in general. At best, this kind of person can be a visionary and a crusader, campaigning against injustice and inspiring others to do the same. But the perfectionist compulsion puts the person in a situation of constant inner tension — between the perfect ideal and a level of achievement that seems quite inadequate. A second source of tension arises when the compulsion becomes stronger: the person begins to confuse the ideal with the reality and to imagine that he or she is already more perfect than others — and then becomes critical of everybody in a carping and negative way.

Anger is a big issue for people of this type. They are dissatisfied with almost everything around them; so they become angry and resentful that people and things won't change for the better. But, as far as these people are concerned, to show anger would not be 'right'. So the anger is crushed down, in such a way that the compulsive perfectionist is not aware of it. The anger leaks out at times in the person's tone of voice or in bouts of irritability.

Other people find these perfectionists hard to put up with at times. But they themselves are their own worst critics. They seem to hear an inner voice that constantly calls them to task for failing to do better. So they are constantly blaming themselves for failing to live up to the high ideals they have set themselves. They assume that there is some law of God or nature that requires that they always conform to the ideal; they don't realize, or they forget, that it is *they* who are making this impossible demand on themselves.

Perfectionists tend to be fascinated with evaluations — ways of checking whether they 'have got it right'. They also spend a lot of time trying to get things in order and tidy, and they find it hard to take when others 'mess up' the place which they have tidied up. Furthermore, they are fussy about being on time for appointments, and upset when others are more easygoing about time. People of this type like to help others by solving their problems — for instance by giving a long list of careful instructions to somebody who has asked for advice. They are inclined to think that others won't be able to manage without such help.

SECTION TWO: A QUESTIONNAIRE

In the second two-hour session on the Enneagram the time should be divided between input time and sharing time. By way of input I suggest that you read out the list of questions given below, allowing about forty seconds for a response after each question. Assuming that the participants know themselves well enough to answer the questions with some accuracy, this should help them a lot. Taken in conjunction with the outline of the different types given in the previous session, the answers to the questions may enable them to identify their own particular dominant compulsions; or at least the answers should lessen the range of their choice by indicating one or two or three types on which they can concentrate.

I have laid out the questions in such a way that it will not be immediately obvious to the participants which questions refer to which of the compulsions. This means that the participants will not be answering in the light of their presuppositions about the different types. So the questions offer a second and independent approach to the problem of locating one's personal dominant compulsion.

Distribute answer sheets modelled on my diagram — 108 numbered boxes, laid out in twelve rows of nine columns. Each box corresponds to one of the list of questions; and in it the participant marks 'y' (=yes) or 'n' (=no). In case of doubt the space is left blank. When the list of questions has been gone through, the 'yes and 'no' scores in each column can easily be totted up.

Enneagram Questionnaire

1. Fairness is a very important value for me.
2. A lot of people look to me for help, comfort, and support.
3. I see myself as a competent person.
4. I often feel misunderstood by others.

1	2	3	4	5	6	7	8	9
10	11	12	13	14	15	16	17	18
19	20	21	22	23	24	25	26	27
28	29	30	31	32	33	34	35	36
37	38	39	40	41	42	43	44	45
46	47	48	49	50	51	52	53	54
55	56	57	58	59	60	61	62	63
64	65	66	67	68	69	70	71	72
73	74	75	76	77	78	79	80	81
82	83	84	85	86	87	88	89	90
91	92	93	94	95	96	97	98	99
100	101	102	103	104	105	106	107	108
'Yes'								
'No'								

249

5. I really like my privacy.
6. I make a good team member.
7. I often entertain others by telling amusing stories.
8. I react more strongly than others against hypocrisy and sham.
9. I am a good mediator or arbitrator.
10. I often blame myself for not doing better.
11. I am reluctant to ask help of others.
12. I am impatient with people who won't make up their minds.
13. I am very sensitive to beauty.
14. I find it difficult to give things away to others — and especially to give away my time.
15. I am a faithful friend.
16. I like to look on the bright side of things.
17. I don't believe in giving in too easily to others.
18. I am a peaceful, easy-going type of person.
19. I'm inclined to be a crusader or campaigner for good causes.
20. I sometimes feel worn out looking after others.
21. I get a lot of satisfaction from getting a project well done.
22. I am an artistic kind of person.
23. I often feel somewhat disgusted by the glib ideas put forward by others.
24. I find it hard to make major decisions.
25. I enjoy planning the future.
26. I feel obliged to struggle for the rights of 'my people'.
27. People sometimes find me colourless and uninteresting.
28. I don't like to waste time, yet I find there's never enough time to do what needs to be done.
29. I am fairly well able to look after my own needs.
30. I seem to work harder than most of those around me.
31. There is a good deal of tragedy in my life.
32. I had a rather lonely childhood.
33. There is a lot of anxiety in my life.
34. People sometimes criticise me for being dissipated and lacking in application.
35. I am not afraid to confront others.
36. I engage in exciting sport to liven up my life.
37. I tend to judge others, to blame them for not being better.

38. I occasionally feel really annoyed by others' lack of appreciation of all I do for them.
39. Others often rely on me to organise them.
40. I like to express my feelings by means of symbols.
41. I enjoy thinking for its own sake.
42. I distrust people who go against those in authority.
43. I get very enthusiastic over new projects.
44. I really hate to lose a contest.
45. I am solid, well rooted, and grounded.
46. I like to review things and evaluate my performance and that of others.
47. When I see somebody in difficulty I come to the rescue almost automatically.
48. I like to look my best.
49. I seem to feel more deeply about things than most other people.
50. At my best I sometimes have brilliant insights.
51. I like to have clear rules about how to live and behave.
52. I'm inclined to gorge myself on food or other pleasures.
53. I enjoy getting my way by bluffing my opponent.
54. I have a sense of being in harmony with nature and its rhythms.
55. When I'm right I put up strong arguments to support my case.
56. I spend a lot of my free time caring for others.
57. I'm not too scrupulous about rules or regulations when there is an important task to be done.
58. I bear suffering with quiet dignity.
59. I tend to be rather silent in a group.
60. I set high store by the virtue of prudence.
61. I like to keep people from getting too serious.
62. Others sometimes say I push people around.
63. I hate to get into conflict with others.
64. I feel a duty to keep my place tidy and feel guilty if I fail to do so.
65. I often pay compliments to others.
66. People sometimes accuse me of being opportunistic or even ruthless.
67. Other people sometimes accuse me of being distant or haughty.

68. I am often afraid that I don't know enough in order to decide or act.
69. I like to know whose side a person is on.
70. I'm inclined to daydream about the past or the future.
71. I don't see much future for those who are soft.
72. I admire the solid traditional values of the past.
73. I criticise myself so as to head off the criticism others might make of me.
74. I'm proud of my ability to help people.
75. At times I have to push others a bit in order to get the job done.
76. At times I'm inclined to be morbid, moody, or brooding.
77. I buy a lot of books, especially on some subject in which I have specialised.
78. It upsets me when people don't obey the rules.
79. I have a rather playful and happy-go-lucky character.
80. I believe in being strong and assertive.
81. I postpone decisions that would give rise to conflict.
82. I'm restless and often feel a desire to move on.
83. I'm usually the one who takes the initiative in writing to or phoning friends.
84. I'm a man or woman of action, not much interested in exploring feelings.
85. At my best I am highly intuitive.
86. I am sometimes accused of being out of touch with the real world of life and action.
87. I find it takes a lot out of me to exercise authority over others.
88. I enjoy parties.
89. I can be a good leader and enjoy it.
90. When I am really 'up against it' I am strong and determined, refusing to give up despite the odds.
91. I like to get the details right.
92. I feel a bit guilty when thinking about my own needs and desires.
93. I dislike being beaten in any competitive situation.
94. I have a highly developed spiritual sense.
95. I get really upset when others question my ideas or convictions.
96. People sometimes accuse me of being dogmatic or prejudiced.

97. I'm grateful for my happy childhood.
98. I don't like to show weakness and vulnerability.
99. I hate to be asked to do more than one thing at a time.
100. I'm fussy about being punctual myself and I'm upset when others are late.
101. My friends tend to take my love and care too much for granted.
102. I have clear goals and I usually achieve them.
103. I sometimes feel as though I were on stage, acting a part.
104. The idea that knowledge is power really rings true for me.
105. I feel that those who betray the group must be dealt with severely.
106. I work in fits and starts.
107. I often challenge people or institutions.
108. People find me 'switched on' at times and 'switched off' at other times.

Ask the participants to tot up the 'yes' and 'no' answers in each column, and to jot down the results at the bottom of each column. Those who had a high 'yes' score in column 5 should look again at the outline of the 'Five' to see if the pattern fits them; similarly, a high 'yes' score in column 2 is an indication that the person may belong to the 'Two' category; and so on. I am not claiming that this short questionnaire will, on its own, show which dominant compulsion a person is subject to. But it can prove useful by narrowing the range of options and supplementing the outline of the types given earlier.

It is important to allow about an hour in this session for sharing by the participants, since the purpose of this introduction to the Enneagram is not merely the gaining of knowledge but also the promotion of good communication among the group. At this point it is likely that many of the participants will already have a good idea which type they belong to. These should be encouraged to go off in little groups ('Ones' together, 'Twos' together, etc). Ask them not to get involved in theoretical discussion but rather to share their experiences; in doing this they may follow the guide questions given in the next paragraph. There will probably be some who are still unable to make up their minds about which group to go to; these can be invited to stay with the facilitator to get some further clarifications. The facilitator must resist the temptation to give further new input at this point. The aim should be to get as many as possible into small sharing groups as soon as this is reasonably possible.

Some groups may be happy to share in a very unstructured way their experiences of yielding to, or resisting, their typical compulsions. Others may find it useful to take up each of the following questions, and having taken some time to work out answers for themselves, to share their answers with each other.

— What is my attitude to *time?* (e.g. to being on time, to spending or wasting time; do I find time heavy on my hands or do I find myself with not enough time, etc.) And how does my attitude on these points compare with that of other people whom I know well?

— What is my attitude to *helping* others — when is it a burden, and when is it a pleasure, etc? How does this compare to that of other people?

— How do I feel and behave in regard to those who are in *authority* over me?

— What is my attitude to *confrontation* with others?

SECTION THREE:
USING THE ENNEAGRAM FOR PERSONAL GROWTH

The third two-hour session on the Enneagram should be divided in such a way that half of it is given to input and half to sharing among the group. I suggest that the input should deal with two topics — the 'wings' (which can be explained briefly in about twenty minutes) and the 'arrows' (which can be introduced in about forty minutes). There is a good deal of material here; and people may get swamped if they try to take in all of it within an hour. But at this stage most of the participants should have a good idea of which type they belong to; so you can suggest that each person skip lightly at first over those aspects which do not concern his or her own character.

The 'Wings'

This is an important topic even though an introductory explanation does not take very long. It has been found that in practice nobody belongs purely and simply to just one of the basic types. We all find in ourselves elements of various compulsions. However, closer reflection shows that each person has one primary compulsive pattern and one secondary one — and that the secondary one is invariably one of the 'neighbouring' types. This means that the person who is primarily a 'Two' (a compulsive helper) will have a secondary compulsion which is typical *either* of the 'One' (the perfectionist) or the 'Three' (the compulsive worker). Similarly, the person who is primarily a compulsive optimist (the 'Seven') will have a secondary compulsion which is characteristic of the 'Six' or the 'Eight'. This is expressed by saying that the 'Seven' has a 'wing' in the 'Six' space or in the 'Eight' space. (Show this on the chart, and give further instances.) The advantage of speaking about a 'wing' is that it helps one to realise that the secondary compulsion is always one of the immediate neighbours. So, for instance, the 'One' cannot have a 'wing' in the 'Five' space, but only in the 'Two' space *or* the 'Nine' space (and not in both).

The implications of all this are quite significant. It means that in practice there are not just nine types of personality; there are eighteen types — the 'One' with a 'wing' in 'Nine', the 'One' with a 'wing' in 'Two', the 'Two' with a 'wing' in 'One', the 'Two' with a 'wing' in 'Three', and so on. Furthermore, the 'wing' may be more prominent for one person and less so for another; so there is an infinite variety of possibilities, made up from various combinations. This consideration provides an answer to the very understandable concern which many people have about being 'pigeonholed' into just one of a small number of character types. (Note that members of the group may have many opinions or questions about these matters; try to avoid theoretical discussion but instead encourage them to work in small groups to share their own experiences and their reflections on them; and be sure to allow time for this sharing.)

The Arrows: Yielding to the Compulsion or Fighting it

There is a further reason why people with similar compulsive patterns may differ very considerably from each other in their behaviour and character. It is because some people yield to the compulsion while others resist it; and this leads to an enormous difference between their two characters. One of the most valuable effects of a study of the Enneagram is that it throws a lot of light on how we can become more or less free of the compulsive patterns which have been governing our lives. This is where knowledge of the Enneagram really begins to 'pay off' — and where, in my opinion, it is more valuable than other systems used to describe different character types.

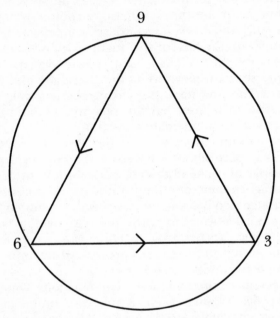

Fig. 11

Begin this part of the input by displaying a chart (Fig. 11) on which there is a circle with the nine numbers on it, and on which you draw arrows from the 'Three' to the 'Nine', from the 'Nine' to the 'Six', and from the 'Six' to the 'Three'. You then go on to explain the relationship between these three types of compulsion (which were the first ones described in the first session). The arrows show where each of these three compulsions tends to drag one if it is not opposed. Point out that the challenge for each of us is to resist the compulsion by going *against* these arrows. This is best explained by taking each case in turn as outlined below;

256

I shall devote one paragraph to each type, indicating where the arrow tends to lead one, and what is involved in going against the arrow. As you explain each of them, point to the appropriate arrows on the chart. Allow about four minutes to cover the material on each of the nine types.

For the 'Three' (the compulsive worker) the highest value is success; and what the 'Three' most avoids is failure. But failures do happen and if the 'Three' allows the compulsion to go unchecked then these will give rise to a sense of futility and frustration. The result is that the 'Three' is inclined to slide towards the indolent behaviour of the 'Nine' (— point this out on the chart). What the 'Three' has to learn above all is to come to terms with the fear of failure. This will allow such a person to be less hard-driving, more sensitive to others' needs and feelings, and more respectful of their rights. All this is likely to come about only when the person turns inward and recognises that it is the fear of failure and desire for success that is the dominant driving force in his or her life. An important step for the 'Three' in resisting the compulsion is to move against the arrow towards the 'Six' position. (Point out the direction on the chart). This involves greater respect for other members of the group (instead of pushing them) and more respect for rules and regulations (instead of subordinating them to the task in hand). In this the 'Three' is coming to accept that there are higher values than success.

For the 'Six' (the compulsively loyal person) the highest value is loyalty. What the 'Six' most wants to avoid is deviance from the group. If 'Sixes' allow themselves to yield frequently to the compulsion then they allow their anxiety and insecurity to push them into compulsive and destructive activity, acting rather like a neurotic 'Three'. In order to act against the compulsion they need instead to move towards the position of the 'Nine'. This means not yielding to anxiety but nurturing instead whatever element of tranquility they can find within themselves. So they come to be more at ease with themselves, less threatened by others. They become more sympathetic towards others — and much more tolerant. They resist the temptation to label others as being 'for me' or 'against me' and in this way they promote and experience harmony. Trust in themselves grows hand in hand with increasing trust of others. Instead of relying on authorities for security, the 'Six' now finds inner resources of peace and stability. Increasingly, such transformed 'Sixes' are able to offer support to others — and this brings them many real friends.

For the 'Nine' (the peace-seeker) the highest value is peace and harmony; and the thing most to be avoided is conflict. When such people slide along with their compulsion they subordinate the real needs of others to their own inner composure; they become quite lazy and neglectful of others and even of their own health, cutting themselves off more and more from the real world and its demands. Eventually they become overwhelmed by despair at their failure and/or by the anxiety which they have repressed up to now. To escape this, they begin to act like a very anxious and panicky 'Six', full of guilt directed at themselves and anger against others whom they label as 'enemies'. They seek security now in outside authorities and may become the victim of scruples. What 'Nines' really need to do is to move instead towards the space of the 'Three', becoming involved in work which gives them a sense of vitality and creativity. It also gives them something to stand for and to stand over; they have a feeling of achievement, which strengthens their sense of their own identity. 'Nines' who move against the compulsion by acting more like the 'Three' also become more con-cerned about what others think and feel about them. Setting out to impress others, they become less inclined to think that they themselves are of little importance. They grow in a sense of their own self-worth and come to be more in touch with their own deep feelings of love — for themselves and for others.

Now display a chart (Fig. 12) showing arrows leading from 'Two' to 'Eight', from 'Eight' to 'Five', from 'Five' to 'Seven', from 'Seven' to 'One', from 'One' to 'Four', and from 'Four' to 'Two'. These arrows show the direction in which each of these compulsions drag the person; and the challenge is to go against the direction of the arrows.

The highest value for the 'Two' (the compulsive 'helper') is the ability to give. What this person avoids most is the acknowledgement of his or her own needs. The temptation for the 'Two' is to keep repressing these needs until they can

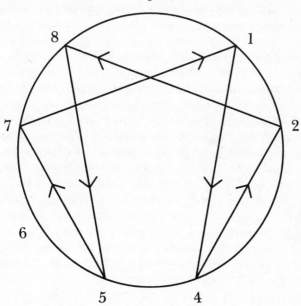

Fig. 12

no longer be resisted; then they come out in a destructive way, through an outburst of aggression. The anger and hatred which had been bottled up are now poured out against those who have not given the 'Two' the love that he or she was looking for; and this happens in such a violent way that it makes the situation even worse. So, through yielding to the compulsion, the 'Two' begins to act like the 'Eight'. (Point out the arrow on the chart.) In order to fight against the compulsion, the 'Two' needs to move against the arrow, that is, in the direction of the 'Four'. This means learning to be more aware of one's own special character and particular needs; and learning to be more assertive about what one really wants, instead of expecting others to know this without being told. It involves acknowledging those feelings that are apprehended as negative, rather than repressing them. The 'helper' must learn to *ask* at times for understanding, care, and attention — instead of trying to manipulate others into giving them without being asked.

259

For the 'Four' (the compulsively special person) the highest value is uniqueness or being special; and what such people wish most of all to avoid is being 'ordinary'. They are tempted to withdraw from real life into their inner world — a world of feelings and imagination. If they give way regularly to their compulsion they become more and more introspective and morbid. Then they find themselves getting lost in despair. In a desperate effort to avoid this, they may begin to act like a 'Two'. (Point this out on the chart.) As a 'Two', they can be clinging on to somebody else; or they despair of 'saving' themselves and begin to project their problems on to others and then find some satisfaction in rescuing these other people. This is an unhealthy direction for the 'Four'. What the 'Four' needs to do in order to go against the compulsion is to move towards the 'One' position, instead of giving in to morbidity and hopelessness they begin to fight against the evil they experience around them. This turns them outward to the real world and helps them to put their special gifts at the service of others.

Being right is the highest value for the 'One' (the compulsive perfectionist); and what this person wants most to avoid is anger. The perfectionist who gives way to the compulsion becomes more and more intolerant, judgmental, and critical — and therefore gets into conflict with others and feels misunderstood by them. This sense of being different and misunderstood pushes the person towards the 'Four' position, which is not healthy for the 'One'. Perfectionists may also retreat to the 'Four' position, because they feel totally swamped by all the work that is to be done, and/or overwhelmed by self-hatred for being evil and a failure; so the best way out seems to be to give up in despair. What 'Ones' need to do instead is to live out of the 'Child' part of themselves, the part that is more spontaneous. This involves a movement towards the 'Seven' position. They begin to enjoy parties and may become witty entertainers there. Light-hearted activity helps to dissipate their repressed anger; and this sets them free of the constant pressure to change other people and the world. They become more tolerant of others, and more friendly with them. All this helps to liberate them from the compulsion to be perfect and make everything else perfect. It makes them more objective also, because they begin to accept reality as it is rather than seeing it exclusively in terms of what they think it ought to be.

'Feeling fine' is the highest value for the 'Seven' (the compulsive optimist); and what this type of person most wishes to avoid is pain. When 'Sevens' yield regularly to the compulsion they get more and more manic and out of control. Their hopes and plans have then no hope of working out. Frustration builds up and the 'Seven' begins to slide towards the worst aspects of the 'One' — the resentment and poorly repressed anger of the person who thinks things should be perfect. The 'Seven' then becomes aggressive and perhaps impulsively violent. In order to resist the compulsion the 'Seven' needs instead to move towards the 'Five' space. They develop reflective capacity and face up more objectively to reality. They begin to go deeper and to experience greater inner peace and security. They are then able to accept that pain and evil are part of the reality of human life. As they become more free of the compulsive need to gratify themselves and avoid pain at all costs, their capacity for enjoyment is transformed into a contemplative gratitude for life in its fullness.

For the 'Five' (the compulsive observer) the highest values are perceptiveness and wisdom. What the 'Five' tries most to avoid is emptiness — and this is to be done by observing and understanding reality. The danger is that he or she will substitute thinking for doing, and even for reality. Those 'Fives' who slide along with their compulsion find it carries them in the direction of the 'Seven'. At that stage these 'Fives' have retreated further from reality and are seeking to avoid the pain of the real world. So they may plunge into irresponsible and/or aggressive behaviour, or alternatively into escapes such as looking at one video after another. In order to go against their compulsion the 'Fives' need to move towards the position of the 'Eight'. This means that instead of withdrawing from life they become engaged. They may not know everything that could be known about the matter in hand, but they have come to accept that they probably know at least as much as others. Furthermore, they now realise that the way to learn more is to become more involved rather than merely observing from outside. And by

261

becoming assertive and involved in action like the 'Eight' they get in touch with their own 'gut centre' which may be a source of deeper wisdom than their heads, on which they have relied too exclusively in the past.

For the 'Eight' (the compulsively aggressive person) the highest value is strength; and what is most to be avoided is weakness. When such people yield to their compulsion they become very aggressive and destructive. This gives rise to so much opposition that they feel the need to be less impulsive and to plan their actions more carefully. So they tend to retreat towards the 'Five' position. This is not a healthy move for them, since it is not motivated by concern for others. It is rather an effort to save their own skins by being more cunning in their use of power. Furthermore, it cuts them off more completely from other people. What people of this type need to do is to move towards the 'Two' position. This means giving up the effort to control and dominate those around them, and beginning instead to take care of them. It means adapting to others, trying to please them. At its best it means that these 'Eights' become willing to sacrifice themselves generously for others. So they grow in respect for the people with whom they come into contact; and they become deeply loving people, much more in touch with their own hearts, and therefore able to touch the hearts of others. In this way their love for power finds a fulfillment that they could not have dreamed of when they were under the sway of the compulsion: they come to realise that the greatest power of all is not to be in control of others but to love them unselfishly.

SECTION FOUR:
POLITICAL AND RELIGIOUS ASPECTS

I suggest that the fourth two-hour session be divided in two. In the first hour the participants will have the opportunity to see what light the Enneagram throws on the way they behave in political matters. The second hour will be a time of quiet reflection in which each person will have time to put into an explicitly religious context the insight that may have come as a result of this introduction to the Enneagram.

I first heard of 'The Three Cs' as an exercise which we learned and taught in psycho-social workshops in Africa.[2] We used to say that the three 'Cs' represent three words beginning with the letter 'C' — 'Cooperate', 'Campaign for awareness' and 'Confront'. But I found that the words 'campaign' and 'confront' seem rather militant to some people; so I now prefer to say that the three 'Cs' stand for 'Cooperate', 'Canvass' and 'Challenge'. The exercise can be used when a group have a certain practical goal in mind but find that its attainment is being blocked. The members of the group are asked to list those who agree with this goal; and then to plan a process of *cooperation* with these people. Next, they list those who seem to be indifferent but who would derive some benefit from having this goal attained; and then the group go on to plan ways to *canvass support* from these people. Finally they list those who are blocking the achievement of the goal; and they plan ways to *challenge* these individuals or groups.

Within the past couple of years I have come to believe that 'The Three Cs' should be seen not just as one out of many exercises that are useful in planning. I now see these three approaches — cooperation, canvassing support, and challenging — as lying at the heart of any political activity that is to be both effective and respectful. And the crucial discernment that has to be made is *which* one of these three approaches is appropriate on any particular occasion. Very often I have seen excellent projects fail because the leaders challenged others when they should have been cooperating with them or canvassing their support. On other occasions I have seen good plans come to nothing because the leaders assumed that as committed Christians they were obliged to cooperate with everybody; so they wasted their energy trying to cooperate with those who were blocking the project.

A shrewd political assessment of the situation is required if one is to know whether to challenge, to cooperate, or to canvass support. But if I am trying to make such a political assessment, my judgment will be clouded by prejudices or compulsive elements in my own personality. For instance, I might be the kind of person who is afraid to challenge anybody; or, alternatively, I might be an aggressive kind of person who challenges people when that is quite inappropriate. At this point it will be evident that the Enneagram has political implications. There is no need for me to spell this out in detail, since it is the kind of material that people can find in their own experience. And the sharing of such personal experience can be very valuable, interesting, and even exciting. However, I shall mention some examples to indicate the kind of thing I have in mind.

John is a very gifted person who has been elected as a member of the local council in his area. But he is a 'Nine' by temperament, which means that he is inclined to avoid situations of conflict. So when he finds himself in a situation that clearly requires that he challenge somebody else, he is very uncomfortable. To escape this, he is inclined to find excuses or even to allow his judgment of the situation to become clouded; he deludes himself into thinking that another effort at cooperation may have the desired effect. So, how does he overcome this weakness? Since studying the Enneagram he has begun to tackle the difficulty at two distinct levels. Firstly, he is working to overcome the compulsion by 'going against the arrow', which means committing himself wholeheartedly to various projects, and investing a lot of his energy in their success. This makes it more likely that he will challenge those who block the attainment of the goals he has set himself. Secondly, John has teamed up with another member of the local council, somebody who is an 'Eight'. This companion is much more ready to challenge others — in fact too eager at times to do so! Each of them has succeeded in attaining a much more balanced outlook, by sharing their impressions and being willing to learn from the other.

A second example: Joan is a religious sister and a member of a 'Justice and Peace' committee. She is a 'One' and is therefore inclined to be something of a crusader, always wanting to change the world. Now that she has become aware of the compulsive elements in this tendency, she has begun to take herself less seriously, to act more like the 'Seven'. This does not mean that she has abandoned the various good causes in which she had been involved. But now she concentrates more attention on the 'fun side': for instance, she plays a very active part in the festivals and parties which marginalised groups organise for themselves. This helps to give a balance to her life and to her political activity.

It is important that the resource-person should not spend too much time talking to the group. Having given two or three examples of the kind I have just mentioned, ask the participants to divide into small groups and to spend about half an hour exploring their own political experiences. They can then go on to consider how knowledge of the Enneagram may, in the future, help them to be more objective in discerning the most appropriate type of political activity, whether it be cooperation, canvassing of support, or challenging what they consider to be wrong. It will be helpful if each small group brings back one or two practical examples to the large group.

Religious Context

It is obvious that the Enneagram has very important religious implications. It throws a lot of light on how we can grow and where the grace of God needs to work in us in regard to our personal development, our community relationships, and our political commitments. All this is such a delicate matter that in this introduction to the Enneagram I think it is best to allow participants to explore these areas for themselves in a quiet and gentle way. So I suggest that you invite them to spend the final hour of the fourth session in a guided meditation on Psalm 139.

Having begun in the usual manner by helping the group to sit in a correct posture and centring themselves, lead the meditation by reading some passages from the psalm, against a background of quiet meditative music. If you feel it is appro   te, you may wish to make some connections betwe   Enneagram and the words of the psalm. For ins   icipants may have adverted to the
                     personality patterns were deter-
                    ; or they may have seen the hand of
                  such remarks might be recalled or
                er. But, on the whole, I think it may be
              nd more effective — to allow the words
           eak to the participants without any overt
          ne prayer with the Enneagram:

265

God, you examine me and you know me
you know everything I do;
from far away you understand all my thoughts,
you see me, whether I am working or resting;
you know all my actions.

Even before I speak
you already know what I will say,
you are all around me, on every side;
you protect me with your power;
your knowledge of me is overwhelming,
too deep for me to understand.

Where could I go to escape from your spirit?
Where could I get away from your presence?
If I went up to the heavens, you would be there;
if I lay down in the world of the dead, you would be there.
If I flew away beyond the east,
or travelled to the farthest point in the west
you would be there to help,
with hand outstretched to lead me.
I could ask the darkness to hide me,
or the light around me to turn into night,
but even the darkness is not dark for you,
and the night is as bright as the day;
darkness and light are the same to you.

You created my inmost being;
you put me together in my mother's womb.
Trembling, I praise and thank you,
as I marvel at the wonder of your action.
You saw me before ever I was born,
you saw my bones take shape,
you watched as my body grew
in the secrecy of my mother's womb.
You counted out all my days
before ever I came to live them.

God, how incomprehensible are your thoughts,
how many of them there are!
To count them would be like counting grains of sand
and if I could finish, your mystery would remain.

Examine me, God, and know my heart,
Delve deep and see my inmost thoughts;
show up whatever deceit is in me,
and guide me on the way to fullness of life.

NOTES

1. Those who wish to study the topic in more depth could read one of the following books: Don Richard Riso, *Personality Types: Using the Enneagram for Self-Discovery*, Boston (Houghton Mifflin Company: 1987); Maria Beesing, Robert J. Nogosek, and Patrick H. O'Leary, *The Enneagram: A Journey of Self Discovery*, Denville N.J. (Dimension Books: 1984). There are also in circulation several sets of privately published tapes and notes on the Enneagram.

2. See Anne Hope and Sally Timmel, *Training for Transformation: A Handbook for Community Workers*, Gwero, Zimbabwe (Mambo Press: 1984), Bk 2, pp 104-6.

9

Where Does God Come In?

In the previous eight chapters of this book I have been exploring some of the human or worldly values that are characteristic of the person who walks in the footsteps of Jesus. In this chapter I shall propose a way of understanding the relationship between these *human* values and our response to *God*. I hope that this will help to overcome the difficulty that many people have in integrating their relationship to God with their deep moral and political commitments.

SECTION ONE: LEVELS OF SPIRITUALITY

It may be helpful to recall the diagram of three interlocking circles which I used in the introduction to indicate the different aspects of spirituality. Our relationship with God is not represented by any specific section of that diagram. This is not because God is outside our spirituality but precisely because our relationship with God suffuses *all* of our spirituality. One might think of God as being beneath and above the whole picture. God is always present to us in our efforts to be more human. The only question is whether or not we are present to God in these efforts — in our successes and even in our failures.

Spirituality is a rather vague word. Its meaning can include almost any activity we engage in or any of our attitudes or commitments or feelings. Because it can mean nearly anything, the danger is that it will come to mean nothing in particular. In order to try to 'pin it down' a little I suggest we make a distinction. We can distinguish between, on the one hand, a spirituality as a religious *tradition* into which people may be 'formed' or moulded, and, on the other hand, spirituality as a set of *personal attitudes* and commitments. I shall spell out these two meanings in turn.

Spirituality as a Tradition

In one sense a spirituality is a particular religious tradition that may have existed long before you were born, a tradition which moulds your religious sensibilities and attitudes in a particular way. When we speak of the 'Puritan' tradition we are referring to a spirituality which inculcated a certain strictness and even severity in moral and religious attitudes. Similarly, a Zen Buddhist spirituality is one that inculcates a deep peace and detachment in those who live according to this way of life. These are traditions into which people may be born; but there may also be a tradition of spirituality which one freely *chooses*. For instance, some people choose to live in a religious community because they are attracted by its Franciscan or its Ignatian spirituality; more recently, a lot of people have taken up the spirituality of the fraternities of Charles de Foucauld. Nowadays quite a lot of Christian or post-Christian people have experimented with various versions of Indian spirituality — for instance with yoga or transcendental meditation.

Before ever there was a Franciscan tradition of spirituality there was Francis, trying to live an authentic human life and to be open to God. So if we want to understand what spirituality is, it is not enough to look at the traditions. We have to look at the personal stories and dramas of founding figures — people who tried to live authentically and to be open to God — at Catherine Macauley and John Calvin, at Ignatius Loyola and Teresa of Avila and John Wesley, at The Buddha and Charles de Foucauld and Julian of Norwich. These are individuals who stand at the source of different traditions of spirituality.

Spirituality as Personal

Almost all of us have been moulded in one or another tradition of spirituality — though we may not have been aware of it. We may be well on in life before we realise that something which we had always assumed was 'the right thing to do' is in fact simply the way we learned to act as children; it was part of the tradition in which we (but not others) were moulded. But any such tradition, no matter how powerful it be, becomes fully effective only when a person begins to appropriate it personally. So each of us has to look at his or her own personal experience of spirituality. We can fully understand the stories of the great founder figures, and the different traditions which they began, only to the extent that these find echoes in our own *personal* experience of trying to be fully human and responsive to God or to the call of the transcendent. So spirituality in its most basic sense is a deeply personal thing.

From a personal point of view, my spirituality is that which from within me and beyond me calls me to be more authentically human, more fully all that God has destined me to be. I say it is a call that comes from *beyond* me because as a Christian I believe that the Holy Spirit speaks to my spirit, inviting me to a fulfillment beyond all my imagining. But the call also comes from *within* me because the Spirit does not remain outside but moves and moulds me, so that the voice of the Spirit becomes my own inner voice as well (cf Rom 8:16). This joint call of the Holy Spirit and of the deepest part of my own spirit is an invitation to me to respond. And, if I choose to answer authentically, my response will have two distinct moments:

— A contemplative moment; for instance, allowing myself to be moved by the beauty of nature, or by the mystery of another person, or by the experience of God's providence, or by the experience of solidarity with people who are poor or powerless.

— An active moment; for instance, helping poor people or working to promote peace, or to care for our planet.

My spirituality is more than just a call; it also includes the *power* or strength to respond. So it might be described as that which leads me beyond my present limitations towards what I am called to be. Ultimately, my spirituality will be the 'shape' of my spirit. For I am confident that, as I allow myself to be led, I am growing and becoming what I am called to be. I now experience a wide gap between that destiny and my present inadequate stance or 'shape'. But my life's task is to allow the gap to be narrowed by God's grace and my own response, so that eventually I grow into my destiny. Then this part of God's creation will be complete; and my every action and response will be that of the person God has known and loved from the beginning and has led to perfection 'with leading strings of love' (Hos 11:4).

Having explored the distinction between spirituality as a tradition and spirituality as personal, we can now move on to look at a further distinction that needs to be made. This is the distinction between spirituality as a relationship with God and spirituality as a set of attitudes towards the world. We can begin by looking at Moses. Obviously he had a spirituality (though he probably did not use that term); and it can be summed up in the two words Yahweh and Exodus:

— 'Yahweh' was the God revealed to Moses as the one who is always near to help;

— the 'Exodus' was the journey out of slavery through the desert into the Promised Land.

It is a misleading question to ask which of these two was the more important; to give priority to one or other would involve us in what the philosophers call 'a category mistake', putting into the same category two things that are not comparable. For Moses felt himself called by God to lead the people out of slavery into a land of their own. His relationship to Yahweh developed in and through his involvement in the Exodus events. The religious challenge for Moses was to trust Yahweh, to believe that God was on his side in the struggle for political freedom. So both the political aspect and the religious aspect were integral to the spirituality of Moses.

I believe that the situation for us today is similar. If we develop a healthy spirituality it is bound to have two dimensions: a living relationship with the God who comes close to us, and a practical earthly commitment to human liberation in one form or another. This conclusion is supported by the accounts people give of their own spirituality. When I ask people what the word 'spirituality' means to them I get two kinds of answer. On the one hand, many people respond in terms of their relationship to God and Jesus Christ; this is the strictly religious dimension of spirituality. On the other hand, quite a lot of people speak about such things as their commitment to peace-making, or to seeking justice for the oppressed, or to the building of community; or they refer to their search for personal authenticity, or their sense of being at one with nature; these are included in what I call the moral-political dimension of spirituality. For most Christians an integral spirituality seems to embrace *both* of these kinds

271

of experience. In practice the two are closely linked. But I find it helpful to distinguish between the two, purely for the purposes of analysis — and I base this distinction on the fact that they correspond to two different levels of transcendence. I shall try to explain what I mean by this.

Two Levels of Transcendence

Spirituality is not confined to one particular set of actions such as praying or reflecting; rather it is concerned with the unfolding of the deeper dimensions of *everything* I do or say or feel. I use the word 'unfold' to indicate that the deeper significance is already present in a latent way, though it may not be articulated clearly. For instance, if a beggar comes to the door, your response may seem to be determined by convenience or your established habit; but it is very likely that your response will reflect your basic attitude to poverty and to the victims of society. These attitudes 'transcend' your immediate convenience or concerns. So I would see them as part of your spirituality. Another example: I walk alone each morning. My obvious and immediate purpose is to get fresh air, to get my energy flowing, to take in the beauty of the surroundings, to be away from distractions. But there is also a deeper purpose: the walk puts me in touch with myself, it brings me some sense of being integrated and at peace. So I see this quiet walk as very important from the point of view of my spirituality. It helps me to 'transcend' or go beyond my immediate concerns in order to ensure that I have a coherent purpose and direction in my life. And it helps me lessen the gap between my professed values and the way I live in practice.

This is the first level of transcendence; it is the point where we have gone beyond immediate concerns and desires and are in touch with the underlying moral or political values that shape our lives. These values determine the 'worldly' (or 'human') aspect of our spirituality, giving it its own unique complexion. For instance, the spirituality of one person may give a central role to service of the poor, while that of another may give more weight to peace-making, or to ecological issues, or to animal suffering.

There is a second level of transcendence which we touch when we advert to the fact that it is *God* who is calling us to respond to values such as justice, authenticity, respect for

272

people and nature, etc. Where the first level of transcendence carried us beyond the everyday to the deeper values, the second level carries us beyond the values to God, the source and end of all value. This may seem complicated, but it becomes more clear when we recall the example of Moses. His commitment to the liberation of his people and his hope for the Promised Land gave a purpose to his life and enabled him to judge whether or not his activity was worthwhile. This is the first level of transcendence. But behind his commitment and hope was his awareness of a loving and powerful God who called him, spoke to him, led him, challenged him, even punished him — but who was always there as the source of his commitment and his hope.

This relationship with God is what I am calling the second level of transcendence. It is not in competition with the first level. It is not as though the spirituality of some people is based on the struggle for justice while that of others is based on a relationship with God. For God is beyond the world and cannot therefore be in competition with any 'earthly' value such as justice or care for the earth. To ask us to choose between God and human values is to reduce God to the position of an idol, something worldly that has been turned into an ultimate value.

Precisely because God is transcendent, beyond the world, our way to God involves commitment to 'worldly' values. We see this not only in the life of Moses but also in that of Jesus. Compassion, simplicity, integrity, gentleness and concern for the common people, especially for the outcasts and those in trouble — these were the values to which Jesus devoted himself. And this was the way in which he carried out the will of the One who sent him. What God asked of him was that he be faithful to the task he had come to do *in the world* — faithful even unto death.

The transcendent God who became present and active in the life of Jesus becomes present in our world also, by calling us to the deeply human values that Jesus stood for. As followers of Jesus we learn that our relationship with God cannot be detached from our relations with other people and the world. For it is human values such as gentleness, justice, fidelity, and integrity that provide the *terrain* on which we travel on our journey to God, the *topics* for our

273

dialogue with God, and the *occasions* for our failures, for our experience of forgiveness, and for our ever-fragile and ever-renewed hope of reaching God.

I conclude this section by recalling again the two levels or aspects of spirituality.

— Firstly, there is our attempt to live a fully human life, a life after the pattern of Jesus, a life permeated by such values as personal responsibility, respect for others, and transformation of society.

— Secondly, there is our experience of being in personal contact with God in and through our commitment to such a fully human life — and also in our inadequacies and failures in this commitment.

My hope is that both the more theoretical-reflective material and the practical exercises and resources of this book will help those who read and use it to experience how close is the link between these two aspects of an authentically integrated spirituality.

SECTION TWO: NOT MY WILL BUT YOURS

Despite the close link between the 'worldly' (or 'human') aspect of spirituality and the explicitly divine aspect many religious people seem on occasion to experience a tension or even a conflict between the two. I can illustrate this by means of an example. Sister Mary has announced that she wants to leave the school in which she is teaching successfully in order to go and share the life of the poor people of a slum area. Those who have been elected to be responsible for the community are not happy about this. Even the members of her own community have begun to criticise her for wanting to 'do her own thing' in going to live with the poor. They say she should sacrifice her own wishes in the interests of the children she is teaching and in obedience to the will of those who are in charge of the community.

It is not helpful to articulate the issue in this way, in terms of a simple choice between self-fulfillment and self-sacrifice. The difficulty stems from the fact that though each of these concepts has a valid meaning, both can very easily be misunderstood when they are used in the context of spirituality. I want to suggest that all that is best in the two concepts can be brought together in the notion of self-transcendence.

274

In order to explain what I mean I shall start with the Gospel. Jesus willingly laid down his life for his friends (Jn 15:13); he even made us his friends by giving his life for us (Rom 5:8). This is obviously *self-sacrifice* of the highest order. But death was not the end of Jesus. He committed his life into the hands of the God he called 'Abba' — and God raised him to a new life (Rom 15:15). His self-sacrifice was the passage into the fullness of human life — into *fulfillment.*

In his teaching Jesus brought out the same idea. The seed that is to bear fruit must fall into the ground and die; and the person that tries to hold on to life will lose it (Jn 12:24-25). But the death of the seed is not an end in itself; rather it is the necessary means by which the seed achieves its purpose. The new life of the plant is a fuller life than that of the seed, and similarly Christ's new life beyond death is a more fully human life than he had before. What is promised is more than just restoration of the old life. There is rather a *self-transcendence*, a going beyond the old in order to attain its fulfillment.

It is only against this background that we can understand correctly the Agony prayer of Jesus: 'Not my will but yours be done'. This act of commitment was the climax of hours of struggle in prayer. The Gospels make it perfectly clear that what Jesus was struggling to do in that prayer was not to *abandon* his own deepest will but to be *faithful* to it — despite the horror and shrinking he experienced in face of the prospect of his utter rejection and death.

Distortions

The Christian teaching on the need for generous self-sacrifice became impoverished because people failed to see the link between Christ's life, death, and resurrection. Furthermore, it got distorted by a kind of dualism which exaggerated the difference between this life and the next. It was assumed that only the life hereafter was really important — and even that our happiness in the next life was in proportion to our renunciation and suffering in this life.

Some years ago I was preaching in a small village in Ireland and I commented on the Scripture reading which spoke of Christian joy. I said that if we expect to be joyful in heaven we must surely be able to be joyful in this life. Somebody must

275

have mentioned what I said to one of the priests in the parish because a few days later he said to me: 'some of the people misunderstood your sermon— they thought you said that you cannot be happy in heaven if you are not happy in this life'. That was quite close to what I had said; but the priest was so sure that the idea was wrong that he assumed I had been misunderstood!

Just as the idea of self-sacrifice has got distorted, so too has the idea of self-fulfillment. One reason for this is that it developed in a Western culture which is profoundly marked by individualism. People in the West have to a large extent lost the sense of community. As a result the notion of personal fulfillment is understood in a very self-centered way — even at times in a selfish way.

In sharp contrast to this, the Christian concept of the human good does not subordinate the person to the community nor the community to the individual. Rather, we understand the community to be composed of uniquely important individuals. When I seek to do 'the right thing' I cannot do so on the assumption that it is to be found either through a selfish commitment to following out my own ideas, or through an unlimited sacrifice of my own needs to the needs or the will of others.

How then are we to resolve the apparent conflict between self-fulfillment (meeting my own needs) and self-sacrifice (meeting the needs of others)? For the Christian who follows the practice and the teaching of Jesus there lies at the heart of spirituality a resolution to this tension: self-giving can be experienced as the noblest form of self-fulfillment. This is not a self-giving which relinquishes the need for self-fulfillment; rather it attains a truly human fulfillment through self-transcendence — through freely going beyond what would normally be understood as one's own self-interest.

How does this view stand up in the case of the supreme sacrifice made by such a person as Maximilian Kolbe, who in a Nazi concentration camp generously offered himself to be killed instead of another prisoner? What moved him to give himself this way was not just his awareness of the other prisoner's need to escape death, but also a certain personal call experienced by Kolbe — a call to a noble fulfillment. At that moment he felt called to give a final meaning and value

276

to his own life by sacrificing himself. He was laying down his life for his friend, as Jesus did.

Kolbe did not sacrifice himself in the sense of subordinating himself entirely to the other. There is a deep human instinct which assures us that to give one's life for another or for a noble cause may at times be the highest way of fulfilling oneself. The Christian who reflects on the death and resurrection of Christ finds there an explicit expression of that profound truth and a model to follow in living it out.

God's Will — or Mine?

At first sight all this may seem to be a philosophical issue rather than one that concerns spirituality. But I have spent time on it because the notion of self-transcendence helps to resolve an issue that arises very frequently for religious people, namely, an apparent conflict between 'my own will' and 'God's will'.

The religious person wants to do 'the will of God'. But 'God's will' is not something different from what is ethically 'the right thing'; it is not normally discovered in some way that is independent of the discernment we undertake to find out what is the morally correct thing for us to do. That in turn involves a balancing of different values — the needs of the community, my own needs, and the call I experience to fulfill myself by giving myself generously (but not rashly or blindly) to others.

However, the committed Christian is not content to engage in a purely ethical evaluation of the situation. Alongside this there is the need to *pray* about it, to ask God for the wisdom that enables one to choose correctly. In prayer we often go even further: we ask to be shown what is 'the will of God'. Even though 'God's will' may *in fact* be the same thing as 'the right thing', nevertheless the *mode* in which it is discerned can have a very different flavour for the person who discerns it in prayer than it has for one who sits down 'to work it out'. If I spend an hour contemplating a scene in the life of Jesus I may find afterwards that I have a strong sense of being called to some specific line of action in my own life — for instance, to seek reconciliation with somebody whom I have hurt, or, on the other hand, to challenge somebody who has wronged me. Anybody who prays seriously will have had the experience

277

of receiving such 'answers' through prayer. There is a real sense in which such inspiration comes from 'beyond' me; the least one can say is that it comes from a deeper part of my spirit, a part that is more open to the movement of the Spirit of God. I discussed this issue a little more fully — and in a more experiential manner — in chapter 2, especially the part where I wrote about 'listening to Jesus'.

How can we know?

Alongside this process of discerning through prayer we *also* have to engage in a more general moral discernment about what we ought to do, how we ought to respond to the various 'calls' we experience. The general norms that govern our behaviour establish certain limits but they do not normally tell us which is the best of the many concrete choices open to us. There is no substitute for wisdom which is both a gift and something we must strive to develop.

Those who are trying to grow in practical wisdom may perhaps derive some benefit from an insight I got a couple of years ago. I came to realise that each of us has a kind of thermometer which we can use to help us discern whether in fact what we are doing is the will of God. The 'thermometer' is myself, what is happening to me. If I want to know whether I am doing the work God wants me to do, it is not sufficient to ask the question: 'am I doing good work, are people bene-fitting from what I am doing?' A second and more important question is: 'in doing this good work am I growing in the love of God, growing in the sense of God's presence in my life and work, growing in freedom of spirit, and in openness to others?' That, in practice, is the real test. Unless I can say 'yes' to this second question then I have to think seriously about changing either my work or the way I am doing it.

What I am saying is that the criterion by which I can assess whether I am doing God's will is the extent to which I am fulfilled by the work, rather than the extent to which my work is helping others. But the 'fulfillment' I have in mind here is not a narrow individualistic furthering of my own interests. It is rather the flourishing of the deepest part of me which is an openness to God, to other people, and to the world.

The most profound element in my personality is a call and inclination to self-transcendence. Not a transcending of

278

myself in the sense of abandoning my present personality and interests. It is not a question of giving up my desire to grow and flourish. Rather it is coming to realise that I am most fulfilled, most true to myself, when I give myself generously to others. And this is not some abstract theological principle to be accepted in faith and followed blindly. It is a matter of experience. I want to stress this last point strongly. For me as a Christian it must be a matter of *experience*, as it was for Christ, that 'my food is to do the will of the one who sent me' (Jn 4:34). Like Christ I must be able to say from experience that 'I have a baptism in which I am to be immersed and what a great tension I am experiencing until that fulfillment comes about.' (Lk 12:50).

So I myself am the 'thermometer'; I have to judge by my own deepest experience. But this 'thermometer' has to be used judiciously. For instance I can expect that when I take on a new task I may well experience personal disruption and confusion for quite some time. Therefore, what I have to measure is not how I find the work at any given moment but rather what is happening to me over a significant period of time — perhaps a few months or longer. We can be quite sure that God does not want any one of us to be completely weighed down or broken in spirit by our work, our life-style, or even by our companions.

I venture to offer a rule of thumb that may help us to apply this principle in practice. Suppose I find that I am over-worked or hassled or so pressured that I cannot pray properly, or I am not able to be open to the people around me. For anything up to six months I may be entitled to blame others for putting me in that situation. But if I continue like that after about six months then I have to take responsibility for it myself. It may not be my fault that I got *into* the situation; but six months should be long enough for me to realise what is happening and to discover some way *out*. The way out does not necessarily have to involve leaving the situation entirely; it may be a matter of finding others to share the load, or of learning techniques to prevent the load weighing me down.

A Risk

I am very aware that there is a danger in what I am saying here. There is an obvious risk of abuse and self-deception. Since the 'thermometer' is really myself, my own assessment of my own experience, it is quite possible that I may be mistaken; I may even delude myself. I may be making poor decisions and justifying them to myself and others by invoking my incorrect evaluation of the effects on my life. Occasionally we see people who are obviously out of touch with themselves, people who are probably deceiving themselves; and no doubt this happens in some degree to all of us.

We may be tempted to solve the problem by seeking some more 'objective' standard of judgment — for instance the considered judgment of a superior or advisor. But there is no easy way to avoid this difficulty. Handing myself over entirely to the judgment of another is not a way out; in fact it may even make it worse. For my judgment about whom to trust may itself be clouded; and the assessment by the other person of what is right for me may also be mistaken. Of course I must ask advice of others. And if I have a 'religious superior' I am committed to having a high degree of trust in that person's judgment. But in the last analysis I have to take responsibility for my own decision to accept or reject the judgment of another person.

Since I cannot evade the responsibility, I can only do my best to avoid self-deception. What this means in practice is to ensure as far as possible that my heart, my affectivity, is truly converted. This change of heart leads on to a change of mind. As St Paul says, 'offer yourselves as a living sacrifice to God and . . . let God transform you inwardly by a complete change of your mind. Then you will be able to know the will of God, what is good, what is pleasing to God, and what is the perfect thing to do' (Rom 12:1-2).

Letting Go

I conclude these reflections by recalling a personal experience I had very recently. I was a member of the facilitation team for an international assembly of lay missionaries. The keynote address was given by the well-known spiritual writer Gerard Hughes S.J. He concluded it with this 17th century Hindu prayer:

280

Take Lord unto Thyself my sense of self.
Let it vanish utterly.
Take Lord my life; live Thou thy life through me.
I live no longer Lord, but in me Thou livest.
Aye, between Thee and me, God,
  there is no longer room for 'I' and 'mine'.

I was very moved by the talk as a whole, but some deep part of me reacted strongly against this little concluding prayer. It seemed so unreal: what could it possibly mean for me to 'vanish utterly'? That afternoon when we resumed the working sessions of the assembly a very difficult issue arose. I found myself floundering in the facilitation; some strong members of the group were unwilling to follow the procedure I was proposing. Eventually, I was 'rescued' by another member of the facilitation team, and things began to move smoothly again.

Late that night I went for a walk alone under the stars. I found my heart almost bursting with happiness over what had happened. There was also some pain, of course: that I hadn't got my way, that I had been shown to be weak, that I needed to be rescued. But that pain was suffused with a deep joy — joy that the group had resolved the difficulty and that my colleague had the courage and skill to intervene when she did. I knew that God was having a busy time all during this assembly, ensuring that it went well; but at that moment I felt that God had taken a little time out just to teach me the meaning of the Hindu prayer which I had rejected that morning. Now I knew in a very practical way what it meant for me to lose my sense of self and to 'vanish utterly'. It implied being able to let go (for that moment at least) of my own concerns, my own self-importance. It meant being able to rejoice in all the good things that had happened as a result of my 'failure'. It meant experiencing fulfillment in self-sacrifice — to such an extent that I couldn't even begin to think of it as a 'sacrifice' in any conventional moral sense. It was an experience of self-transcendence.

SECTION THREE: RESOURCES

In this section I include a hymn, a poem, a short dialogue with God, and a song. The hymn is the well-known one which sums up much of what I have been saying in the past nine chapters; it is entitled 'Walk Humbly with Your God.[1]

Chorus:
This is what Yahweh asks of you, only this:
that you act justly, that you love tenderly,
that you walk humbly with your God.

I

My children I am with you such a little while,
and where I go now you cannot come.
A new commandment I give to you:
as I have loved you, so love each other.

II

Do not let your hearts be troubled;
trust in God now, and trust in me.
I go to prepare a place for you,
and I shall come again to take you home.

III

Peace is the gift I leave with you,
a peace the world can never give.
If you keep my word my Father will love you,
and we will come to you to make our home.

This poem is by the Irish poet Brendan Kennelly; it speaks of the hope that keeps us going in spite of everything.[2]

Begin

Begin again to the carolling birds,
To the sight of light at the window,
Begin to the roar of morning traffic
All along Pembroke Road.
Every beginning is a promise
Born in light and dying in dark,
Daily deception and exultation
Of Springtime flowering the way to work.
Begin to the pageant of queueing girls,
To the lonely arrogance of swans in the canal,
To bridges linking the past and future,
To old friends passing though with us still.

Begin to the treasures that we have squandered,
To the profit and loss, the pleasure and pain,
Begin to the knowledge that to-morrow
Is another beginning for every man.
Begin to the loneliness that cannot end
Since it perhaps is what makes us begin,
Begin to wonder at unknown faces,
At crying birds and the sudden rain,
At branches stark in the winter sunlight,
At seagulls foraging for bread,
At couples sharing a sunny secret
Alone together while making good.
Begin to the surge of the waking city,
To familiar streets that are always strange,
To words of greeting in the Dublin morning
Proving that we have come through again.
Blessed with the promise and disappointment
That make the minutes of every day,
We step into the streets of morning
Walking the pavements of come-what-may,
Though we live in a world that thinks of ending,
That always seems about to give in,
Something that will not acknowledge conclusion
Insists what we forever begin.

The following dialogue, entitled 'Covenant', was written by
Margaret Halaska. It suggests something of the unconditional
and infinitely patient love of God:

God knocks at my door, seeking a home for Jesus.
'The rent is cheap', I say.
'I don't want to rent, I want to buy', says God.
'I'm not sure I want to sell,
but you may come in and look around.'
'I think I will', says God.

'I might let you have a room or two.'
'I like it,' says God, 'I'll take the two.
You might decide to give me more some day.
I can wait', says God.

'I'd like to give you more but it's a bit difficult —
I need some space for me.'
'I know', says God, 'but I'll wait;
I like what I see.'

'Hm, maybe I can let you have another room;
I really don't need that much.'
'Thanks', says God, 'I'll take it;
I like what I see.'

'I'd like to give you the whole house, but I'm not sure . . . '
'Think about it', says God, 'I wouldn't put you out;
your house would be mine and Jesus would live in it.
You'd have more space than you ever had before.'

'I don't understand at all.'
'I know', says God, 'but I can't tell you about that;
you'll have to discover it for yourself;
that can only happen if you let him have the whole house.'

'A bit risky', I say.
'Yes', says God, 'but try me.'

'I'm not sure; I'll let you know.'
'I can wait', says God. 'I like what I see.'[3]

This final song, as the title indicates, is also about taking a
risk. It is the one of which I have been writing in this chapter — the risk of giving up a narrow notion of self-fulfillment
in order to seek self-transcendence. The words and music of
this song were written by my missionary colleague, Pádraig
Ó Fátharta.[4]

Risking

I

Take a little risk, it's worth the gamble,
Plunge right in with no preamble,
Take a chance on the dance, believe in living,
Move with the beat with no misgiving,
Let the Spirit call the tune.

Chorus:
As the fish believe in water,
As the birds trust in the air,
As the sunflower is the daughter
Of the sun, without a care.

II

Afraid of starting a conversation,
Afraid of causing a sensation,
Afraid of the day, afraid of the night-time,
Hesitating, waiting for the right time
— But the right time is today.

III

Gilt-edged bonds for life insurance,
And cash in the bank for reassurance.
The strength for helping not expended,
The gift in the fist but not extended
— 'What would the neighbours think of me?'

IV

The seed in the pod is well contented,
The chick in the egg is well defended,
But it pecks at the shell for transformation,
The seed lets go for a new creation
— Shed your shell and become free.

V

Cocoon and shelter have their reason,
They serve their purpose for a season.
But comes a time to leave enclosure,
Comes a time to face exposure,
To the sunshine and the rain.

VI

Courage to commit the heart in caring,
And courage to take one's stand in sharing,
To join in the noise and enter silence,
Savour the joys, endure the violence,
To smile with life and really be.

NOTES

1. Words (based on Scripture) and music by Mary McGann.

2. Taken from *Good Souls to Survive*, Dublin, (Allen Figgis and Co. 1967), 60-61.

3. I have adapted the wording slightly. I have been unable to trace the copyright holders of this material.

4. Previously unpublished. I hope to include a recording of the song in the resource materials which are to be made available to accompany this book.

Appendix

Getting Started with a Group

Variety of Starting-Points

In this appendix I propose to make some practical suggestions about how to get started in working with a group. It can be done by offering an introductory seminar/workshop. The way this is described and 'sold' may vary from person to person and from group to group. Some will be interested in a training programme for leaders. For others, the key phrase may be 'how to build (basic) communities'. Others may be attracted to the idea of working together to develop a holistic spirituality. There may be people who would welcome an introduction to the use of participative methods. And there are some whose main interest is in ensuring that the Church becomes an effective promoter of justice. Obviously, an introductory seminar/workshop could not meet any of these needs fully. But it could be the start of a training programme that would meet all of them.

The content of the introductory seminar can be very much the same whichever one of these 'selling-points' is being catered for. The reason for this is that in all of the above cases the first priority should be to help the group to listen respectfully to each other and to share openly their experiences, their feelings, their convictions, and their faith. There is little point in talking about justice unless the participants are being helped to do each other the fundamental justice of listening respectfully to each other, and cooperating together. Again, it is almost impossible to explain satisfactorily what a community means, except to people who are actually experiencing community. And finally, those who are looking for ways of training leaders need to become aware that it is not a matter of learning a technique by which they will train others; what is on offer is a way in which all can learn together about leadership.

What is on offer — and for whom?

The organisers of the seminar (and of any follow-up training programme) need to be clear in their own minds about what they are offering — and about the expectation of the group they hope to work with. It is important to remember that some groups are not really ready for, or interested in, the kind of material suggested here. They may be looking for a few lectures and a bit of discussion, with little real experiential work. So, long before one offers to put on a seminar or workshop, it is essential to clarify what the group really wants.

I much prefer to run a workshop or a workshop/seminar rather than the kind of seminar that consists mainly of lectures — because I am convinced that this is a better form of adult education. But I cannot force people to agree with me on this point. If it is clear after some discussion that they just want lectures I may decide not to take on the work; alternatively, I may go along with their wishes in the hope that it will lead on to something more experiential.

There is need for care in choosing the groups with whom one is willing to work. At times I have been invited to work with a group of people who belong to the upper 'fishbowls' (to use the image explained in chapter 6). My experience is that if an experiential approach is adopted when the majority of the group are people of this type, they may reinforce each other's prejudices, rather than allowing themselves to be challenged on issues of justice. The model of education proposed here works best with people who find themselves saying: 'ah, that is what I have been trying to do', or: 'this may help me to do more effectively what I have been trying to do'. It does not work well with people who feel very threatened by the approach or its implications — for instance, the need to relinquish power.

Generally I am reluctant to run workshops for people who are mainly wealthy, powerful or privileged, unless I am really convinced that they are willing to embark on radical changes. Even then, I have found it is best to ask such people to take part in mixed workshops where they can meet less privileged

288

people on a basis of equality. The facilitators can then give an opportunity to those who feel oppressed to challenge those who hold power. It is far more effective to have the challenge coming not from the facilitators but from the participants themselves.

Preparations

I think it is most important that any seminar or workshop that is put on should be planned and facilitated by a team rather than by one individual. In this way they can model for the group the kind of teamwork and participative approach they are promoting.

The facilitating team should allow themselves at least one full day together prior to the beginning of the workshop. This is for immediate planning; it presupposes that most of the background preparations are already done, e.g. the preparation of 'inputs' (talks) and of other resource materials (pictures, materials for exercises etc.) If some or all of the members of the team have travelled a long way, they should allow extra time for relaxation before their planning sessions. It is very important that they should not be harassed, tired, or preoccupied at the beginning of the workshop. Their calmness will help to allay the anxiety of the participants. If the members of the team are not used to working together they will probably need a longer time for the immediate preparation; for they will have to get used to each other's style, and strengths and weaknesses.

Occasionally the team may include somebody who does not have much experience of using participative methods. In that case it is very important that the members have reached consensus beforehand about their methodology. Otherwise the participants in the seminar/workshop are almost bound to get a confused message; and as the time goes on they may be disturbed by conflicting approaches within the team.

One of the first things to be done in the planning is to check that all the necessary materials have been brought along or made available. These include:
(1) adequate supplies of newsprint, i.e. large sheets of inexpensive paper;
(2) plenty of felt pens which are not dried up;

(3) masking tape and/or 'blue-tack' for sticking the paper to the walls;

(4) some writing material and pens for participants who failed to bring their own;

(5) a typewriter and stencils or photocopier for doing a report (it is very satisfying if a report can be prepared during the seminar and made available as the participants are departing);

(6) a reliable tape recorder with fresh batteries and/or plugs that fit the available sockets; and suitable tapes, e.g. for hymns or background music;

(7) a video-recorder and T.V., and video-tapes if they are to be used;

(8) equipment for simulations, or other exercises, arranged in proper order;

(9) pictures, posters, headings, etc required for any 'inputs' (talks);

(10) any handbook or manual (or any other reading material) that is required as resource material for the team or the participants;

(11) light card and pins for name cards (there is no need to buy name badges — they are expensive and generally too small);

(12) two light cushions or pillows that may be needed for one of the opening exercises as described below — if it is decided to use this exercise.

I learned the hard way how important it is for the facilitation team to inspect the rooms offered for the working sessions to ensure that they are suitable; some years ago the hall in which we were to work remained locked until the very last moment — and then I found it was a tiered lecture-hall, totally unsuited for this kind of work. Try if possible to ensure that the room is not too big. It is difficult to work in a very large hall because the group tends to feel lost, and to lose cohesion, and also because the acoustics are generally poor. If there is no other location available, it may be possible to improve things by the use of screens to cut off one section of the hall as a working area. The facilitation team should ensure that any rostrum, podium, or large desk is removed.

The team should also make sure that there are sufficient upright chairs for the group; arm-chairs are too bulky, and too conducive to dozing! The chairs should be arranged in a fairly tight circle, and extra chairs should be removed. Do not use desks or tables — they act as barriers. To sit in a circle without the protection of a desk or table leaves people feeling just a little vulnerable and is an invitation to them to be open to each other. Make sure that there is adequate wall-space or stands for the display of newsprint and posters. Lights, heaters (or fans) and electrical sockets also need to be tested. It is important to try out all the electrical equipment brought by the team, to make sure that the fittings are correct. This will lessen the chance of things going wrong when the equipment comes to be used during the seminar/workshop.

At these initial planning sessions the team should look through the list of participants in order to have some idea of the make-up of the group. The strengths of the different participants should be noted in so far as they are known. The team should also try to anticipate any problems or difficulties that are likely to arise for individual participants or in the relationships between groups.

The next step for the team is to make sure that they all have the same set of aims for the seminar — and also that they are agreed in general on the way these aims are to be met. This can be a major task if the team has not worked together previously — and particularly if there is a significant difference in the approach to group-work which the different members have learned. On the other hand, if all the members of the team are used to working together the task is likely to be much easier; but it is important to check out that all have the same understanding of what they want to do and how they are to approach the task.

Once it is clear that there is agreement on goals and methodology, the team can go on to share their ideas about the over-all format of the seminar/workshop — for instance, by outlining what they see as the major elements that will go into the beginning, the middle and the end. They need to allocate the time in such a way that important elements do not get squeezed out — or squeezed in — at the end. However, it is not a good idea to prepare a fixed timetable at this stage; they need to wait until they hear the expectations of the participants, and get a 'feel' for the major issues as they emerge in the group.

It often happens that organisers of a seminar or workshop ask the participants to send in *beforehand* a list of their expectations. That may be helpful insofar as it invites the participants to think about the topics. But, in my experience, it is a very serious error to plan a workshop on the basis of such prior responses. For the fact is that people are not consistent; their ideas — and more especially their feelings and their interests — may change quite significantly when they come together. It often happens that a really generative issue emerges in the course of a seminar or workshop — something that did not have a high priority for the participants beforehand. It is essential for the facilitation team to remain open to the likelihood that this may happen — and to be willing to move with it.

Having got some kind of tentative outline for the seminar, the facilitation team can then prepare a detailed plan for the opening session and for at least the morning of the first day. They should also have a good idea of what they may propose for the afternoon of the first day — though what is actually done that afternoon may have to be left a bit open, in order to take account of 'where the participants are at'. When planning any session it is, of course, essential that it be clearly specified *who* will do *what* — and *when* exactly it is to be done. I give below some suggestions about what may be done in these early sessions of the seminar/workshop.

Welcome

The participants are welcomed when they first arrive and every effort is made to help them feel at ease. One or two of the facilitators should take responsibility for this. This means that the planning session of the team should not drag on until the last minute, when participants are arriving. Some of the participants who have arrived early should be invited to become involved in welcoming those who come later; this will give them a sense of 'ownership' of the whole event.

In what follows I shall assume that the seminar is to begin in the evening, after a meal. Shortly before the evening meal all those who have arrived are registered. This should be a friendly and informal meeting with no element of officiousness. Participants should not be given name-badges at this stage. But the facilitators should ensure they have a name card for everybody who has come. The card should be about 10 cm by 8 cm, and a straight pin should go with it. On the card the person's name should be clearly written, with a felt pen, in large block capitals (make the letters about 3 cm high). These cards will be given to the participants during the opening session. Normally, the name used will be the person's first name or Christian name — but this depends on the wish of the person. It is better to check with the person about the name to be used. Do not lightly assume that you know the person's wishes in this regard. I have often found that at a workshop a person may wish to use a form of his or her name different from the one commonly used.

In general I would prefer to play down the use of titles such as 'Father', 'Reverend' or 'Sister'; but it is important to be sensitive to the wishes of the person. For instance, the person's title or family name may be written in smaller letters on the card in addition to the name that is in large letters. Where more than one person in the group has the same name, it is important to help people distinguish between them by adding an initial or a second name in somewhat smaller letters.

The Opening Session

People who have rushed to get away and have travelled to the seminar/workshop are likely to be tired when they arrive. Nevertheless, it is better if at all possible not to postpone the opening session to next morning. This is because having it the first evening helps people to feel settled and at ease. But, in order to facilitate those who are tired, the workshop should begin as soon as possible after the completion of the evening meal; and the opening session should be fairly short and snappy — lasting about one hour.

The opening session begins with a lively prayer or hymn. Then both the participants and the team should be formally welcomed (briefly) by one of the sponsors of the workshop. After that the team takes over. If possible they should arrange that each member of the team has some public role to play on the first evening, even if it is a very brief role; this will help the participants to know who are on the facilitation team.

Having briefly acknowledged the welcome, the facilitator quickly moves on to the first exercise which has been planned.

This will be some exercise to help the group get to know each other's names and some other information about each other. There is a wide variety of such exercises to be found in hand-books for group work. It is good to experiment a little, so as not to be confined to just one technique. Here I shall describe one such exercise, one that I have found helpful for different kinds of groups.

The facilitator asks the group to break into two. The simplest way to do this is to ask those on the facilitator's left side to go into another room, with another one of the facilitation team, while the other half of the group stays in the same room. (Alternatively, the facilitator may ask the people themselves to form two groups, making sure that as far as possible they join a group that contains people whom they do not know.) The remaining members of the facilitation team spread themselves out between the two groups.

In each of the two sub-groups the leader asks everybody to stand up, away from the chairs, and briefly explains that the aim of this exercise is to help people to get to know each others' names as quickly as possible. The leader explains that he or she will throw a small cushion to a member of the group and say his or her own name (e.g. 'My name is Joan'). The person who has been thrown the cushion then throws it to somebody else, and says his or her own name; and so it goes on. After a short time the leader announces a change in the procedure. Now the person who throws the cushion says the name of the *other* person — the one to whom the cushion is thrown. After some minutes of this, another variation may be introduced, namely, the person *to* whom the cushion is thrown must name the person who threw it. The whole exercise is conducted in a lively and light-hearted way.

A third member of the facilitation team checks to ensure that both groups are moving through the exercise at more or less the same pace. At a suitable time (not too long . . .) this third person suggests to the two leaders that the two groups be brought together again. When they come together the over-all facilitator (or another member of the team) moves them quickly into the next part of the exercise. The group which has stayed in the room forms a circle, facing *outward*. The other group forms another circle around the first group, and facing *inward*. So the members of the two groups are facing each other in two concentric circles.

The facilitator welcomes them back and explains briefly that this next stage of the exercise is to help members of the two sub-groups to get to know each other a bit better. The people in the two rings are asked to circle around in opposite directions while lively dance music is played; when the music stops, each person will stand where he or she is, facing somebody in the other circle; they will then be given a topic on which to speak to the person facing them, and to listen to that person. So the music begins and the participants dance around each other. When the music stops, the people who find themselves opposite each other are invited to say who they are and where they come from. Then a topic for sharing is announced, e.g. 'The happiest day in my life was . . . ' or 'I came to this seminar because . . . ' They are given a short time to speak and to listen. Then the music begins again and the dance resumes. This goes on until about five or six topics have been covered, so that each person should have met five or six of the people in the other circle. The topics chosen should not be too heavy. Some of them should be rather amusing and topical. A number of them should be topics that encourage people to share their feelings, rather than just their thoughts. It is better not to have any deeply controversial topic, though a mildly controversial subject can liven things up for the group. Suitable topics, in addition to the two given above are:
— 'my favourite food'
— 'a funny thing that happened to me'
— 'what I like about men is . . . '
— 'something that frightened me very much'
— 'what I like about myself is . . . '
— 'the best thing about women is . . . '
— 'the kind of music I like best'

It is important to move on from this exercise before the group gets tired or bored. (One of the most important things for a facilitator to learn is to be able to judge when to move on in situations like this.) While the group are still standing, the facilitator explains that there is a third brief part to the exercise. The name cards are distributed at random; each participant is asked to find the person whose card he or she

295

has been given, and attach the card to the person's clothes with the pin which is provided. When this is complete, the facilitators make sure that all participants, including themselves, have got a name-card displayed.

Everybody then sits down in a circle. The facilitator thanks the participants for their cooperation, and hands over to another member of the facilitation team, who proposes to the group that before they retire it will be helpful if they can choose members for three service committees. These are:

(i) A Prayer Committee whose task it will be to organise the community prayer life, in liaison with the facilitation team; they will not be expected to do all the preparation themselves; rather they will see that the gifts of others in the group are used for the good of the whole group.

(ii) A Report Committee whose task it will be to ensure that a record is kept of the various exercises of the seminar/ workshop to help participants recall what happened and so that they may be able to use the exercises later, if they found them helpful. It is useful if this group contains two or three people who can type well.

(iii) A Social Life Committee, who will organise recreation during the time the group is together. They will also take responsibility for time-keeping, and for ensuring that the hall is tidy. They should also make sure that there are some medical facilities for anybody who might become sick.

The facilitator puts up three sheets of newsprint on the wall, one for each of the committees. Members of the group are encouraged to volunteer for one of the three committees. People should not pressure others into joining a committee; a certain amount of informal nomination of others is acceptable, provided the freedom of the person to say 'no' is really respected; it is for the facilitator to check that the person is really willing to volunteer.

It is best to take volunteers for all three committees at the same time; otherwise all the most willing people might volunteer for the first committee leaving the others weak. The number of members on each committee may vary somewhat; three would be a minimum number. Sometimes it may be appropriate for members of the facilitation team to 'sound out' some talented participants beforehand, suggesting that they volunteer for a particular committee;

however, the whole thing should not be set up beforehand in a manipulative way.

When the committees have been chosen, the facilitator informs the group that each committee can keep in touch with one member of the facilitation team who will act as a liaison or link-person, to ensure that there is an integrated approach in the seminar/workshop as a whole. The names of these liaison people are announced, and a quick arrangement may be made for a preliminary meeting of each of the three committees with its liaison person. The prayer commitee should be told that the facilitation team will take responsibility for morning prayer next day, so as to allow the committee time to do its planning.

The working session is drawn to a close by the announcement of the time of meals next day and the time of the opening session; then a final hymn is sung. Then light refreshments are offered to all.

The First Full Working Day

Every effort should be made to start work promptly next morning. But the members of the facilitation team should resist the temptation to take on the role of time-keepers; at most they should quietly encourage the Social Life Committee to play this role.

Over the past four or five years I have found it very helpful to start each morning of a workshop or a seminar with some body exercises. Occasionally, some of the participants found this a bit odd at first; but almost invariably they came to appreciate it. The exercises should be carefully chosen so that nobody feels they are too demanding. A ten-minute package of very simple bio-energetic exercises (stretching and moving) can make people more aware of their bodies and of where they are carrying tension, and will help to release some of the tension and the energy that has been blocked; they may also help the participants to feel more 'grounded' or 'rooted' on the Earth. At the very least, they help to wake people up and to relate more easily to the other members of the group.

Each morning, after the exercises, it is good to have some quiet reflective time — perhaps a fifteen-minute prayer period (normally prepared by volunteers at the request of the Prayer Committee). However, on this first full day of the seminar/workshop it can be very useful to have a much more extended time of prayer and reflection, given over to faith-sharing. In my experience this changes the whole mood of the group and leads to a much greater depth in all the work that follows. The following is one way in which this can be done.

After the body exercises the participants are invited to sit down very quietly with their backs straight and both feet planted firmly on the ground. They are then led through an 'awareness-and-quieting' exercise — to help them find some inner peace, and get into a mood where they can really open themselves to listen to the Word of God.

There are three steps in the faith-sharing exercise — a time for personal prayer, a time for sharing in small groups, and a time for some general sharing. It is best to begin by having about three fairly short passages from Scripture (and, possibly, from other sources too) read out by different readers. *After* the reading pass around sheets of paper on which the texts have been written out. The passages will be ones that have been carefully chosen beforehand (in this case by the facilitation team) to suit the occasion.

The facilitators may feel inclined to choose some challenging texts so as to start the seminar on a strong note. But I have found that it is better to hold over such passages for a couple of days. On this first morning many of the participants will still be feeling quite insecure and fragile, wondering how they will cope in the group. The kind of passages which will be of greatest benefit to them are ones which bring reassurance. They will be helped by hearing God say to them: 'You are precious, you are called by name, you are uniquely important, you need not be afraid, you are not forgotten but are chosen, you are protected and loved by God with a love greater than that of a mother for her baby, your name is carved on the palm of God's hand (Is 41:8-14; 43:1-2: 44:21-22: 46:3-4: 49:14-16; Eph 1:11-12). If it seems appropriate, a second theme, closely related to the previous one, could be included — the idea that each person here has been given a great task by God (e.g. Is 42:6-8; 43:18-21; 49:1-6; Jer 1:4-8).

Allow about thirty to forty minutes for personal prayer on these passages. Then ask people to form groups of four in

which they share in turn (without being interrupted or probed) on their answers to any of these questions:
— What touched or moved me in the prayer?
— What insight did I get?
— Did I feel drawn to any action?

Each person should have five or six minutes to share in the small groups. When all have spoken there may be a little time for some responses and dialogue. After about thirty minutes the members of the small groups are invited to form a large circle for about fifteen or twenty minutes. There is no question of giving 'reports' from the groups. Some very gentle facilitation is called for, to evoke an atmosphere of silence into which a few people may occasionally drop a few words, or a short prayer. Then the group disperses for a break. The whole event, including the body exercises, will have occupied the best part of two hours. It is time well spent.

After a break, the group comes together and this time they are invited to divide into local groups (or vocational groups, e.g. medical workers), for about forty-five minutes to prepare (on newsprint) short reports for the whole group about their experiences and the needs they feel have to be met in their area or sphere of work. These reports are then presented to the whole group, with a short pause after each one and a few moments for people to ask for clarification on any particular point; it is better not to get into discussion on the reports, as this makes the session very long-drawn-out. In any case, it is likely that at least some of the reports will have to be carried over into the afternoon.

When the reports have all been presented, the participants can be asked: 'In the light of what you have heard from members of this group, and of your own previous experience, what would you now hope to get out of this seminar/ workshop?' People should be asked to take about five minutes to jot down their answers to this question; but they may need to be reminded that their answers should, of course, be related in some way to the advertised theme of the seminar. In mixed groups of about five or six, the participants can share their responses. Then, in the large group, the main headings should be 'drawn out' from each small group by one of the facilitation team, while another member of the team writes them down (in large writing) on sheets of newsprint.

299

To draw the session to a close another member of the team should ask everybody to reflect personally for a moment to see if they have any reservations they would like to share, i.e. anything they would like not to happen. These are written up on another sheet of newsprint. The team then explains to the group that they will work on this material and report back to the group on it next morning. In the meantime, if there is still time available on this first day, the facilitators may propose that, after a break, the group should begin work on some topic which is obviously related to the expectations of the group; preferably this should be something light, perhaps an exercise of the kind I have suggested in various chapters of this book.

The day's work provides the facilitation team with a great lot of material which they will take away and work on that evening. A crucial part of any workshop — and perhaps especially of this introductory seminar/workshop — must be the effort of the facilitators to show that they are taking full account of the expectations, hopes, and concerns of all the participants. So the task of the planning and facilitation team is to come back next morning to the whole group with an outline plan which is obviously a response to the expectations and reservations expressed by all the participants. The outline plan which the facilitators put forward for the seminar does not have to cover every item listed by the participants. The team may have to explain that some of the expectations cannot be met in this particular workshop, though they could be met in a more advanced one, later on. Other items on the list may be omitted from the workshop on the grounds that they were expressed by only one or two people in the group, or because they do not fit in with the nature of the workshop as advertised. It may also be useful to say about a particular item that the facilitators are unable to respond to the request at this time but that other participants may be able to do so outside the formal sessions, or even during a formal session later in the workshop.

Once the first day is over, the seminar/workshop should be fairly easy to plan. I do not think it would be appropriate for me to try to spell out here the topics that should be covered — even though, as I noted previously, the content covered may be quite similar in most such seminars. There are just three bits of general advice I wish to give:

1. Resist the temptation to 'cover' a lot of material by means of talks. The group may find the talks interesting but talks are not so likely to bring about the kind of conversion that is important. No matter how good a talk is, it tends to silence people, to make them feel that they do not know much about the subject; in fact it often happens that an audience feels more ignorant and helpless after a really good lecture. So I think that one talk a day is the very most that should be given.

2. If at all possible ensure that the group work comes *prior* to a talk by a resource person rather than after it. After a talk the group work is more likely to be discussion. This can of course be useful but group exercises are generally much more effective. It is helpful to have a talk which draws together some of the themes that have been raised in the group work.

3. Make sure to allow sufficient time towards the end of the seminar for planning by the group of the next step they would like to take; and allow about half a day at the very end for an evaluation and celebration by the whole group. The evaluation should focus attention not so much on the detail of particular talks or exercises as on such general questions as 'What, for me, was the fruit of the seminar?' or 'What am I taking away from this seminar?